INTERNATIONAL LAW AND CANNABIS

INTERNATIONAL LAW AND CANNABIS

Regulation of Cannabis Cultivation for Recreational Use under the UN Narcotic Drugs Conventions and the EU Legal Instruments in Anti-Drugs Policy

Volume I

Piet Hein van Kempen
Masha Fedorova

intersentia
Cambridge – Antwerp – Chicago

Intersentia Ltd
8 Wellington Street | Cambridge
CB1 1HW | United Kingdom
Tel.: +44 1223 736 170
Email: mail@intersentia.co.uk
www.intersentia.com | www.intersentia.co.uk

Distribution for the UK and Ireland:
NBN International
Airport Business Centre, 10 Thornbury Road
Plymouth, PL6 7PP
United Kingdom
Tel.: +44 1752 202 301 | Fax: +44 1752 202 331
Email: orders@nbninternational.com

Distribution for Europe and all other countries:
Intersentia Publishing nv
Groenstraat 31
2640 Mortsel
Belgium
Tel.: +32 3 680 15 50 | Fax: +32 3 658 71 21
Email: mail@intersentia.be

Distribution for the USA and Canada:
Independent Publishers Group
Order Department
814 North Franklin Street
Chicago, IL 60610
USA
Tel.: +1 800 888 4741 (toll free) | Fax: +1 312 337 5985
Email: orders@ipgbook.com

International Law and Cannabis. Regulation of Cannabis Cultivation for Recreational Use under the UN Narcotic Drugs Conventions and the EU Legal Instruments in Anti-Drugs Policy

ISBN 978-1-78068-870-1
D/2019/7849/105
NUR 828

GPRC
Guaranteed
Peer Reviewed
Content

British Library Cataloguing in Publication Data. A catalogue record for this book is available from the British Library.

PREFACE

What legal avenues are there to regulate cannabis cultivation and trade for recreational use? This question has generated heated discussions in various societies, in political and academic discourses. Several states are considering or have adjusted their legal and policy approaches towards a more lenient regulation of cannabis cultivation and trade for the recreational user market. These discussions have been the overture for two academic studies that we have conducted recently.

The first study focused on the question to what extent are domestic initiatives involving regulation of cannabis cultivation for recreational use compatible with the relevant UN narcotic drugs conventions and European Union law. It was this question that took centre stage in the political discussion in the Netherlands at that time. The results of this study were presented to the Minister of Justice and Security in the Netherlands in 2014.[1] Because of the limitation of this first study to the framework of UN and EU law regulating drugs only, we decided to complement our research by involving international law more broadly and by looking more specifically at the positive human rights obligations.

The second study covered two questions. First, to what extent can regulation of cannabis for recreational use, for the sake of health, safety and crime control, be considered a positive human rights obligation resulting from the right to health, the right to life, the right to physical and psychological integrity and the right to privacy. In the event this obligation can be established, the second question concerned the hierarchical relationship between these positive human rights obligations and the obligations arising from the UN drugs conventions and EU anti-drugs laws. This second study was presented to politicians in the Netherlands in 2016.[2] Since that time, the developments in the Netherlands have progressed to the extent that the government has decided to set up an experiment for legal supply of cannabis to point-of-sale for recreational use. The legislation concerning this experiment is being prepared as we speak.

---

1 Piet Hein P.H.M.C. van Kempen & Masha I. Fedorova, *Internationaal recht en cannabis. Een beoordeling op basis van VN-drugsverdragen en EU-regelgeving van gemeentelijke en buitenlandse opvattingen pro regulering van cannabisteelt foor recreatief gebruik*, Deventer: Wolters Kluwer, 2014.

2 Piet Hein P.H.M.C. van Kempen & Masha I. Fedorova, *Internationaal recht en cannabis II. Regulering van cannabisteelt en -handel voor recreatief gebruik: positieve mensenrechtenverplichtingen versus VN-drugsverdragen*, Deventer: Wolters Kluwer, 2016.

Due to the topical nature of the issue and the ongoing discussions on national and international levels, we decided to make our both studies available to a broader academic forum to which end these books have been translated and updated:

- Piet Hein. P.H.M.C. van Kempen & Masha I. Fedorova, *International Law and Cannabis I. Regulation of Cannabis Cultivation for Recreational Use under the UN Narcotic Drugs Conventions and the EU Legal Instruments in Anti-Drugs Policy*, Cambridge: Intersentia, 2019.
- Piet Hein P.H.M.C. van Kempen & Masha I. Fedorova, *International Law and Cannabis II. Regulation of Cannabis Cultivation and Trade for Recreational Use: Positive Human Rights Obligations versus UN Narcotic Drugs Conventions*, Cambridge: Intersentia, 2019.

For the fine translation work we are indebted to Mr. Paul de Wit, *Dutch Translations*, London. We are also grateful to the publishing house Intersentia for their patience and support in publishing the two books.

All errors are our own. The sources have been updated and all the websites were accessible on 1 January 2019.

Piet Hein van Kempen and Masha Fedorova

CONTENTS

LIST OF CASES

PERMANENT COURT OF INTERNATIONAL JUSTICE

INTERNATIONAL COURT OF JUSTICE

COURT OF JUSTICE OF THE EUROPEAN UNION

SUPREME COURT OF THE NETHERLANDS

FEDERAL COURT OF CANADA

LIST OF ABBREVIATIONS

CESCR	Committee on Economic, Social and Cultural Rights
CJEU	Court of Justice of the European Union
CND	Commission on Narcotic Drugs
CSC	Cannabis Social Clubs
ECommHR	European Commission of Human Rights
ECOSOC	Economic and Social Council
ESC	European Social Charter
ECSR	European Committee of Social Rights
ECtHR	European Court of Human Rights
EU	European Union
ECHR	European Convention on Human Rights
GA	General Assembly
GC	Grand Chamber
I-ACionHR	Inter-American Commission on Human Rights
I-ACtHR	Inter-American Court of Human Rights
ICJ	International Court of Justice
ICTY	International Criminal Tribunal for the former Yugoslavia
ILC	International Law Commission
INCB	International Narcotics Control Board
ICCPR	International Covenant on Civil and Political Rights
ICESCR	International Covenant on Economic, Social and Cultural Rights
HRC	Human Rights Committee
OJ	Official Journal (of EU)
CoE	Council of Europa
SC	Security Council
Trb.	Tractatenblad
UN	United Nations
UNODC	United Nations Office on Drugs and Crime
UDHR	Universal Declaration of Human Rights
UN	United Nations
WHO	World Health Organization
WTO	World Trade Organization

CHAPTER 1
INTRODUCTION

1.1. RATIONALE FOR AND PURPOSE OF THE BOOK

The policy of tolerance regarding the sale of cannabis (marijuana/hemp/weed, grass[1] and hash[2]) in so-called coffee shops[3] in the Netherlands continues to confront society, the authorities and supporters and opponents of this policy with difficult questions. An important issue is that the cultivation of cannabis to supply coffee shops does not form part of the policy and is therefore completely illegal. This is sometimes referred to as the back-door problem (as deliveries to a coffee shop would take place at the back door). The resulting ambivalent situation around coffee shops leads to much dismay and discussion, including in the Dutch parliament. That discussion is partly about arguments and concrete plans of Dutch municipalities to arrive at regulated cannabis cultivation, as well as initiatives in other countries, which aim to provide such regulation. The discussion led to a promise by the Dutch Minister of Justice and Security to the Parliament to have the recent national and international developments and schemes in the area of cannabis cultivation assessed in the light of international legal frameworks arising from the UN narcotic drugs conventions and from relevant EU law.[4] Until now, the position of the Dutch government on legalizing or regulating in another way the cultivation of cannabis for recreational use

---

1 Marijuana – also called weed – consists of the dried and crumbled female flower tops of the cannabis plant and is greenish brown in colour (information obtained from the Trimbos Institute website www.trimbos.org). The cannabis plant is also referred to as hemp. Note: all websites referred to in this book were last accessed 1 January 2019.

2 Hashish – also called hash – consists of compressed cubes or slices of cannabis resin and its colour varies from yellow to light brown to black (information obtained from the Trimbos Instituut website www.trimbos.org).

3 Sales outlets licensed by the municipality in the Netherlands where the sale of alcohol is prohibited but the sale of cannabis in small amounts to adults for personal use is permitted. All the references in this book are meant in this way. Other possible retail locations will be referred to more generally as retail shop or points-of-sale.

4 *Kamerstukken II* 2012–2013, 24 077, nr. 310, p. 2 (Drugbeleid; Brief van de Minister van Veiligheid en Justitie) (i.e., *Dutch Parliamentary Documents II* 2012–2013, 24 077, no. 310, p. 2 (Drug policy; Letter of the Minister of Security and Justice) and *Kamerstukken II* 2012–2013, nr. 312, p. 28 (Drugbeleid; Verslag algemeen overleg) (i.e., *Dutch Parliamentary Documents II* 2012–2013, no. 312, p. 28 (Drug policy; Report on general consultations).

has been based on the findings in a report of the T.M.C. Asser Institute from 2005.[5] The conclusion of this report is that under international law there is no room to permit the cultivation of cannabis for the supply of retail shops. The above-mentioned arguments and initiatives from within municipalities and also in other countries were the reason to carry out the further analysis of international law and an assessment based on this law.[6] That is what we do in this research. This does not involve only the above-mentioned problems of supplying coffee shops, but also new developments, such as joint cultivation and consumption in so-called Cannabis Social Clubs.

1.2. DEFINITION OF THE CENTRAL PROBLEM

Against the background outlined above, the key question of this research is the following:

> To what extent are initiatives regarding the legalization, decriminalization, policy-based tolerance and/or other forms of regulation of cannabis cultivation for recreational use compatible with applicable international law as laid down in the UN narcotic drugs conventions and in European Union law?

To arrive at a substantiated answer to this question, the book first provides an elaborate account and analysis of relevant international law. First, we will look at the Single Convention on Narcotic Drugs 1961, as amended by the Protocol of 1972 amending the Single Convention on Narcotic Drugs, and the Convention against Illicit Traffic in Narcotic Drugs and Psychotropic Substances 1988.[7] Furthermore, European law is relevant, in particular the so-called Schengen acquis (Agreement and Implementation Agreement), the Joint Action on illegal drug trafficking of 1996 and the Framework Decision on Illegal Drug Trafficking of 2004.[8] With respect to all these international instruments, the book focuses more specifically on the ensuing obligations for the states parties regarding

---

5 T.M.C. Asser Instituut, *Experimenteren met het Gedogen van de Teelt van Cannabis ten Behoeve van de Bevoorrading van Coffeeshops – Internationaal rechtelijke en Europees rechtelijke aspecten*, Den Haag: 2005 (i.e., Asser Institute – Centre for International & European Law; *Experimenting with tolerating the cultivation of cannabis for the supply of coffee shops – aspects of international and European law*, The Hague: 2005).

6 See for example *European Drug Report 2013: Trends and developments*, European Monitoring Centre for Drugs and Drug Addiction, 2013, p. 62, available on: http://www.emcdda.europa.eu/publications/edr/trends-developments/2013.

7 For acknowledgement of sources and further information on these instruments see Chapter 2.

8 For acknowledgement of sources and further information on these instruments see Chapter 3.

cannabis, on the content and scope of exceptions to these obligations (such as the exception of medical and scientific purposes) and on judgements, findings and views of the international bodies appointed to supervise these instruments. As for this latter point, we concern ourselves particularly with the International Narcotics Control Board (INCB), the Commission on Narcotic Drugs (CND) and the European Court of Justice (ECJ). The resulting international legal framework provides a foundation for the assessment of the arguments and initiatives relating to cannabis cultivation both in the Netherlands and in other countries. The following two sub-questions act as a guideline in the assessment:

1. Do the arguments furnished by municipalities in the Netherlands and the modalities that they propose for permitting cannabis cultivation for recreational use provide any reason to conclude that there is any room under international law for legalization, decriminalization, policy-based tolerance and/or other forms of regulation of such cultivation? If yes, to what extent and in which respect? If no, why not?
2. Do the bills, acts and laws in countries other than the Netherlands regarding cannabis cultivation for recreational use and the arguments put forward to that end and the official positions taken give rise to the conclusion that there is any room under international law for legalization, decriminalization, policy-based tolerance and/or other forms of regulation of cannabis cultivation for recreational use? If yes, to what extent and in which respect? If no, why not?

By answering these sub-questions, we aim to arrive at a detailed and precisely substantiated answer to the main question. Dealing with the question of legal permissibility of cannabis cultivation in relation to the many specific arguments and initiatives also has the effect that certain analyses are sometimes repeated in slightly different contexts in various parts of the book.

1.3. RELEVANT DEFINITIONS

This book contains many terms also found in other literature and documents, where they do not always have the same meaning. In order to avoid misunderstandings as much as possible, it is worthwhile to specify the meaning of some of these terms and other concepts used in this book.

1.3.1. ROOM UNDER INTERNATIONAL LAW

The concept of 'room under international law' refers to legal possibilities left by the UN narcotic drugs conventions (which are decisive for the drug control regimes of all countries that signed the conventions) and European law (within which the member states of the European Union have to operate) to states parties to legalize, decriminalize, tolerate by virtue of a policy and/or otherwise regulate the cultivation of cannabis.

1.3.2. LEGALIZATION, DECRIMINALIZATION, POLICY-BASED TOLERANCE AND/OR OTHER FORMS OF REGULATION OF CANNABIS CULTIVATION

To produce a refined and comprehensive analysis, we chose to differentiate between the four possible regulation modalities of cannabis cultivation, namely legalization, decriminalization, policy-based tolerance and/or other forms of regulation. First and foremost, we must observe that the use of terminology for the modalities of regulating cannabis cultivation in the political debate and the media often varies and is not always conceptually pure. Moreover, the relevant terminology for this research is used with variation within academic literature, where the specific use sometimes depends on the pertinent discipline. There tends to be less confusion about the use of the term 'legalization' than about the slightly less specific concept of 'regulation', whereas the terms 'decriminalization' and in particular 'tolerating' are used in rather diverging ways. We will therefore need to clarify the following.

Legalization in this research means that prohibited conduct (an act or omission to act) is declared legal. The conduct then no longer contravenes the law, from that moment on it is legally allowed and permitted. This does not affect the possibility that conditions may be attached to that conduct. In that case, the legalization can be said to be *regulated*. For example, the use of alcohol in the Netherlands is legal in itself, but that does not alter the fact that legal restrictions apply to both the supply and the demand side of the market, where the authorities have the power to act in case these restrictions are violated.

Decriminalization is less far-reaching than legalization. In this book, decriminalization means that conduct which is prohibited under criminal law is removed from the sphere of criminal law. The conduct as such is no longer subject to criminalization, but is still prohibited by virtue of legislation not related to criminal law. In other words, decriminalization does not yet mean that the decriminalized conduct is legal and/or permissible from now on. The conduct is still deemed undesirable and it can be subject to action other than under criminal law, for example through administrative law or civil law. One example of decriminalization is that a provision from the Road Traffic Act is no longer enforced under criminal law but only via administrative law.

Policy-based tolerance in this book refers to the situation that a form of conduct which has been criminalized is explicitly tolerated by the Public Prosecution Office and the administrative authorities, on the basis of documented policy. That tolerance is therefore subject to explicitly formulated rules, assumptions and criteria. Policy-based tolerance can involve tolerance on a criminal and administrative level. *Policy-based penal tolerance* means that the Public Prosecution Office refrains in general from prosecution for conduct covered by the formulated rules, assumptions and criteria on the basis of documented policy. The possibility for such tolerance in the Netherlands has its origin in the expediency principle (Article 167(2) of the Dutch Code of Criminal Procedure). If there is a policy of non-prosecution, the investigation policy is adjusted accordingly. For example, on the basis of the Instruction regarding the Dutch Opium Act (*Aanwijzing Opiumwet*[9]), the Public Prosecution Office now tolerates the sale of cannabis in coffee shops if a coffee shop acts in agreement with the relevant policy (the so-called 'AHOJGI' criteria[10]); if that is the case, the authorities will not start criminal proceedings against the coffee shop. Incidentally, the Instruction regarding the Dutch Opium Act differentiates between a policy of tolerance and low investigation priority. A policy of tolerance refers to the positive decision not to investigate and prosecute offenders, since the interest of criminal law enforcement must give way to a higher identifiable public interest such as public health. According to the Instruction regarding the Dutch Opium Act, the assignment of a low investigation priority to certain categories of offences is based in general on the assessment of the relative seriousness of the offences versus considerations of capacity. This distinction will not be discussed in this book. To the extent that such a policy of prioritization is based on explicitly formulated rules, assumptions and criteria, and the result is that the relevant offences are scarcely prosecuted if at all, this would be covered by the category of policy-based penal tolerance in the context of this book. Finally, a few comments about *policy-based administrative tolerance*. This is the case if the administrative authorities in general refrain from acting against situations and conduct that comply with the formulated rules, assumptions and criteria, on the basis of a documented policy. For example, if the municipality issues a licence to a coffee shop, this would be a case of administrative tolerance.

---

9 See for this policy, College van procureurs-generaal openbaar ministerie, 'Aanwijzing Opiumwet (2015A003)', *Stcrt.* 2015, 5391 (i.e., Board of Procurators General of the Dutch Public Prosecution Office, 'Instruction regarding the Dutch Opium Act (2015A003)', Dutch Government Gazette, 2015, 5391), with effect from 1 March 2015.

10 AHOJGI are the first letters of crucial elements in the conditions imposed on coffee shops: they are not allowed to put up posters/displaying promotional material (*a*fficheren); sell *h*ard drugs, cause nuisance (*o*verlast); admit access to and sell to minors under 18 (*j*eugdigen); sell or stock large (*g*rote) quantities (no more than 5g per person per transaction/no more than 500g in stock); and refuse access to and sell to anyone but citizens (*i*ngezetenen) of the Netherlands). Municipalities can determine whether to allow coffee shops, and if so, how many shops. They may impose additional rules with regard to coffee shops.
See also https://www.government.nl/topics/drugs/toleration-policy-regarding-soft-drugs-and-coffee-shops.

The fourth and last term in the subdivision is *other forms of regulating*. Regulating means subjecting to provisions, rules and/or conditions. As we have seen above, decriminalization and policy-based tolerance go hand in hand with regulating and this can also be the case with legalization. When we speak of 'and/or other forms of regulating' in this book, this covers both a situation where legalization is accompanied by regulation and the situation where there is no legalization, decriminalization or policy-based tolerance, while the government still provides a regulating system for cannabis cultivation for recreational use in one way or another. The objective of using this term is therefore to cover all possible forms of regulation of cannabis cultivation for personal use.

1.3.3. CULTIVATION AND THE RELEVANT ACTS

This book focuses explicitly on the question whether regulation of the *cultivation* of cannabis intended for recreational use can be permissible, given the obligations with regard to fighting drugs assumed by the Netherlands under international law. This involves planting, growing or cultivating. The act of *cultivating* only refers to growing the plant with the name cannabis. The obligations under international law, however, also refer to all sorts of other acts. Many of these play a role in cannabis cultivation that takes place for example to supply retail shops, or in the context of a Cannabis Social Club. Apart from cultivation, this will also involve production (including the separation of flowering and fruiting cannabis tops and cannabis resin from cannabis plants), manufacture (further processing), possession, offering for sale, distribution and selling and possibly extraction and/or preparation. A separate discussion of these acts will often be impractical, given the correlation between these acts. For example, in many cases the acts mentioned presuppose the possession of cannabis. Consequently, the discussion of the relevant obligations with regard to cannabis *cultivation* in many cases is also relevant for the production, manufacture, possession, delivery, offering, distribution and selling of flowering and fruiting cannabis tops and cannabis resin from the cannabis plants. Because the focus in this book is on cultivation of cannabis for recreational use, we only mention and discuss other acts particularly in relation to the question whether legalization, decriminalization, policy-based tolerance and/or other forms of regulating cannabis cultivation for recreational use is permissible.

1.4. FOCUS AND LIMITATIONS

This book is as strictly legal as possible. First, this means that we are not going to assess the arguments of a factual, social and/or political nature which are presented by Dutch municipalities and put forward in literature on the accuracy of their content or their validity. This book is only about the question whether the arguments put forward – be they factual or legal in nature – could legitimize the regulation of cannabis cultivation under the UN narcotic drugs conventions and the EU laws on drugs. To that end, the book contains a legal analysis and assessment on the basis of the text, the system and the rationale of the UN narcotic drugs conventions and the EU laws on drugs, and also based on the history of deliberations, official comments and the legal literature on the subject. It will also take into account the relevant rules of international public law for the interpretation and operation of the conventions. So if, for example, it is argued that regulating cannabis cultivation makes it easier to fight organized crime effectively, we will not evaluate whether this is factually true. We will assume that the argument is valid and from that starting point we will only assess whether the UN narcotic drugs conventions and the EU laws on drugs permit proceeding to such regulation on the basis of this argument.

The book is also as strictly legal as possible in the sense that we will not let any personal opinions about the desirability of legalization, decriminalization, policy-based tolerance and/or other forms of regulating cannabis cultivation for recreational use play any part (at any rate not consciously) in the discussion. In the Dutch and international legal academic debate about regulating cannabis cultivation, many people present themselves clearly as advocates of or alternatively opponents of such regulation with the relevant arguments and assertions. In order to keep our assessment as purely legal as possible, we will steer clear of such courses. This also means that we will not pass judgment on the question of legal policy whether the Netherlands – if the study showed that permitting cannabis cultivation contravenes the UN narcotic drugs conventions and the EU laws – should play a pioneering role internationally with regard to permitting cannabis cultivation.

This legal approach is also limited in scope. It only concerns itself with the question to what extent municipal plans and initiatives in other countries to legalize, decriminalize and/or explicitly tolerate cannabis cultivation are compatible with the relevant UN narcotic drugs conventions and the EU laws on drugs. These conventions and laws are of paramount importance to the assessment. That is why the international discussion about human rights and cannabis use as well as fighting this use is not dealt with here. This means that we will not address the question whether cannabis use is protected by the fundamental rights and freedom such as a right to privacy, the right to freedom of expression or the right to freedom of belief and religion. Nor will we look at the question whether fundamental economic, social or cultural rights – such as the right to participate in cultural life, the right to self-determination, the right to enjoy the advantage of scientific progress, the right of children to be protected against drugs and the right to health – entail possibilities or even obligations for states to apply a different drug policy and whether the regulation of cannabis cultivation could be a part of that.

1.5. METHODOLOGY

The book involves desk-research. The legal sources that are fundamental to this discussion are the UN narcotic drugs conventions and EU drug instruments mentioned above in section 1.2. In order to examine arguments for regulated cannabis cultivation for recreational use, we primarily rely on domestic and international documents and studies.[11] For the legal analysis of provisions in the international drug instruments, we use the interpretation methods recognized in public international law: the textual, contextual and systematic, teleological and historical methods of interpretation. Therefore, of relevance are the texts of the conventions, their systems and/or the context within which their provisions are found and the rationale of the conventions, and alternatively the drafting history, the official commentaries on the conventions and relevant literature.[12] Relevant opinions and views of supervisory judicial institutions and other bodies are also taken into account in our analysis. For a more detailed discussion of the methodology see Chapter 2.[13]

1.6. DESIGN OF THE BOOK

Chapter 2 offers an overview and analysis of the international conventions created in the context of the United Nations to reinforce the international drug control system. More specifically, two UN narcotic drugs conventions are discussed in detail, also in the light of the central research question: the Single Convention and the Illicit Traffic Convention. Chapter 3 provides an overview and analysis, again in light of the central question, of the relevant EU laws on drugs: the Schengen acquis (Agreement and Implementation Agreement), the Joint Action of 1996 and the Framework Decision of 2004. Chapters 2 and 3 together form the framework of international law that is the source of the obligations assumed by the Netherlands with respect to cannabis cultivation.

---

11 E.g. Letters, notes and reports from 25 Dutch municipalities provided for by the Dutch Ministry of Justice and Security, see more specifically Piet Hein P.H.M.C. van Kempen & Masha I. Fedorova, *Internationaal recht en cannabis. Een beoordeling op basis van VN-drugsverdragen en EU-regelgeving van gemeentelijke en buitenlandse opvattingen pro regulering van cannabisteelt voor recreatief gebruik*, Deventer: Kluwer, 2014, Chapter 4; and further studies such as Beau Kilmer, Kristy Kruithof, Mafalda Pardal, Jonathan P. Caulkins & Jennifer Rubin, *Multinational overview of cannabis production regimes*, RAND Europe/ WODC, 2013. See also European Monitoring Centre for Drugs and Drug Addiction, *Cannabis legalization in Europe. An overview*, Luxembourg: Publications Office of the European Union, 2018.

12 By 'convention' we mean here (and only here) the instruments created within the European Union as well.

13 See section 2.1.2.

Chapter 4 contains an account and categorization of the arguments and initiatives both in Dutch municipalities and in other countries for regulating the cultivation of cannabis for recreational use, so as to assess the arguments and initiatives systematically on the basis of the international legal framework. Finally, Chapter 5 contains the conclusion: what do the findings from the previous chapters mean for the question whether there is any room under international law to legalize, decriminalize, tolerate by virtue of a policy and/or otherwise regulate the cultivation of cannabis for supplying retail shops, in the context of Cannabis Social Clubs or via other modalities involving recreational use of cannabis by third parties?

CHAPTER 2

OBLIGATIONS UNDER INTERNATIONAL LAW REGARDING CANNABIS

UN Narcotic Drugs Conventions

2.1. INTRODUCTION

Cannabis first became subject to international control through the *International Opium Convention* of 1925 (the '1925 Convention').[1] This convention – to which the Netherlands was also a party – limited itself to regulation in connection with international trade. It did not prohibit the production of cannabis as such and did not impose any obligations on states with regard to the domestic trade in cannabis or its consumption.[2] After the Second World War, the United Nations took over the supervision of multilateral drug control from the League of Nations.[3] This led to a stricter control with a wider scope. The three most important instruments created for this purpose are:

1. *Single Convention on Narcotic Drugs, 1961*[4] as amended by the *Protocol amending the Single Convention on Narcotic Drugs, 1961* of 1972;[5]
2. *Convention on Psychotropic Substances, 1971;*[6]
3. *United Nations Convention Against Illicit Traffic in Narcotic Drugs and Psychotropic Substances, 1988.*[7]

The second convention – the 1971 Convention on Psychotropic Substances – has no particular relevance for this book. Admittedly, delta-9-tetrahydrocannabinol (THC) is a psychoactive substance mentioned in Schedule II of the convention

---

1. Geneva, 19 February 1925, League of Nations Treaty Series, vol. 81, pp. 318–358. This treaty expired on 13 December 1964 with the entry into force of the *Single Convention on Narcotic Drugs, 1961* which will be discussed later (see Article 44(1) under c).
2. UNODC, *A Century of International Drug Control*, Vienna: United Nations, 2008, p. 55.
3. UNODC, *A Century of International Drug Control*, Vienna: United Nations, 2008, p. 7.
4. New York, 30 March 1961.
5. Geneva, 25 March 1972.
6. Vienna, 21 February 1971.
7. Vienna, 20 December 1988.

and occurs in cannabis, but because it is not common practice to extract that substance from cannabis, and such an extraction is not what this book is about, this convention will not be considered further. That will certainly not be the case for the other two conventions: they are key to this chapter.

2.1.1. VARIATION BETWEEN PARTIES TO THE CONVENTION

In the discussion of these conventions, we must take into consideration that the interests and policy insights of the states parties can vary considerably. For example, a distinction can be made between *cultivating states* (countries where the organic material needed for drugs is grown), *manufacturing states* (countries where synthetic production takes place), *strong control states* (countries that are culturally opposed to drug use and suffer from the consumption of drugs in their territory), *weak control states* (countries that consider drug control to be an internal affair and regard foreign intervention as a breach of their sovereignty), and *neutral states* (countries that have no clear-cut interests regarding drug control either way).[8] This implies that the conventions in principle cannot be interpreted from the point of view of just one state or a certain category of states. It also means that a trend with regard to a relaxation or tightening of drugs policy in a group of states does not imply that that trend manifests itself generally among the parties.[9] The continuum of parties ranges from countries with very liberal cannabis legislation to states where the death penalty for the illicit trade in cannabis is carried out.[10] Within the United Nations and among the member states, there are movements advocating tightening the repressive drug control regime for cannabis as well as developments towards relaxing this very regime.[11] This matters in two ways.

---

8 See for example Jay Sinha, *The History and Development of the Leading International Drug Control Conventions*, Ottawa: Library of Parliament, Parliamentary Research Branch, 2001, pp. 19–20, with reference to: William B. McAllister, 'Conflicts of Interest in the International Drug Control System', in: William O. Walker III (ed.), *Drug Control Policy: Essays in Historical and Comparative Perspective*, University Park, Pennsylvania: Pennsylvania State University Press, 1992, pp. 148–151.

9 See also David R. Bewley-Taylor, 'Towards revision of the UN drug control conventions. The logic and dilemmas of Like-Minded Groups', *Series on Legislative Reform of Drug Policies*, No. 19, March 2012, pp. 1–16, which Article reveals major differences between groups of states with respect to the way in which they perceive the UN narcotic drugs conventions.

10 Patrick Gallahue, Ricky Gunawan, Fifa Rahman, Karim El Mufti, Najam U Din & Rita Felten, *The Death Penalty for Drug Offences: Global Overview 2012*, London: International Harm Reduction Association, 2012, e.g. pp. 17, 22, 29.

11 See David R. Bewley-Taylor, 'The Contemporary International Drug Control System: A History of the UNGASS Decade', in: John Collins (ed.), *Governing the Global Drug Wars*, London: London School of Economics, 2012, pp. 49–55, in particular p. 53. See also Tom Blickman, 'European Cannabis Policies Under Attack', *TNI Briefing*, April 2002,

It illustrates that the consensus about the importance and meaning of the UN narcotic drugs conventions may not be as strong today as it was at the time they came into force. It also demonstrates clearly that one should not just assume that a country's national insights about the admissibility or desirability of certain interpretations and implementation of the convention's provisions are widely shared.

2.1.2. INTERPRETATION OF THE CONVENTION AND OTHER CONCEPTS OF PUBLIC INTERNATIONAL LAW

To interpret and explain the conventions and their provisions, we will use methods of treaty interpretation generally accepted in public international law as expressed in Article 31 of the Vienna Convention on the Law of Treaties, Article 38 of the Statute of International Court of Justice (ICJ) and Guideline 3.1.5.1 of the Guide to Practice on Reservations to Treaties of the International Law Commission.[12] For the interpretation and explanation of the UN narcotic drugs conventions we will therefore in the first place use the convention text, the convention system and/or the context of the provisions and the rationale for the convention, and in the second place, the preparatory history (travaux preparatoires), the official UN Commentaries[13] on the conventions and relevant literature.

With regard to the UN Commentaries, it must be noted that these date back to approximately the same period as the conventions they refer to. In other words, these Commentaries are not very recent, but that does not mean that they are obsolete. After all, the texts of the conventions they relate to have remained the same, even though the meaning of provisions in the convention

available on: http://www.undrugcontrol.info/en/issues/cannabis/item/2400-european-cannabis-policies-under-attack.

12 Included in Report of the ILC on the Work of its 63rd session, General Assembly, Official Records, 66th Session, Supplement n° 10, Addendum 1, *UN Doc.* A/66/10/Add.1. (2011); see also the comments there on Guideline 3.1.5.1 on pp. 359 ff.

13 The UN Commentary on the Single Convention (United Nations, *Commentary on the Single Convention on Narcotic Drugs, 1961*, New York: 1973) was created under the supervision of the United Nations' Secretary-General to implement ECOSOC Resolution 914 D (XXXIV), *UN Doc.* E/RES/1962/914(XXXIV)D, 3 August 1962: '1. Requests the Secretary-General to prepare a legal commentary on the Single Convention, giving an interpretation of the provisions of the convention in the light of the relevant conference proceedings and other material'. The UN Commentary on the Protocol (United Nations, *Commentary on the Protocol Amending the Single Convention on Narcotic Drugs, 1961*, New York: 1976) was also created under the responsibility of the UN. In the same sense as the Commentary on the Single Convention, the UN Commentary on the Illicit Traffic Convention (United Nations, *Commentary on the United Nations Convention Against Illicit Traffic in Narcotic Drugs and Psychotropic Substances*, Vienna: 1988) was created to implement ECOSOC Resolution 1993/42, *UN Doc.* E/RES/ 1993/42, 27 July 1993.

may change as a result of state practice or generally accepted interpretations of the Convention. In this chapter, we will also look at whether these changes have occurred in the UN narcotic drugs conventions.[14] Where there are no such changes, the UN Commentaries are relevant in any case. In view of the way in which these Commentaries were created, and given the fact that they rely considerably on the preparatory history of the conventions, as subsidiary means for the determination of public international law they are in line with Article 31 ('A special meaning shall be given to a term if it is established that the parties so intended') and Article 32 of the Vienna Convention on the Law of Treaties ('the preparatory work of the treaty') and also Article 38(1)(d) of the ICJ Statute: ('the teachings of the most highly qualified publicists of the various nations, as subsidiary means for the determination of rules of law').

The assessments of international bodies designated to supervise the implementation of the conventions – such as the International Narcotics Control Board (INCB) and the Commission on Narcotic Drugs (CND) – are not referred to in the interpretation and explanation of the conventions and their provisions in first instance. These assessments will be discussed independently later. This approach makes it possible to come to a legal and independent assessment of the content and scope of the obligations under the conventions first, so that the insights of these bodies do not influence the assessment from the very beginning. The assessments of these bodies are not without importance, we admit, and that is why they deserve our attention, but as we will explain later, this does not mean that they are always decisive by definition.[15]

Where more specific doctrines of public international law play an important part – for example with regard to state practice and reservations – we rely on both relevant literature and the work of the International Law Commission (ILC). This commission was set up by the United Nations in 1948 to promote the development and codification of international law. The work of the ILC is generally seen as the authoritative representation of the content of international law as reflected in the generally recognized sources of public international law. In addition to, amongst others, the Vienna Convention on the Law of Treaties, we will therefore also refer to the work of the ILC.

2.2. CONVENTION ON NARCOTIC DRUGS 1961 AS AMENDED BY THE 1972 PROTOCOL

The Single Convention on Narcotic Drugs, 1961, as amended by the Protocol amending the Single Convention on Narcotic Drugs, 1961 (Single Convention) is

[14] See section 2.5.
[15] See the introduction to section 2.4.

essentially a continuation and extension of the international legal infrastructure for drug control that was developed between 1909 and 1953.[16] This convention has two fundamental goals. It aims to ensure that narcotic drugs are available for medical use if they are indispensable for alleviating pain and suffering and also for scientific purposes.[17] At the same time, the convention aims to guarantee that the use of narcotic drugs is exclusively restricted to those medical and scientific purposes.[18] To this end, the convention intends to make an effective contribution to combating the serious evil that is addiction to narcotic drugs on a personal level, as well as the many social and economic dangers that it presents to mankind.[19] In short: the convention focuses on eliminating the circulation of narcotic drugs for purposes other than medical or scientific ones.

To achieve these fundamental objectives, the original Single Convention of 1961 aimed to implement changes to the existing international control regime in three areas. Its introduction implied the replacement of many multilateral drug treaties with one convention, led to a reduction of the number of international treaty bodies concerned with the control of narcotic drugs, and also intended to put stricter controls on the production of opium and to increase international control to include the cultivation of cannabis plants among other things.[20] A more pronounced prohibitive approach manifested itself, for example in various obligations to resort to criminal law, also with regard to cannabis. The aim of the 1972 Protocol was to specify more clearly certain obligations for states, including with regard to combating cultivation, production, trade in and consumption of cannabis.[21] At the same time, the Single Convention shows itself to be a compromise between the various interests of different categories of states.[22] The question now is what those obligations

---

16 Senate Canada, *Cannabis: Our Position for a Canadian Public Policy. Report of the Senate Special Committee on Illegal Drugs*, 2002, p. 451. For a short overview of that earlier infrastructure, see T. Blom, *Opiumwetgeving en drugsbeleid*, Deventer: Kluwer, 2008, pp. 1–19; Tom Blom, *Drugs in het recht, recht onder druk*, Deel 1 (diss. Rotterdam), Deventer: Gouda Smit, 1998, pp. 29–56; and for the discussion that preceded the Single Convention Adolf Lande, 'The Single Convention on Narcotic Drugs, 1961', 16 *International Organization* 4 (1962), pp. 776–797; Jay Sinha, *The History and Development of the Leading International Drug Control Conventions*, Ottawa: Library of Parliament, Parliamentary Research Branch, 2001; David R. Bewley-Taylor & Martin Jelsma, 'Fifty Years of the 1961 Single Convention on Narcotic Drugs: A Reinterpretation', *Series on Legislative Reform of Drug Policies*, No. 12, March 2011.

17 See the Preamble to the Single Convention.

18 See also United Nations, *Commentary on the Single Convention on Narcotic Drugs, 1961*, New York: 1973, p. 110.

19 Ibid. See also David R. Bewley-Taylor & Martin Jelsma, 'Fifty Years of the 1961 Single Convention on Narcotic Drugs: A Reinterpretation', *Series on Legislative Reform of Drug Policies*, No. 12, March 2011, p. 1.

20 UNODC, *A Century of International Drug Control*, Vienna: United Nations, 2008, p. 61.

21 Ibid, p. 63.

22 For such categories, see section 2.1.1 above.

entail, what the scope of these obligations is and to what extent these obligations permit any exceptions. The following applies to the amended Single Convention, unless it is explicitly stated that it concerns the original Convention.

2.2.1. THE STATUS OF CANNABIS IN THE SINGLE CONVENTION

The Single Convention defines 'cannabis' as 'the flowering or fruiting tops of the cannabis plant (excluding the seeds and leaves when not accompanied by the tops) from which the resin has not been extracted, by whatever name they may be designated'.[23] This includes the tops from both female and male plants, whether they are dried or not.[24] This is often called weed or marijuana. 'Cannabis plant' means any plant of the genus Cannabis. 'Cannabis resin' means the separated resin, whether crude or purified, obtained from the cannabis plant.[25] This is often referred to as hash or hashish. The term 'cannabis' will be interpreted in a broad sense hereafter, namely cannabis plants, cannabis resin and the flowering or fruiting tops of the cannabis plant. If cannabis is interpreted only in the latter strict sense in accordance with the Convention definition, we will explicitly state this. Incidentally, the Single Convention only refers to cannabis as a – legal or illegal – narcotic drug: it does not apply to the cultivation of the cannabis plant exclusively for industrial purposes (fibre and seed) or for horticultural purposes, as explicitly stipulated by Article 28 of the Single Convention.[26]

The extent to which the provisions of the Convention are applicable with regard to a certain 'narcotic drug' ('drug') depends on the Schedule or list, annexed to the Convention, in which the drug has been included. The Convention has four Schedules: I, II, III and IV.[27] Cannabis – in the sense of flowering and fruiting tops of the cannabis plant – and cannabis resin are included in Schedule I as well as Schedule IV. That means that the narcotic drug cannabis comes under the strictest regime the Convention provides for.[28]

---

23 Article 1(1)(b) of the Single Convention.

24 United Nations, *Commentary on the Single Convention on Narcotic Drugs, 1961*, New York: 1973, p. 2.

25 Article 1(1)(c) and (d) of the Single Convention respectively.

26 Article 2(9) of the Single Convention also states that – under strict conditions – parties are not required to apply the provisions of this convention to drugs which are commonly used in industry for other than medical or scientific purposes. For example, the production of *Coca Cola* qualifies for this exception; see David R. Bewley-Taylor & Martin Jelsma, 'Regime change: Re-visiting the 1961 Single Convention on Narcotic Drugs', 23 *International Journal of Drug Policy* 2012, pp. 72–81 on p. 78.

27 Article 1(1)(u) of the Single Convention.

28 Less stringent regime applies to Schedule II, which is not relevant here, and Schedule III deals with preparations.

The objective of this classification was to encourage states to apply the strictest control measures to cannabis.[29] Therefore, there is no recognition at all of the differentiation between so-called soft drugs and hard drugs. Narcotic drugs in Schedule I are subject to all generic measures of supervision under the Convention.[30] Since flowering and fruiting tops of the cannabis plant and cannabis resin are also included in Schedule IV, additional special obligations pursuant to Article 2(5) of the Single Convention also apply. Furthermore, in respect of flowering and fruiting cannabis tops and the cannabis plant and leaves, Article 28 of the Single Convention[31] (control of the cannabis plant) and Article 22 of the Single Convention[32] (cultivation of the cannabis plant among other items) for the cannabis plant apply as well. The reason to place cannabis – together with heroin for example – in the most serious category of narcotic drugs via Schedule I and Schedule IV was because this drug was widely misused.[33] The representative of the United States even called cannabis 'extremely dangerous'.[34] It was not until later that the World Health Organization (WHO) acknowledged that cannabis can have medical value.[35]

Moreover, the Single Convention provides for a procedure to transfer narcotic drugs from one Schedule to another or to delete it from a Schedule altogether.[36] The Commission on Narcotic Drugs (CND)[37] can do this with a majority decision following a recommendation to that effect by the WHO. The reclassification or deletion can be challenged by every state party before the Economic and Social Council (ECOSOC), which will then make the modification the subject of a new study. ECOSOC may confirm, change, or revoke the decision by the CND with a majority decision, which will be final. Given the existence of this possibility to make changes, we will always indicate

---

29 See David R. Bewley-Taylor & Martin Jelsma, 'Regime change: Re-visiting the 1961 Single Convention on Narcotic Drugs', 23 *International Journal of Drug Policy* 2012, pp. 72–81, pp. 76 and 77; see also p. 80, where they note that this classification came about without a solid basis.

30 Article 2(1) of the Single Convention.

31 Article 2(6) and (7) of the Single Convention.

32 Article 2(6) of the Single Convention.

33 Jay Sinha, *The History and Development of the Leading International Drug Control Conventions*, Ottawa: Library of Parliament, Parliamentary Research Branch, 2001, p. 22.

34 United Nations, 'Conference for the adoption of a Single Convention on Narcotic Drugs, New York, 24 January–25 March 1961, Official Records, Volume II', *UN Doc.* E/CONF. 34/24/Add.1, p. 107.

35 See also James H. Mills, 'Science, Diplomacy and Cannabis: The Evidence Base and the International Drugs Regulatory System, 1924–1961', in: John Collins (ed.), *Governing the Global Drug Wars*, London: London School of Economics, 2012, pp. 28–29.

36 For the possibilities and the procedure, see Article 3 of the Single Convention. See also Robin Room & Sarah McKay, *Roadmaps for Reforming the UN Drug Conventions*, Oxford: Beckley Foundation Press, 2012, p. 11.

37 For more information on this, see section 2.2.5.

hereafter what the effects would be in terms of the obligations if cannabis were to be deleted from a Schedule. Incidentally, as far as we could see, not a single country has to date tried to transfer cannabis to another Schedule or to have it deleted from the Schedules by means of this procedure.[38]

2.2.2. THE SINGLE CONVENTION'S OBLIGATIONS REGARDING CANNABIS

i. General

It follows from the foregoing that the obligations regarding cannabis have four legal bases: 1. the inclusion of flowering and fruiting tops of the cannabis plant and cannabis resin in Schedule I (Article 2(1)); 2. the inclusion of flowering and fruiting tops of the cannabis plant and cannabis resin in Schedule IV (Article 2(5)); 3. the applicability of special provisions for cannabis plants (Article 2(6) and (7)); 4. the applicability of special provisions for flowering and fruiting tops of the cannabis plant and cannabis leaves (Article 2(6)). These obligations will be discussed below. To that end, it is useful to clarify a few terminology issues.

ii. The Concepts of Cultivation, Production and Manufacture

The Convention uses terms such as cultivation, production and manufacture. These have different meanings, and not all the Convention's obligations apply to all these activities. *Cultivation* of drugs is differentiated from production and manufacture in the Convention. In the case of cannabis, the term cultivation only covers the cultivation or growing of the cannabis plant.[39] Other activities regarding cannabis are not included, although cultivation – together with trading – is a form of illicit traffic[40] if this takes place contrary to the Convention. These other activities can be production or manufacture. According to the UN Commentary, production refers to more agricultural activities, whereas

38 Also UNODC, *A Century of International Drug Control*, Vienna: United Nations, 2008, p. 82. There seems to be an intention to discuss the modification of the Schedules regarding cannabis during the UN General Assembly Special Session on Drugs (UNGASS) 2016; see Marie Nougier, 'Informal Drug Policy Dialogue Report. Warsaw, Poland, 14th to 16th February 2013', May 2013, p. 27, available on: http://www.diogenis.info/ckfinder/userfiles/files/Informal%20Drug%20Policy%20Dialogue%20in%20Warsaw_FINAL.pdf. However, this is not considered likely to succeed by Scenario Team appointed by the Organization of American States, *Scenarios for the Drug Problem in the Americas 2013–2025*, Washington: Organization of American States 2013, p. 48.

39 See Article 1(1)(i) of the Single Convention.

40 See Article 1(1)(l) of the Single Convention.

manufacture involves more industrial activities.[41] *Production* in the definition of the Convention – insofar as this is relevant here – means the separation of cannabis (in the sense of flowering and fruiting tops of the cannabis plant) and cannabis resin from the plants from which they are obtained.[42] Admittedly, the removal of the leaves from the cannabis plant is covered by Article 28 of the Single Convention, but at present this cannot be classified as production or manufacture, because cannabis leaves are not included in a Schedule. If cannabis leaves were to be included in one, then their removal would not constitute production but manufacture instead.[43] *Manufacture* covers all processes, other than production, by which drugs may be obtained and includes refining as well as the transformation of drugs into other drugs.[44]

a. Obligations Regarding the Flowering and Fruiting Tops of the Cannabis Plant and Cannabis Resin because of the Inclusion in Schedule I

With regard to the obligations that apply to the narcotic drugs on Schedule I, a rudimentary distinction can be made between general obligations, obligations to furnish information, obligations to limit manufacture and import, obligations to introduce a licensing system for drugs for medical or scientific purposes, the obligation to prohibit possession, obligations related to criminal law, obligations to prosecute and obligations to take measures to combat the abuse of drugs. The deletion of cannabis – that is to say: flowering and fruiting tops of the cannabis plant and cannabis resin – from Schedule I (and consequently from Schedule IV[45]) would mean that these obligations would no longer be applicable. If, however, it was only a question of transferring cannabis from Schedule I to Schedule II, nearly all generic obligations remain valid: only the obligations in paragraphs 2 and 5 of Article 30 about the trade in and the dispensation of drugs (for medical or scientific purposes) would no longer apply.[46]

I. General Obligations: Article 4 of the Single Convention

Article 4 of the Single Convention contains the most important general obligations. Because of this provision, the states parties must take the

---

41 United Nations, *Commentary on the Single Convention on Narcotic Drugs, 1961*, New York: 1973, pp. 26–27 (no. 1–2).

42 Article 1(1)(t) of the Single Convention.

43 United Nations, *Commentary on the Single Convention on Narcotic Drugs, 1961*, New York: 1973, p. 18 (no. 7) and p. 246 (no. 2).

44 Article 1(1)(n) of the Single Convention.

45 See Article 2(5) of the Single Convention.

46 For that matter, a transfer from Schedule I to Schedule II would mean that cannabis would need to be deleted from Schedule IV (see Article 2(5) of the Single Convention); see section 2.2.2.ii.b. for the question what the consequences of the deletion from Schedule IV would be.

necessary legislative and administrative measures – in short – to implement the Convention (which is a normal obligation under public international law), to cooperate with other states in the execution of the provisions of the Convention (see also Articles 35 and 36 of the Single Convention) and – '[s]ubject to the provisions of this Convention' to 'limit exclusively to medical and scientific purposes the production, manufacture, export, import, distribution of, trade in, use and possession' of drugs such as cannabis. Because this provision is not very specific in how these obligations should be fulfilled, the states parties have considerable discretion for their own individual approach. That does not alter the fact that it would not be compatible with the text of this provision to legalize the cultivation of cannabis for example or permit it in any other way.

The UN Commentary on Article 4 of the Single Convention also states that parties are not allowed to legalize the possession of drugs for anything other than 'medical or scientific purposes'.[47] In section 2.2.3.i. – where this exception will be discussed at length – we will see that this exception has a restricted if not very restricted meaning, which was chosen deliberately and explicitly, and that the phrase 'medical purposes' is to be interpreted rather narrowly from a linguistic point of view. It will also become clear there that cannabis cultivation, delivery and trafficking with a view to supplying the so-called retail shops cannot be subsumed under this medical and scientific exception. Consequently, Article 4 of the Single Convention rules out the legalization of cannabis cultivation for retail shops with a view to recreational use, since this cultivation implies the possession of flowering and fruiting tops of the cannabis plant and/or cannabis resin at some point. However, the prohibition of legalization which ensues from Article 4 of the Single Convention, does not in itself entail an obligation of criminalization, as restrictions can also be imposed by means of administrative law, for example. Later on, however, we will show that the required legislative measures also need to include criminalizations.[48]

II. Obligations to Furnish Information and the 'Estimate System'

Another general obligation is the obligation of Article 18 of the Single Convention to furnish information to the Secretary-General that the CND may request as being necessary for the performance of its functions.

More importantly, there is also an obligation to provide information under the system provided for by the Convention, which system aims to keep strict

[47] United Nations, *Commentary on the Single Convention on Narcotic Drugs, 1961*, New York: 1973, p. 113 (no. 25).

[48] See also United Nations, *Commentary on the Single Convention on Narcotic Drugs, 1961*, New York: 1973, pp. 111–113 (nos. 15–25).

control over all stages of the drug economy, the so-called 'estimate system' in the Articles 12 to 21bis of the Single Convention.[49] This system also enables states to guarantee that narcotic drugs are sufficiently available for medical and scientific purposes.[50] Article 19 of the Single Convention requires states to furnish the International Narcotics Control Board each year with estimates on the quantities of drugs to be consumed for medical and scientific purposes; and on the stocks of drugs to be held as at 31 December of the year to which the estimates relate. The obligation also applies in connection with all narcotic drugs of Schedule I and therefore also to flowering and fruiting tops of the cannabis plant and cannabis resin.[51]

Furthermore, the states parties are required by virtue of Article 20 of the Single Convention to furnish the INCB with statistical data about, among other things, the production, manufacture, consumption,[52] import and export, seizure and stocks of drugs.[53] The statistical data are to show whether the country has exceeded the limits for the quantities of manufactured and imported drugs (see below). The data should also provide insight into the extent of the illicit trafficking, the effectiveness of enforcement and/or whether the possibility to obtain drugs on medical prescription is being abused.[54]

III. Limits to Quantities as Regards Manufacture and Import

Next, Article 21 of the Single Convention (in the context of the 'estimate system') imposes limits on the manufacture and import of drugs or – insofar as this is relevant here – flowering and fruiting tops of the cannabis plant and cannabis resin.[55] Roughly speaking, this means that the total quantities

---

49 See United Nations, *Commentary on the Single Convention on Narcotic Drugs, 1961*, New York: 1973, p. 263 (no. 1) and also p. 155 (nos. 1–2) and p. 221 (no. 1).

50 T.M.C. Asser Instituut, *Experimenteren met het Gedogen van de Teelt van Cannabis ten Behoeve van de Bevoorrading van Coffeeshops – Internationaal rechtelijke en Europees rechtelijke aspecten*, Den Haag, 2005, p. 7 (i.e., Asser Institute – Centre for International & European Law; *Experimenting with tolerating the cultivation of cannabis for the supply of coffee shops – aspects of international and European law*, The Hague, 2005).

51 See also United Nations, *Commentary on the Single Convention on Narcotic Drugs, 1961*, New York: 1973, p. 221 (no. 3); but quantities of cannabis that are governed by Article 49 are excluded: see p. 226 (no. 9), p. 228 (no. 6), p. 230 (no. 3).

52 According to Article 1(2) of the Single Convention, a drug is considered as 'consumed' 'when it has been supplied to any person or enterprise for retail distribution, medical use or scientific research'. The term consumption is construed accordingly.

53 For the definition of production and manufacture see above in section 2.2.2.ii.

54 United Nations, *Commentary on the Single Convention on Narcotic Drugs, 1961*, New York: 1973, p. 243 (no. 2).

55 Harvesting cannabis leaves (without the tops) of cannabis plants in itself does not constitute manufacture nor production, as these leaves are not included in the Schedules; see United Nations, *Commentary on the Single Convention on Narcotic Drugs, 1961*, New York: 1973, p. 246 (no. 2) and p. 255 (no. 1).

of manufacture and import of flowering and fruiting tops of the cannabis plant and cannabis resin may not exceed the quantities needed for medical and scientific purposes, for the manufacture of other drugs and preparations and other substances for the export, for replenishing stocks and for special purposes.[56] For each of these possibilities, these are quantities allowed under the Convention. The obligations to furnish information under the Convention and the related 'estimate system' to keep international control of the quantities of drugs circulating in the states parties and which are allowed to be available there, show that the Convention aims to keep control of drugs in an explicit and accurate manner and how it wants to restrict their availability forcefully.

IV. Licensing System for Producers, Manufacturers and Traders

The manufacture of, trade in and distribution of drugs is only allowed insofar as this happens for purposes recognized under the convention: medical and scientific (and special) purposes.[57] In order to supervise this – and by extension the drug economy – the Convention requires that states only permit the manufacture (Article 29) and the trade and distribution (Article 30)[58] when a licence has been granted, unless these activities take place in a state-owned company. To this end, states will have to create a licensing system with supervision and inspection by virtue of Article 34 of the Single Convention. Of course, the granting of permits is only possible for the purposes recognized under the Convention. This is clear not only from the system of the Convention (see in particular Article 4(c) see above under 2.2.2.i.), but also from the requirement that licensees must have adequate qualifications 'for the effective and faithful execution of the provisions of such laws and regulations as are enacted in pursuance thereof' (Article 34 (a)). The implication of this is also that granting permits for the cultivation of drugs – and therefore of flowering and fruiting tops of the cannabis plant and cannabis resin – for purposes other than the recognized purposes for medicine and science is not possible within the framework of the Convention. Such manufacture therefore constitutes a breach of the Convention's provisions.

V. Ban on Possession of Drugs: Article 33 of the Single Convention

Article 33 of the Single Convention stipulates that the states parties must not permit the possession of drugs – and that includes (insofar as this is

---

56 See for more information on this section 2.2.3.i.

57 Ibid. See also United Nations, *Commentary on the Single Convention on Narcotic Drugs, 1961*, New York: 1973, p. 263 (no. 1).

58 Moreover, Article 31 imposes special limitations on international trade – export – of drugs.

relevant here) flowering and fruiting tops of the cannabis plant and cannabis resin – without legal authority. According to the UN Commentary, this provision must be taken in relation to Article 4 of the Single Convention. Therefore, legal permission can only be given for the recognized purposes of a medical and scientific nature[59] and not for recreational use. However, because of the link to Article 4 of the Single Convention, this is about more than simply 'not permitting' (as this might still suggest that the state only needs to abstain from granting permits, but is not required to use a ban)[60]: the states parties must restrict possession exclusively to medical and scientific purposes according to Article 4(c) of the Single Convention. This implies activity on the part of the state and therefore that it must prohibit possession for recreational use.[61] The UN Commentary even states that it is clear that Article 33 of the Single Convention implies an obligation of seizure if drugs are found on a person for non-medical or non-scientific personal use.[62]

Even if one ignored this supposed obligation of seizure, the foregoing still means that possession – and consequently for example also cultivation and distribution – for personal recreational use is not to be permitted and must be[63] prohibited outside the medical and scientific purposes.[64] This is the case then *a fortiori* in relation to retail shops. As noted before, cannabis cultivation, delivery and trade with the objective of supplying retail shops implies the possession of flowering and fruiting tops of the cannabis plant and/or cannabis resin at some point, so that Article 33 of the Single Convention in that respect also blocks the way towards legalizing, tolerating by virtue of a policy or otherwise regulating such supply other than for the above-mentioned recognized purposes. Seeing that allowing possession is not permitted under the Convention, it would appear that a policy-based tolerance or even actually permitting any possession is not allowed.

Article 33 of the Single Convention does not contain any explicit obligation to criminalize possessing or holding cannabis, but if there is evidence of intent, Article 36 of the Single Convention requires that this is criminalized

59 United Nations, *Commentary on the Single Convention on Narcotic Drugs, 1961*, New York: 1973, p. 402 (no. 1).

60 See in that sense and therefore at any rate contrary to the UN Commentary: David R. Bewley-Taylor & Martin Jelsma, 'The Limits of Latitude. The UN drug control conventions', *Series on Legislative Reform of Drug Policies*, No. 18, March 2012, p. 5.

61 See also United Nations, *Commentary on the Single Convention on Narcotic Drugs, 1961*, New York: 1973, p. 113 (no. 22).

62 United Nations, *Commentary on the Single Convention on Narcotic Drugs, 1961*, New York: 1973, pp. 402–403 (nos. 3 and 6) and p. 113 (no. 24). For more information about this see later in this section (2.2.2.i.a.VIII).

63 The question whether that should be a prohibition under criminal law will be discussed below under vi.

64 See also Alfons Noll, 'Drug abuse and penal provisions of the international drug control treaties', 29 *Bulletin on Narcotics* 4 (1977), pp. 41–57 (para A).

(see below for more information). Incidentally, the possession of cannabis leaves (without the tops) does not need to be prohibited, as these are not mentioned in the Schedules.[65]

VI. Obligations to Criminalize and Penalize: Article 36 of the Single Convention

The Convention contains an obligation to criminalize a wide range of deliberate acts regarding drugs, including – to the extent that it is relevant here – flowering and fruiting tops of the cannabis plant and cannabis resin. The obligations apply only to acts that are contrary to the provisions of the Convention: permissible acts relating to medical and scientific purposes are not covered by it. Apart from that, criminal law strongly influences the Convention's perspective on drug problems. This is also the case with regard to cultivation.

Article 36(1) of the Single Convention requires each party to ensure that 'cultivation, production, manufacture, extraction, preparation, possession, offering, offering for sale, distribution, purchase, sale, delivery on any terms whatsoever, brokerage, dispatch, dispatch in transit, transport, importation and exportation of drugs contrary to the provisions of this Convention, and any other action which in the opinion of such Party may be contrary to the provisions of this Convention, shall be punishable offences when committed intentionally'. Acts committed unintentionally, for example culpable conduct, are therefore outside the scope of this obligation.[66] Strictly speaking, since the cannabis plant as such is not included in the Schedules, the obligation to criminalize cultivation does not apply directly to cultivation of the cannabis plant.[67] However, to the extent that growing cannabis plants leads to the cultivation of flowering and fruiting tops of the cannabis plant and/or cannabis resin, the growing of cannabis plants does fall under Article 36(1) of the Single Convention. The above implies that the obligations of criminalization from Article 36(1) of the Single Convention impede the legalization or decriminalization of cannabis cultivation, delivery and trafficking with the objective of supplying retail shops. The obligation of criminalization does not apply to acts with regard to cannabis leaves (without tops), since these leaves are not included in the Schedules and consequently do not qualify as drugs.[68]

---

65 United Nations, *Commentary on the Single Convention on Narcotic Drugs, 1961*, New York: 1973, p. 403 (no. 8) and also p. 246 (no. 2) and p. 255 (no. 1). See for more information section 2.2.2.ii.d.

66 United Nations, *Commentary on the Single Convention on Narcotic Drugs, 1961*, New York: 1973, p. 403 (no. 8) and also p. 428 (no. 2).

67 See in this respect the obligations not necessarily related to criminal law in the Articles 22 and 28 of the Single Convention and for more information below in this section (2.2.2.ii.c).

68 United Nations, *Commentary on the Single Convention on Narcotic Drugs, 1961*, New York: 1973, p. 427 (no. 7).

In addition to this, consumption was knowingly excluded from Article 36 of the Single Convention, so that there is no obligation of criminalization under the Convention with regard to that either.[69]

It is worth noting that there is a discussion going on about the question whether intentional possession of drugs should be punishable no matter what, or only if it is intentional possession with a view to distribution.[70] In the latter case, possession by drug users for personal recreational use would not come under the obligation of criminalization. In itself, the literal text of Article 36 of the Single Convention offers no departure points for such an interpretation. After all, in this Article intentional possession is covered by the obligation of criminalization without any reservations. Moreover, criminalization of the possession of drugs for personal consumption is more consistent with the rationale and the system of the Convention, which aims to eliminate completely the circulation of narcotic drugs for purposes other than medical or scientific ones.[71] It is remarkable, however, that this obligation does not extend to drug use as such. Because drug use at any time also implies the possession of drugs, it can be argued, given the system of the Convention, that there is no obligation of criminalization for intentional possession of drugs purely for personal consumption.[72] A systematic look at Article 36 of the Single Convention does not inexorably lead to this tolerant interpretation: after all, it is perfectly conceivable that one criminalizes possession but not consumption, because that way persons who have been shown to have consumed drugs are not going to be incriminated at any rate and enforcement would then be limited to checks on the presence of drugs and is not aimed at applying drugs tests to persons to check whether they have consumed drugs either. Be that as it may, it would not make much difference. Even if one chooses to adopt the liberal interpretation of the Convention system, the fact still remains that states cannot allow the possession of cannabis for purely personal consumption (except for medical and scientific purposes) by virtue of Article 33 of the Single Convention as discussed above. In summary: possession for personal consumption may

---

69 United Nations, *Commentary on the Single Convention on Narcotic Drugs, 1961*, New York: 1973, p. 428 (no. 7). See also Dave Bewley-Taylor & Martin Jelsma, 'The Limits of Latitude. The UN drug control conventions', *Series on Legislative Reform of Drug Policies*, No. 18, March 2012, p. 5.

70 United Nations, *Commentary on the Single Convention on Narcotic Drugs, 1961*, New York: 1973, p. 112 (no. 18) and pp. 402–403 (nos. 1–3).

71 See also Article 4(c) of the Single Convention.

72 See for example Neil Brett Boister, *The Suppression of Illicit Drugs Through International Law*, Nottingham: University of Nottingham, 1998, pp. 86–89; Krzysztof Krajewski, 'How flexible are the United Nations drug conventions?', 10 *International Journal of Drug Policy* 4 (1999), pp. 329–338 on p. 332; David R. Bewley-Taylor & Martin Jelsma, 'The Limits of Latitude. The UN drug control conventions', *Series on Legislative Reform of Drug Policies*, No. 18, March 2012, p. 5.

be decriminalized in that interpretation, but it still cannot be legalized or permitted.

The criminalizations must also extend to intentional participation in, conspiracy to commit these acts as well as preparing for and attempting to commit such acts.[73] What merits special attention is the fact that Article 36(2) of the Single Convention makes these obligations dependent on the limitations of a state party that ensue for that party from its 'legal system and domestic law'. This clause does not derogate from the obligation as such, it only implies that states are not beholden to modify their domestic law concepts to the terminology of the Convention.[74] Nor do they have to change the structure of participation forms to that end, nor the way in which they interpret attempts, while there is no need either to criminalize for example conspiracy in the above-mentioned drug-related acts if that is not a generally recognized legal concept in the domestic system.[75] The fact that this clause has only been included in paragraph 2 implies that such freedoms do not apply with regard to the other obligations, such as the obligations of criminalization in paragraph 1.[76] This is also reflected in the fact that the suggestions to include such a clause for the entire Article[77] or at any rate for the first paragraph as well[78] were not taken on board.

Additionally, Article 36 of the Single Convention stipulates that if it is a serious offence, the party must ensure that it is liable 'to adequate punishment particularly by imprisonment or other penalties of deprivation of liberty.' Therefore, this obligation does not apply to lesser offences.[79] Article 36 of the Single Convention goes on to stipulate all sorts of additional requirements for

---

73 Article 36(2)(a) under ii of the Single Convention. See also United Nations, *Commentary on the Single Convention on Narcotic Drugs, 1961*, New York: 1973, p. 426 (no. 6).

74 United Nations, *Commentary on the Single Convention on Narcotic Drugs, 1961*, New York: 1973, p. 430 (no. 3). See also United Nations, 'Conference for the adoption of a Single Convention on Narcotic Drugs, New York, 24 January–25 March 1961, Official Records, Volume II', *UN Doc.* E/CONF. 34/24/Add.1, pp. 233 and 237, which incidentally show that the Netherlands called for the clause.

75 United Nations, *Commentary on the Single Convention on Narcotic Drugs, 1961*, New York: 1973, pp. 432–433 (nos. 1, 2 and 5–7).

76 Please note that in paragraph 1 (and also paragraph 2) the clause of 'the constitutional limitations' still applies.

77 See United Nations, 'Conference for the adoption of a Single Convention on Narcotic Drugs, New York, 24 January–25 March 1961, Official Records, Volume II', *UN Doc.* E/CONF. 34/24/Add.1, pp. 46, 236 (proposal by India).

78 See United Nations, 'Conference for the adoption of a Single Convention on Narcotic Drugs, New York, 24 January–25 March 1961, Official Records, Volume II', *UN Doc.* E/CONF. 34/24/Add.1, p. 238 (suggestion by Yugoslavia).

79 See also Alfons Noll, 'Drug abuse and penal provisions of the international drug control treaties', 29 *Bulletin on Narcotics* 4 (1977), pp. 41–57 (para A). For information on the provisions of the convention regarding punishment see also below in this section 2.2.2.ii.a.IX.

punishment (paragraph 1(b) and paragraph 2(a)), jurisdiction (paragraph 3), proper administration of justice/*aut dedere aut judicare* (paragraph 2(a) and extradition (paragraph 2(b)).

VII. Obligation of Transposition: Article 36(4) of the Single Convention

The fourth paragraph of Article 36 of the Single Convention states that no provision of the Convention affects the principle 'that the offences to which it refers shall be defined, prosecuted and punished in conformity with the domestic law of a Party.' This clause, according to the UN Commentary, only aims to ensure that none of the provisions in the Convention is self-executing in countries where the constitution provides for the direct operation of international law.[80] The clause thereby rules out that the Convention is used directly as a basis for national action. In this way, the fourth paragraph prevents the remaining elements of Article 36 from being applied directly as criminalization or as prosecuting power for example. That should be provided for by domestic law. Article 36(4) of the Single Convention therefore implies an obligation of 'transposition': the necessity to transpose or implement the obligations of substantive, international and procedural criminal law in the Convention in national criminal law and criminal procedural law. Therefore, it is not the provision's objective to allow parties discretion in creating their own distinctive policy, which is also confirmed in the preparatory history and the UN Commentary on the Illicit Traffic Convention.[81] If this were the case, then the provisions mentioned above in Article 36(1) and (2) of the Single Convention that refer to the national legal system would in fact be superfluous, seeing that its contents would then already have been covered in a wider and more general sense by the fourth paragraph. Also, the system of Article 36 of the Single Convention implies that the fourth paragraph cannot

---

80 United Nations, *Commentary on the Single Convention on Narcotic Drugs, 1961*, New York: 1973, p. 427 (no. 8), p. 440 (no. 3).

81 See United Nations, 'Conference for the Adoption of a Convention against Illicit Traffic in Narcotic Drugs and Psychotropic Substances, Vienna, 25 November–20 December 1988, Official Records, Volume I', *UN Doc.* E/CONF. 82/16, p. 16 (no. 79); and United Nations, *Commentary on the United Nations Convention Against Illicit Traffic in Narcotic Drugs and Psychotropic Substances*, Vienna: 1988, p. 97 (no. 3.131). For a different view, see Tom Blom, *Drugs in het recht, recht onder druk*, Deel 1 (diss. Rotterdam), Deventer: Gouda Quint, 1998, p. 75 (i.e., Tom Blom, *Drugs in legislation, legislation/law under pressure*, Part 1 (dissertation Rotterdam), Deventer: Gouda Smit, 1998, p. 75); see by comparison Jos Silvis, 'De internationale juridische speelruimte voor Nederlands drugbeleid', in: Tom Blom, Hans de Doelder & Dick J. Hessing (eds.), *Naar een consistent drugbeleid. Een congresverslag*, Deventer: Gouda Quint, 1996, p. 220 (i.e., Jos Silvis, 'The room for Dutch drug policy under international law', in: Tom Blom, Hans de Doelder & Dick J. Hessing (eds.), *Towards a consistent drug policy. A conference report*, Deventer: Gouda Quint, 1996, p. 220).

be meant as a clause to create freedom of policy or room for considerations of expediency.[82]

The foregoing does not alter the fact that transposition of the Convention's obligations into national law as necessitated by Article 36(4) of the Single Convention forces each state to interpret the Convention in those places where it allows various interpretations. Moreover, prosecution on the basis of the implemented criminalizations must take place within the nation's criminal procedural law. In that respect too, Article 36(4) of the Single Convention implies that the Convention must be implemented in the national legal system, so that prosecution for the criminalization as required in the Convention will be possible. In this respect as well, the provision does not aim to grant states discretion. The fourth paragraph simply has no bearing on that.

Incidentally: even if the purpose of Article 36(4) of the Single Convention were to protect national legal systems, the expediency principle would still not preclude prosecution pursuant to the obligations under the Convention. The expediency principle (Article 167(2) of the Dutch Code of Criminal Procedure) as a rule does not prevent such prosecutions. The principle only implies that the prosecution authorities have national discretion or are authorized not to prosecute in certain cases, rather than that as such they are required to refrain from prosecution. If the fourth paragraph was meant as a clause to protect national law at all (which is not the case, as we have explained), even then the expediency principle could not be presented convincingly as a national obstacle to prosecution.[83]

VIII. Obligations Regarding Seizure

The Convention contains different obligations regarding seizure. Because these also extend to cannabis in cultivation, delivery and trafficking for retail shops, any form of permission (including legalization and policy-based tolerance) of these acts is ruled out in fact.

The seizure of drugs, substances and equipment used in or intended for the commission of any of the offences referred to in Article 36 of the

82 A comment was made in the Second Chamber of the Netherlands Parliament the other day: 'According to the Single Convention, we must criminalize certain acts but we are free to take into account our own legislation, including the expediency principle.' (*Kamerstukken II* 2012–2013, 24 077, nr. 312, p. 14) (i.e., *Dutch Parliamentary Documents II* 2012–2013, 24 077, no. 312, p. 14). This comment is probably based on an incorrect reading of Article 36(4) of the Single Convention; at any rate, the comment can be based neither on this provision nor on any other from the Single Convention.

83 For this reason, but first and foremost because Article 36(4) of the Single Convention only establishes the need for transposition, we believe that this provision – and, for that matter, the convention (see below in this section 2.2.2.ii.a.IX) – leaves no room for applying the expediency principle. See also Silvis *supra* footnote 81.

Single Convention, is covered by Article 37 of the Single Convention: 'Any drugs, substances and equipment used in or intended for the commission of any of the offences, referred to in article 36, shall be liable to seizure and confiscation.' Therefore, this applies to all acts that the parties are required to criminalize by virtue of Article 36(1) of the Single Convention and not merely insofar as they are 'serious offences'. Whereas the – non-authentic – Dutch text of the Convention stipulates that said equipment 'can' be seized, the UN Commentary assumes that states are required to do so.[84] Although the English text does not imply this absolutely either, any other interpretation is hard to defend. Really, the provision would have no meaning or added value if it referred to a power rather than an obligation, since it is evident that every state has such a power. And this also applies to the seizure referred to in Article 22(2) of the Single Convention (see below). Seizure will need to take place subject to national conditions and conditions relating to human rights; it is not a question of ruthlessly entering everywhere in search of drugs to be seized and confiscated.[85]

Finally – and once more – it must be noted that the UN Commentary states that Article 33 of the Single Convention also clearly implies an obligation of seizure if drugs for (recreational) personal consumption are found on somebody.[86] Although the UN Commentary gives no further arguments for that, it must be established at any rate that such an inherent obligation is in line with the system of the Convention, which after all uses various prohibition obligations and also the 'estimate system' in its attempt to eliminate completely the circulation of illegal drugs.[87,88]

IX. Obligations to Prosecute

One cannot find an explicit statement of a general obligation to prosecute in the Single Convention. The history of deliberations also pays only scant

84 United Nations, *Commentary on the Single Convention on Narcotic Drugs, 1961*, New York: 1973, pp. 442–443 (nos. 1–5).

85 See for example United Nations, 'Conference for the adoption of a Single Convention on Narcotic Drugs, New York, 24 January–25 March 1961, Official Records, Volume II', *UN Doc.* E/CONF. 34/24/Add.1, p. 246 (comments from Denmark and Canada); see also the comments by Yugoslavia, which demonstrate there is an absolute obligation regarding seizure.

86 United Nations, *Commentary on the Single Convention on Narcotic Drugs, 1961*, New York: 1973, pp. 402–403 (nos. 3 and 6) and p. 113 (no. 24). See section 2.2.2.ii.a.V for more information.

87 This is also evident from Article 4(c) of the Single Convention and also from the Preamble where it expresses the desire to limit the use of narcotic drugs to medical and scientific purposes and where measures are taken to achieve these objectives.

88 See also David R. Bewley-Taylor & Martin Jelsma, 'Fifty Years of the 1961 Single Convention on Narcotic Drugs: A Reinterpretation', *Series on Legislative Reform of Drug Policies*, No. 12 March 2011, pp. 1–20 on p. 9.

attention to prosecution, and the same goes for the UN Commentary. Nonetheless, given the object and purpose of the Convention (to combat drugs actively and effectively) and the content of the Convention (a system to ban drugs for recreational use) it is hard to argue that states would not be required to prosecute in the event that acts are committed which the Convention requires to be criminalized.[89] After all, the Convention aims to be an effective instrument to limit behaviours with respect to drugs to medical and scientific purposes exclusively (see Article 4(a) and (c) of the Single Convention). To that end, the parties will have to take the necessary measures 'to give effect to and carry out' the provisions of the Convention; as far as the provisions of the Convention in respect of the obligations of criminalization are concerned, it is hard to claim that such criminalization would then not have to be followed up by prosecution of the offences involved (Article 4 in conjunction with Article 36 of the Single Convention). The importance of prosecutions, sentencing and punishment in this context is also reflected in the fact that states are required to include information about this in their annual reports pursuant to Article 18(1)(a) of the Single Convention.[90]

Furthermore, Article 36(1)(a) and (b) of the Single Convention points out that parties must in principle apply a sanction involving deprivation of liberty in the event of 'serious offences' committed deliberately.[91] This will require prosecution. Under certain circumstances, however, in addition to this or as an alternative to this, states have the discretion to impose measures on 'abusers of drugs' (treatment, education, after-care, rehabilitation and social reintegration). The UN Commentary raises the question in this respect whether or not states parties then also have the discretion to abstain from prosecution. In the answer, it is assumed that the states parties are under an obligation to prosecute, although pursuant to Article 36(1)(b) of the Single Convention they are not required to convict or punish all the acts mentioned in paragraph (a).[92]

89 See also Hub Hennekens, 'Grenzen aan het opportuniteitsbeginsel. Een verkenning in relatie tot het drugsbeleid', in: Jan W. Fokkens, Piet Hein P.H.M.C. van Kempen, Henny J.B. Sackers & Paul C. Vegter (eds.), *Ad hunc modem. Opstellen over materieel strafrecht* (Machielse-bundel), Deventer: Kluwer, 2013, pp. 103–104 (i.e., Hub Hennekens, 'The limits of the expediency principle. An exploration in connection with the drug policy', in: Jan W. Fokkens, Piet Hein P.H.M.C. van Kempen, Henny J.B. Sackers & Paul C. Vegter (eds.), *Ad hunc modem. Essays on substantive criminal law* (Machielse bundle of essays), Deventer: Kluwer, 2013, pp. 103–104).

90 United Nations, *Commentary on the Single Convention on Narcotic Drugs, 1961*, New York: 1973, p. 213 (no. 4).

91 The fact that Article 36(1) of the Single Convention – also with regard to punishment – requires the states parties to provide not only an adequate legal framework, but also applies to specific drug-related offences is reflected in particular in United Nations, *Commentary on the Protocol Amending the Single Convention on Narcotic Drugs, 1961*, New York: 1976, pp. 76–78 (nos. 3–11).

92 United Nations, *Commentary on the Protocol Amending the Single Convention on Narcotic Drugs, 1961*, New York: 1976, p. 77 (no. 5).

What does that mean? Is there a legal possibility to decide against prosecution or does it only mean that while a prosecution must be brought, the judge in the criminal court may impose a treatment measure rather than a sanction involving deprivation of liberty? In terms of the obligations to punish, there is in any case room for non-prosecution for non-serious offences, since there is no specific obligation to punish these offences in Article 36 of the Single Convention. In view of the content and spirit of the Convention, it is hard to maintain that cultivation, delivery and trade in cannabis for retail shops would not qualify as serious offences in the sense of Article 36(1) of the Single Convention. The scale alone on which such cultivation, delivery, trade in and sale to consumers usually takes place cannot be squared with such a light qualification. Moreover, flowering and fruiting tops of the cannabis plant and cannabis resin are included in both Schedule I and Schedule IV, and are therefore some of the most important drugs under the Convention. From this perspective too, it seems as if fairly soon we are looking at serious offences in the case of such drugs (namely when it involves a bigger quantity than is required for personal use). To that extent, there is an obligation to prosecute. So does that obligation not exist if Article 36(1)(b) of the Single Convention applies? As we noted before, the UN Commentary is not entirely clear about this. Yet, it is certain that this provision does not apply to people if they are growers or suppliers of or traders in cannabis. After all, the provision only refers to 'abusers of drugs'. According to Article 36 of the Single Convention, only people who frequently use narcotic drugs qualify as abusers, in other words those who depend on it (addicts). Article 36(1)(b) of the Single Convention therefore does not apply to people who only use drugs occasionally, let alone non-users.[93] If this provision left any room for non-prosecution at all, it would not be useful in the context of cannabis cultivation for third parties.

Furthermore, Article 36(2)(a)iv of the Single Convention stipulates that serious offences referred to in Article 36(1) of the Single Convention committed by nationals or by foreigners 'shall be prosecuted by the Party in whose territory the offence was committed, or by the Party in whose territory the offender is found if extradition is not acceptable in conformity with the law of the Party to which application is made, and if such offender has not already been prosecuted and judgement given' (*ne bis in idem*). By using phrases such as 'should be prosecuted', 'an obligation to prosecute', and 'should [...] try him', the UN Commentary implies that Article 36(2)(a)iv of the Single Convention constitutes an obligation to prosecute.[94] While it is true that this provision refers

93 For a different and broader discussion – without going into the meaning of 'abusers' – see Krzysztof Krajewski, 'How flexible are the United Nations drug conventions?', 10 *International Journal of Drug Policy* 4 (1999), pp. 329–338 on p. 333.

94 United Nations, *Commentary on the Single Convention on Narcotic Drugs, 1961*, New York: 1973, pp. 435–436 (nos. 4–5); see also p. 388 (no. 5), which says that international agreements

to the proper administration of justice in international law in criminal matters, it also literally means that a state's nationals 'shall be prosecuted' by the state in whose territory the 'serious' offence was committed.[95] Apart from this, it is also important that the measures to fight drugs which the parties need to provide, pursuant to the Convention – including criminalizations – focus primarily on drug-related behaviour inside a party's territory. Taking into account the system of the Convention, it would not make sense if, on the one hand, the Convention presupposes an obligation to prosecute persons for 'serious' offences which the Convention requires to be criminalized if they have a cross-border aspect to them, but on the other hand, none at all in those cases where this aspect is absent. As it happens, Article 36(1)(a) and (b) of the Single Convention demonstrates that this is not the case. Moreover, it would be at odds with the object and purpose (active effective fighting of drugs) of the Convention. Since cannabis cultivation, delivery and trade for retail shops must be considered serious offences in principle, it would seem as if Article 36(2)(a) iv of the Single Convention also presupposes an obligation to prosecute persons for those offences.

Considering all that has been noted about prosecution above, one can hardly argue that tolerating cannabis cultivation in order to supply retail shops as a matter of policy is permissible on the grounds of the expediency principle under the Single Convention.[96] This must be regarded as absolutely out of the question with regard to decriminalization or even legalization.

X. Measures Against the Abuse of Drugs: Article 38 of the Single Convention

Finally, it is important – also for the discussion about legalization, decriminalization, policy-based tolerance and/or other forms of regulating cannabis cultivation for recreational use – that under Article 38 of the Single Convention, parties must 'give special attention to and take all practicable measures for the prevention of abuse of drugs and for the early identification, treatment, education, after-care, rehabilitation and social reintegration' of the users. If necessary, they must also provide information to the public 'if there

in the sense of Article 31(15) of the Single Convention 'cannot authorize Parties to fail to carry out other provisions of the Single Convention which relate to drugs in transit, in particular those requiring them to prosecute and punish acts of the illicit traffic in accordance with articles 35 and 36.'

95 In that sense, also see Neil Brett Boister, *The Suppression of Illicit Drugs Through International Law*, Nottingham: University of Nottingham, 1998, p. 186.

96 As discussed above in this section (2.2.2.ii.a.VII), Article 36(4) of the Single Convention does not allow for this either.

is a risk that abuse of drugs will become widespread', in order to prevent drug abuse.

It is interesting that whereas Article 38 of the original Single Convention only applied to 'drug addicts', this provision now has a more general and wider target group in that it refers to 'abusers of drugs'. It is not entirely clear what is meant by drug abuse. In view of the content and system on the Convention, it seems to mean: every use of narcotic drugs other than for medical or scientific purposes. This ties in with the Preamble and also Articles 2(9) and 3(3), (4) and (5) of the Single Convention, in which the term 'abuse' is used. At the same time, it is clear that the measures in Article 38 of the Single Convention are primarily relevant for people whose consumption of drugs can be said to be problematic from a physical, psychological, moral and/or social point of view.[97] At any rate, it has to be about drug users, where in principle the focus is primarily on addicts.[98]

The UN Commentary once more confirms what is already obvious from the Convention with respect to Article 38 of the Single Convention. A system of administrative control, criminalizations and penalties to keep narcotic drugs – including flowering and fruiting tops of the cannabis plant and cannabis resin – away from actual or potential victims is the essence of the Single Convention.[99] That also makes clear that the attention and measures referred to in Article 38 of the Single Convention must counteract any use other than that for medical or scientific purposes. Legalization, decriminalization, policy-based tolerance and/or other forms of regulating cannabis cultivation conflicts with that idea and therefore cannot be justified by Article 38 of the Single Convention either. This approach also implies that parties do not have the freedom to permit cannabis cultivation etc, *de jure* or *de facto* with a view to keeping the soft drugs and hard drugs markets separated.[100] This conclusion is quite separate from the fact that the Single Convention does not exactly recognize cannabis as a lighter narcotic drug, as its inclusion in both Schedule I and Schedule IV actually means it belongs to the most serious category of drugs under the Single Convention.

---

97 United Nations, *Commentary on the Protocol Amending the Single Convention on Narcotic Drugs, 1961*, New York: 1976, pp. 84–89.

98 United Nations, *Commentary on the Protocol Amending the Single Convention on Narcotic Drugs, 1961*, New York: 1976, p. 77 (nos. 4 and 6).

99 United Nations, *Commentary on the Protocol Amending the Single Convention on Narcotic Drugs, 1961*, New York: 1976, p. 83 (no. 1).

100 See for example T.M.C. Asser Instituut, *Experimenteren met het Gedogen van de Teelt van Cannabis ten Behoeve van de Bevoorrading van Coffeeshops – Internationaal rechtelijke en Europees rechtelijke aspecten*, Den Haag:, 2005, pp. 12–13 (i.e., Asser Institute – Centre for International & European Law; *Experimenting with tolerating the cultivation of cannabis for the supply of coffee shops – aspects of international and European law*, The Hague, 2005).

b. Obligations Regarding the Flowering and Fruiting Tops of the Cannabis Plant and Cannabis Resin because of the Inclusion in Schedule IV

In respect of cannabis, the Dutch representative during the drafting of the Single Convention was 'quite willing for it to be placed in Schedule IV'.[101] The inclusion of cannabis in Schedule IV entails that the additional special obligations pursuant to Article 2(5) of the Single Convention also apply to it. Deleting cannabis from Schedule IV would merely mean that only those obligations no longer apply. This concerns two obligations.

First, according to Article 2(5)(a) of the Single Convention, a party must adopt all 'special measures of control' that 'in its opinion are necessary having regard to the particularly dangerous properties' of – to the extent that it is relevant here – flowering and fruiting tops of the cannabis plant and cannabis resin. For example, one can require producers to point out to physicians the dangerous properties and limitations with regard to the therapeutic use of the drug.[102] It is up to the party to decide what is necessary in this context, but it must use this provision in good faith.[103] The party will have to take measures that it deems necessary. If the party is of the opinion that action in the criminal law sphere is indispensable for this, it will have to provide for that action.

Secondly, Article 2(5)(b) of the Single Convention seeks to ensure that parties implement a virtually total ban on flowering and fruiting tops of the cannabis plant and cannabis resin. By virtue of this provision, the party is required to 'prohibit the production, manufacture, export and import of, trade in, possession or use' of any drug from Schedule IV, except when and only if this is necessary 'for medical and scientific *research* '(emphasis added).[104] The exception allowed by the provision is very limited, since it only applies to 'research',[105] so that for example even medical treatment or pain relief are not covered by it, whereas they are permissible under the wider exception of 'medical and scientific purposes'. There was some controversy around the

101 United Nations, 'Conference for the adoption of a Single Convention on Narcotic Drugs, New York, 24 January–25 March 1961, Official Records, Volume II', *UN Doc.* E/CONF. 34/24/Add.1, p. 175.

102 United Nations, *Commentary on the Single Convention on Narcotic Drugs, 1961*, New York: 1973, p. 65 (no. 4).

103 See also Article 26 of the Vienna Convention on the Law of Treaties (*Pacta sunt servanda*).

104 Cultivation is not mentioned explicitly in Article 2(5)(b) of the Single Convention, but a prohibition of the acts that are mentioned in the provisions, such as possession, would also exclude cultivation de facto. The generally applicable Article 22 of the Single Convention does have an explicit bearing on cultivation; see section 2.2.2.ii.c.I below about this.

105 For example, it covers specific authorized controlled clinical trials; see United Nations, 'Conference for the adoption of a Single Convention on Narcotic Drugs, New York, 24 January–25 March 1961, Official Records, Volume II', *UN Doc.* E/CONF. 34/24/Add.1, pp. 3, 33 and pp. 81–82.

question whether the Convention had to require parties to implement such a prohibition,[106] but eventually the Convention here too stipulates that the party only has to implement it 'if in its opinion the prevailing conditions in its country render it the most appropriate means of protecting the public health and welfare'. Once again, the state will not be allowed to abuse this clause and will therefore have to act in good faith.[107] Thus, according to the UN Commentary, a prohibition in the sense of Article 2(5)(b) of the Single Convention can be 'appropriate' for the protection of public health and welfare if the members of the medical profession administer or prescribe narcotics drugs from Schedule IV too easily.[108] The commentary also shows clearly that the underlying assumption of this view is that cannabis can hardly be of any medical value.[109]

Since the obligations in Article 2(5)(a) and (b) of the Single Convention are informed by the assessment of the party – provided this is carried out in good faith – which depends on time and place, the party has the discretion to take knowledge of the effect of cannabis and its threat to society into account when considering whether or not to give substance to these obligations and if yes, in which way that is to be done. In short: a party that sees no reason for it, will not need to apply special control measures in the sense of paragraph (a) or the prohibition of paragraph (b) of Article 2(5) of the Single Convention to cannabis.

c. Obligations Regarding Cannabis Plants: Articles 22 and 28 of the Single Convention

The Convention does not only impose obligations regarding cannabis on the parties by mentioning it in the Schedules, this also happens directly because some provisions concern cannabis. Therefore, these obligations can only be avoided legally either by changing or denouncing the Convention. Denouncing the Convention only to re-join it with the formulation of a reservation with respect to Articles 22 and 28 of the Single Convention, is not possible under the Convention itself, as Articles 49 and 50 of the Single Convention do not allow this.[110]

---

106 United Nations, *Commentary on the Single Convention on Narcotic Drugs, 1961*, New York: 1973, p. 65 (no. 6).

107 United Nations, *Commentary on the Single Convention on Narcotic Drugs, 1961*, New York: 1973, p. 67 (no. 8).

108 United Nations, *Commentary on the Single Convention on Narcotic Drugs, 1961*, New York: 1973, p. 67 (no. 9).

109 United Nations, *Commentary on the Single Convention on Narcotic Drugs, 1961*, New York: 1973, pp. 66–69 (nos. 7–9 and 14–15).

110 See sections 2.2.4 and 4.2.3.

I. General Prohibition of Cultivation of Cannabis Plants if Necessary: Article 22 of the Single Convention

Pursuant to Article 22(1) of the Single Convention, parties must prohibit growing or cultivating the cannabis plant among other things, if 'the prevailing conditions in the country or a territory of a Party render the prohibition of the cultivation of the opium poppy, the coca bush or the cannabis plant the most suitable measure, in its opinion, for protecting the public health and welfare and preventing the diversion of drugs into the illicit traffic'. Paragraph 2 adds an obligation of seizure to this.[111] Article 22 does not require parties to prohibit cannabis cultivation if it only yields relatively small quantities of cannabis.[112] The reason for this is that this would not be necessary to protect 'the public health and welfare'. In other respects, however, these objectives must be interpreted broadly: when public health and welfare in other countries necessitate a prohibition, a party is obliged to introduce it.[113] To this extent, it is relevant to what extent domestic cannabis cultivation leads to export to other countries.

Whether or not a party is obliged to implement a prohibition depends on the question whether this is 'the most suitable measure, in its opinion'. Having said that, the party must be acting in good faith:[114] the actual assessment of the authorities is relevant, not what they possibly pretend.[115] The parties do not have so much freedom of policy as an obligation to assess the situation truthfully. A party without a prohibition that turns out to be incapable of preventing large-scale cannabis production by counteracting cannabis cultivation cannot legitimately claim that a prohibition is not the most appropriate measure, according to the UN Commentary.[116] At the same time, the nature of the prohibition must also be taken into account: the Convention does not require that it is related to criminal law, but if a criminal prohibition is the most suitable measure, it would seem that the party would be obliged to implement it.

The question is what the added value of Article 22 is in comparison with Article 36 of the Single Convention. After all, the latter provision already

111 *Cf.* the discussion of Article 37 of the Single Convention.

112 United Nations, *Commentary on the Single Convention on Narcotic Drugs, 1961*, New York: 1973, p. 275 (no. 2).

113 United Nations, *Commentary on the Single Convention on Narcotic Drugs, 1961*, New York: 1973, p. 275 (no. 3).

114 See also Article 26 of the Vienna Convention on the Law of Treaties (*Pacta sunt servanda*).

115 United Nations, *Commentary on the Single Convention on Narcotic Drugs, 1961*, New York: 1973, p. 276 (no. 8).

116 United Nations, *Commentary on the Single Convention on Narcotic Drugs, 1961*, New York: 1973, p. 276 (no. 8). See also David R. Bewley-Taylor & Martin Jelsma, 'Regime change: Re-visiting the 1961 Single Convention on Narcotic Drugs', 23 *International Journal of Drug Policy* 2012, pp. 72–81 on p. 78.

carries an obligation of criminalization (as a consequence of the inclusion of flowering and fruiting tops of the cannabis plant and cannabis resin in the Schedules) – and therefore a prohibition – of the cultivation of cannabis, among other things. However, as Article 36 only refers to acts that are not allowed by virtue of medical or scientific purposes, it would appear that the prohibition of Article 22 of the Single Convention by comparison does extend to such acts. The preparatory history also points in that direction. It shows that initially a virtually total ban on cannabis cultivation was envisaged, which even implied the exclusion of cultivation of cannabis that did not contain any narcotic substances for the manufacture of fibres and seeds for the textile industry for example.[117] In the end, that was not what was desired, but the optional prohibition on cultivation in Article 22 of the Single Convention was couched in truly very loose language. The wording of this provision also implies that the prohibition in this provision intends to be more general and/or broader than the one of Article 36 of the Single Convention: the phrase 'the diversion of drugs into the illicit traffic' implies that in first instance this is about legal cultivation of cannabis which finds its way into the illegal circuit. This is also borne out by the definition of illicit trafficking in Article 1(1)(l) of the Single Convention, from which it follows that illegal cultivation in itself already constitutes illicit traffic, so that it would be nonsensical to talk about diversion into illicit traffic in Article 22 if that provision were only aimed at illegal cannabis cultivation. Finally, it also follows from Article 22(2) of the Single Convention that the prohibition which the first paragraph refers to constitutes a near total ban which also applies to cultivation for medical or scientific purposes. After all, only 'small quantities required [...] for scientific or research purposes' are excluded from the obligation of seizure included in that second paragraph. In view of Article 2(5)(b) of the Single Convention[118] and also from a linguistic point of view, it must be assumed that 'scientific or research purposes' is more restricted than the exception of 'medical or scientific purposes', so that the prohibition implemented by a party pursuant to Article 22(1) can also include cannabis cultivation for medical or scientific purposes if it does not include cultivation for 'scientific or research purposes' as well. Moreover, that cultivation will have to be small-scale, because it may only yield small quantities.

In view of the aforementioned, Article 22 of the Single Convention currently has no special meaning or relevance for the discussion about

---

117 United Nations, 'Conference for the adoption of a Single Convention on Narcotic Drugs, New York, 24 January–25 March 1961, Official Records, Volume II', *UN Doc.* E/CONF. 34/24/Add.1, pp. 174–175. See also United Nations, *Commentary on the Single Convention on Narcotic Drugs, 1961*, New York: 1973, p. 276 (nos. 4–7); UNODC, *A Century of International Drug Control*, Vienna: United Nations, 2008, p. 61.

118 See section 2.2.2.ii.b.

cannabis cultivation for supplying retail shops. After all, the ban on cannabis cultivation of Article 22 of the Single Convention intends to be an addition to the obligation of criminalization of cannabis cultivation of Article 36 of the Single Convention in case the criminalization required by this provision proves to be inadequate in preventing the diversion of cannabis to the recreational market. Article 22 of the Single Convention therefore is primarily aimed at the (virtually) complete prohibition of cannabis cultivation which may in itself be legal under the Convention. Only if cannabis were to be deleted from the Schedules altogether – in which case Article 36 of the Single Convention no longer applies to cannabis cultivation – could Article 22 of the Single Convention gain relevance: then it can be defended that a state would have to implement a prohibition (not necessarily related to criminal law) of cannabis cultivation, should the authorities consider that to be 'the most suitable measure' to protect public health and welfare. Simultaneously, it is conceivable that the reasons for a state to agree to deleting cannabis from those Schedules implies that quite to the contrary, the state does not see this as the most suitable measure.

II. Control of Legal Cultivation of Cannabis Plants: Article 28 of the Single Convention

It follows from Article 28(1) of the Single Convention that if a party permits the cultivation of the cannabis plant for the production of flowering and fruiting tops of the cannabis plant and/or cannabis resin, that party has to apply the provisions of control mentioned in Article 23. Because this will have to be about cannabis cultivation which in itself is permitted under the Convention (therefore for medical and scientific purposes[119]), this provision is not relevant for the discussion about cannabis cultivation for the supply of coffee shops in the Netherlands. Such cannabis cultivation is not covered by the exception of medical and scientific purposes (see below) and runs counter to the Convention, as becomes clear from Article 36 of the Single Convention for example. In addition to this, where the sale of cannabis to consumers (patients) is based on medical grounds, the conditions of Article 28(1) in conjunction with Article 23 of the Single Convention must be met. This means that a national government agency has to decide who is given a licence for cultivation, on which location the licensee is allowed to cultivate and within which area (in hectares) cultivation is allowed. The agency is also responsible for issuing the licences. Furthermore, the agency will also exclusively take physical possession of the crops of cultivators, and be in charge of wholesale

119 See also United Nations, *Commentary on the Single Convention on Narcotic Drugs, 1961*, New York: 1973, p. 314 (no. 7).

trading and maintaining stocks. Through this agency, deliveries can be made to points of sale (be they commercial or not) of medical cannabis to patients.

d. Obligations Regarding Cannabis Leaves: Article 28 of the Single Convention

Article 28(3) of the Single Convention could be important for this discussion, as it relates to cannabis leaves. Such leaves do not classify as narcotic drugs in their own right under the Convention, since they are not included in the Schedules.[120] Article 28(3) of the Single Convention – which is the only provision in the Convention that is relevant for cannabis leaves – reads: 'The Parties shall adopt such measures as may be necessary to prevent the misuse of, and illicit traffic in, the leaves of the cannabis plant.' This provision does not imply automatically that action should be taken against acts involving cannabis leaves. The obligation to take measures – which does not require a ban per se[121] – only exists if a party (acting in good faith) has to draw the conclusion that it involves misuse (such as the consumption of narcotically very potent leaves or huge quantities[122]) or 'illicit traffic'. Illicit traffic must not be taken here in the sense of the definition in Article 1(1)(l) of the Single Convention, but as trade in breach of national regulations and if export is part of the picture, then also in breach of the applicable foreign regulations.[123] To this extent, it seems that each party is in control of the measures it has to take against trade in cannabis leaves.

At the same time, the UN Commentary assumes that the states parties are at any rate not allowed to permit the uncontrolled use of the leaves. A ground for that obligation can only be found if misuse has a more factual meaning, which can be broader to include more than just acting in contravention of national legislation. It would appear that parties also have to take measures against the cultivation and sale of cannabis leaves – separately or as an ingredient of weed/marijuana – if misuse of those leaves is the consequence. To that extent, the legalization of cannabis cultivation, delivery and traffic for the supply of retail shops would yet run counter to Article 28(3) of the Single Convention. The obligation in this provision is not particularly strict however, because 'abuse' is a rather vague criterion, while there is also room for discretionary policy since

---

120 Article 1(1)(j) of the Single Convention. The cultivation and sale of cannabis leaves with a high content of delta-9-tetrahydrocannabinol (THC) has increased since approximately 2005, according to the Commission on Narcotic Drugs, Report on the fifty-third session (2 December 2009 and 8–12 March 2010), E/2010/28, E/CN.7/2010/18, p. 64 (para 91).

121 See also United Nations, *Commentary on the Single Convention on Narcotic Drugs, 1961*, New York: 1973, p. 316 (no. 4).

122 See also United Nations, *Commentary on the Single Convention on Narcotic Drugs, 1961*, New York: 1973, p. 316 (no. 4).

123 See also United Nations, *Commentary on the Single Convention on Narcotic Drugs, 1961*, New York: 1973, p. 315 (no. 1).

the provision does not require a ban but only measures. This provision is not or hardly relevant for the current practice in the Netherlands. However, if one wanted to get round the obligations in the Convention by using only cannabis leaves for the production of weed/marijuana and hashish,[124] then we believe it takes some effort to argue that this does not constitute abuse in the sense of Article 28(3) of the Single Convention.[125] In that case, the party will have to take the necessary and therefore effective measures against it. This rules out legalization and/or policy-based tolerance of cannabis cultivation for retail shops through cultivation of cannabis plants using just the leaves as a legally viable option. Therefore, this obstacle too can only be avoided by amending or denouncing the Convention.

2.2.3. THE 'MEDICAL OR SCIENTIFIC PURPOSES' AND OTHER EXCEPTIONS

The Single Convention recognizes a few exceptions to the obligations that have been laid down in it. Insofar as the Convention requires parties to realize criminal liability, the obligations can be influenced by national defences (justifications and excuses).

i. Exceptions in the Convention: Medical or Scientific Purposes

Although the Convention – as a consequence of the inclusion of flowering and fruiting tops of the cannabis plant and cannabis resin in Schedule IV – seeks to allow cannabis only if this is needed for 'medical and scientific *research*' (emphasis added) and not directly as a medicine, parties can in principle opt for a less strict regime. Yet even then room for manoeuvring is rather restricted: only to the extent that an act involving cannabis meets the criteria for 'medical or scientific *purposes*' (emphasis added), can this act be permitted pursuant to the Convention.[126] This raises the question what the extent of this exception is. Can it possibly include, for example, cannabis cultivation, delivery and trafficking with a view to supplying retail shops? Before looking into this question, we point out that the Convention also recognizes the exception of 'special purposes' ('special stocks').[127] As this exception is limited to extraordinary needs in

124 Robin Room & Sarah McKay see a few possibilities to this end in their book *Roadmaps for Reforming the UN Drug Conventions*, Oxford: Beckley Foundation Press, 2012, pp. 11–12.

125 In our opinion, the authors mentioned in the previous footnote have overlooked this.

126 The point is that 'research' is a narrower term than 'purposes'; see section 2.2.2.ii.b for the former, and below for the latter.

127 See Article 1(1)(w) and (x), Article 12(4), Article 13(4), Article 19(1)(d) and (2)(d), Article 20(3) and Article 21(1)(e) and (2) of the Single Convention.

connection with government objectives for the Armed Forces or in the event of an emergency,[128] it merits no further discussion here.

The Single Convention does not give a further definition of the exception of medical and scientific purposes recognized in, among other places, the preamble and Article 4(c) of the Single Convention. During the discussions about the creation of the Convention in 1961, the representative of the Netherlands, Kruysse, argued that the term 'medical purposes' could be interpreted in various ways.[129] He maintained that in the Netherlands the concept was used in a very narrow sense and only applied to the administration of medicines to the sick, whereas in other countries it could also include the production of medicines. He therefore made a case for a very accurate definition of the concept. As we noted before, this did not happen because of a lack of consensus about what exactly the definition should cover. The crux of this matter was the question whether that definition should be narrow or very narrow, so either way it is true that the exception was intended to be fairly limited. That is also evident from the discussion about the Convention as such (prohibitive towards recreational drug use, the preamble treats the use of drugs outside the exception of 'medical or scientific purposes' a 'abuse'[130] or even as an 'evil'), the wording of the exception (restricted from a linguistic point of view), the rationale for the Convention (narcotic drugs are to be used exclusively for medical or scientific purposes[131] and must be completely prohibited otherwise) and the Convention system (aimed at the aforementioned complete prohibition, which is reflected among other things in the estimate system, a total ban on cannabis for recreational use which to a large degree is covered by criminalizations).

It is also relevant that the discussion following the Dutch proposal[132] illustrates that the concept was borrowed from the 1925 International Opium Convention, that it was never contested that this includes dental and veterinary medicine as well,[133] and also that narcotic drugs can be

---

[128] See United Nations, *Commentary on the Single Convention on Narcotic Drugs, 1961*, New York: 1973, pp. 30–37 (nos. 1–22). United Nations, 'Conference for the adoption of a Single Convention on Narcotic Drugs, New York, 24 January–25 March 1961, Official Records, Volume II', *UN Doc.* E/CONF. 34/24/Add.1, p. 2 and pp. 189–192.

[129] Kruysse, in the Ad Hoc Committee on Articles 30 and 40–43 of the Third Draft, First Meeting, Monday, 6 February 1961, in: United Nations, 'Conference for the adoption of a Single Convention on Narcotic Drugs, New York, 24 January–25 March 1961, Official Records, Volume II', *UN Doc.* E/CONF. 34/24/Add.1, p. 123.

[130] The English text refers to abuse here and in various other provisions.

[131] This can be seen very clearly in Article 4(c) of the Single Convention.

[132] United Nations, 'Conference for the adoption of a Single Convention on Narcotic Drugs, New York, 24 January–25 March 1961, Official Records, Volume II', *UN Doc.* E/CONF. 34/24/Add.1, pp. 123–124.

[133] See also United Nations, *Commentary on the Single Convention on Narcotic Drugs, 1961*, New York: 1973, p. 111 (no. 13).

used both for direct use and for the production of other medicines. The UN Commentary also shows that parties may permit the medicinal use of narcotic drugs by addicts to alleviate the suffering during withdrawal treatments (kicking the habit) and in cases where the addict is not able to stop using drugs so as to avoid painful withdrawal symptoms and to enable them to lead a normal life.[134] It is clear from the preamble that the exception is there only for the relief of pain and suffering, although the preamble recognizes the importance of research. With regard to research, the preparatory history shows that it can mean specifically authorized controlled clinical trials, which can involve both the narcotic drugs themselves and patients.[135] Insofar as preparatory history and the UN Commentary also deals with 'scientific purposes', this is invariably done in the context of medical interests.[136] The sparse examples provided all relate to such interests. Therefore, it seems that the exception of 'scientific purposes' concerns medicine and medical science. In addition to this, such an interpretation of the exception would be the closest match to the objective of the Convention,[137] in which science as such plays no part, although the availability of narcotic drugs for medicinal use does. We therefore hold the view that the exception 'scientific purposes' is also meant to be interpreted in a rather narrow way and that (in principle[138]) it is restricted

---

134 United Nations, *Commentary on the Single Convention on Narcotic Drugs, 1961*, New York: 1973, p. 111 (no. 11). See also David R. Bewley-Taylor & Martin Jelsma, 'The Limits of Latitude. The UN drug control conventions', *Series on Legislative Reform of Drug Policies*, No. 18, March 2012, pp. 9–10, who argue that the conventions leave room for 'Needle or Syringe Exchange', 'Substitution and Maintenance Treatment', and 'Drug injection rooms'.

135 See United Nations, 'Conference for the adoption of a Single Convention on Narcotic Drugs, New York, 24 January–25 March 1961, Official Records, Volume II', *UN Doc.* E/CONF. 34/24/Add.1, pp. 3, 33 and pp. 81–82. See also p. 177, where a government official remarks that 'the use of cannabis leaves as a flavouring agent in a soft drink could not be considered as covered by the expression "medical and scientific purposes"'. Eventually, this is considered to be 'social' use.

136 See United Nations, 'Conference for the adoption of a Single Convention on Narcotic Drugs, New York, 24 January–25 March 1961, Official Records, Volume II', *UN Doc.* E/CONF. 34/24/Add.1; we searched a PDF version of this document for the string 'scien'. We did the same with the UN Commentary to the Single Convention with regard to those provisions containing the phrase 'scientific purposes'.

137 The same conclusion is reached by T.M.C. Asser Instituut, *Experimenteren met het Gedogen van de Teelt van Cannabis ten Behoeve van de Bevoorrading van Coffeeshops – Internationaal rechtelijke en Europees rechtelijke aspecten*, Den Haag, 2005, p. 7 (i.e., Asser Institute – Centre for International & European Law; *Experimenting with tolerating the cultivation of cannabis for the supply of coffee shops – aspects of international and European law*, The Hague, 2005).

138 See for example Neil Brett Boister, *The Suppression of Illicit Drugs Through International Law*, Nottingham: University of Nottingham 1998, p. 412, who defends the notion that the use of drugs plants among other items as evidence in criminal cases is permissible as such evidence would be of a scientific nature (because, for example, drug content in such plants must be established scientifically). However, we ask ourselves whether it is necessary to rely on the exception for this, because this will involve plants seized from the defendant, which will be destroyed after they have been tested, if necessary only after the criminal proceedings.

to science and more specifically medicine and medical science. Within the limited scope of 'medical or scientific purposes', it is up to the parties to establish the exact meaning of this.[139]

The significance of all this is that in the final analysis, the exception of medical or scientific purposes is limited to the use of narcotic drugs as meaningful and/or effective[140] medicine in concrete cases, the use of narcotic drugs to produce medicines for such cases, and scientific research for the aforesaid medicinal use, the aforesaid production of medicines or medical science. The Convention itself, the preparatory history and the UN Commentary do not provide any departure points for a broader interpretation of the exception. On the contrary: as we said before, everything points to a limited to very limited meaning of the exception, which the parties chose deliberately and explicitly. The term 'medical purposes' must therefore be interpreted very precisely and strictly medically. As it can hardly be claimed that the sale of cannabis products to consumers in retail shops in general takes place for individual reasons serving medical (or scientific) purposes, the regular sale as well as the cannabis cultivation, delivery and trafficking with a view to supplying those retail shops cannot be subsumed under the exception.[141] Even in concrete cases where a retail shop did sell cannabis for a medical purpose to an individual consumer or patient, it would appear that the exception does not apply in principle. After all, the Convention seeks to prevent the situation – most clearly via Schedule IV – where members of the medical profession administer or prescribe narcotic drugs too easily.[142] This implies that the medicinal use of cannabis – a drug included in Schedule IV – if not prescribed by a physician must be prohibited, while it seems that its use on the basis of such a prescription must be limited to cases in which it is necessary.[143]

---

139 INCB, *Report of the International Narcotics Control Board for 2003*, New York: United Nations, 2004, p. 37 (no. 227).

140 Incidentally, it must be noted that the 1971 Convention on Psychotropic Substances explicitly states the requirement of 'usefulness of the substance in medical therapy' if the question is whether narcotic drugs must be included in the international control system (which aims to guarantee the availability for medical and scientific purposes and to fight all other uses); see Article 2(4) of that Convention.

141 Likewise, see T.M.C. Asser Instituut, *Experimenteren met het Gedogen van de Teelt van Cannabis ten Behoeve van de Bevoorrading van Coffeeshops – Internationaal rechtelijke en Europees rechtelijke aspecten*, Den Haag, 2005, p. 13 (i.e., Asser Institute – Centre for International & European Law; *Experimenting with tolerating the cultivation of cannabis for the supply of coffee shops – aspects of international and European law*, The Hague, 2005).

142 United Nations, *Commentary on the Single Convention on Narcotic Drugs, 1961*, New York: 1973, p. 67 (no. 9).

143 See also David R. Bewley-Taylor & Martin Jelsma, 'The Limits of Latitude. The UN drug control conventions', *Series on Legislative Reform of Drug Policies*, No. 18, March 2012, p. 14, who imply that it is not lawful to permit the sale of cannabis under the exception of 'medical or scientific purposes' when in actual fact the sale is aimed at recreational use.

Therefore, the states parties may only permit the supply of cannabis to patients via a retail shop' if that patient uses cannabis on a doctor's prescription. It follows from the above that it could be a case of a withdrawal treatment or addiction care, at least insofar as cannabis use is truly instrumental for that.

This already answers the question whether the exception leaves any room for general arguments that the regulation of cannabis cultivation, delivery and trafficking for the supply of retail shops is beneficial to public health. For example, these arguments can be the following: separation of the soft drugs and hard drugs markets serves public health because it stops cannabis users from getting into contact with hard drugs; by regulating the cannabis market, control on the quality of cannabis can be more effective; by preventing the cannabis market from going underground, cannabis use by minors can be thwarted better. The foregoing implies that such policy-driven arguments cannot be recognized under the exception for various reasons.

This is primarily because cannabis sold to consumers in that case clearly does not serve as a medicine needed by the individual buyer. This means that it is not possible to include the regulation of such sales to consumers – and therefore also the preceding cannabis cultivation, delivery and trafficking – in the rather limited exception of 'medical or scientific purposes'. In this context, it is also important that it is not possible – as we will explain later – to subsume public health policies under the exception by interpreting the Single Convention as a 'living instrument' (sometimes this is also called evolutive interpretation).[144]

However, even if a certain group of consumers does buy cannabis for medical reasons, then secondly there is still the obstacle that such a sale cannot take place freely, because in each individual case it requires the prescription of a physician. Ultimately, there is a third reason: insofar as cannabis is sold to consumers on medical grounds, the actual physical harvesting of crops, the wholesale trading and maintaining stocks among other things, will have to be done by a government agency in the sense of Article 28(1) in conjunction with Article 23 of the Single Convention.[145] Through this agency, deliveries can be made to points of sale (be they commercial or not) of medical cannabis to patients. Under the Single Convention, the supply of cannabis is not allowed to take place directly from grower or commercial traders to retail shops, other commercial enterprises or other private individuals. The extent to which the arguments mentioned and other policy-based arguments are valid, and whether they presuppose methods that in the long run may prove to be less or more sensible than a strictly prohibitive approach is something that we

144 See section 4.2.4.ii.

145 See section 2.2.2.ii.c.II.

cannot and do not want to assess here. We only observe that the Convention represents the latter approach – indeed: 'zero tolerance' – and leaves no room for a policy-based approach that deviates from it.

Besides, in particular where medicinal use of cannabis is concerned, it is important that the term 'medical use' has no fixed meaning, but is dependent on time and place so that developments in medical science can be relevant to what is and is not covered by the exception.[146] Those developments can relate to modern and Western medical science as well as legitimate systems of indigenous medicine such as those in China, India and Pakistan. This does not mean that over time room will become available for the above-mentioned policy-based approaches with regard to public health. It does mean that insofar as cannabis can be used for medical applications or proves to be useful in the future, that application may be permitted by virtue of the exception.

ii. National Exceptions: Defences

The Single Convention makes no mention of any application of national defences in those cases where a person is prosecuted for an act that the Convention requires to be criminalized. While it is true that conventions containing obligations for criminalization do not normally do that, but they do not dispute the applicability of defences in connection with those obligations under the Convention either. In short: national defences are as usual applicable for offences which are based on an obligation for criminalization pursuant to a Convention, provided of course that this application does not contravene the obligation to interpret and implement the Convention in good faith.[147] A person who is prosecuted for cannabis cultivation, delivery and/or trafficking for supplying retail shops will be able to appeal to any applicable defence (justification or excuse). Of course, this also applies if the retail shop itself or for example the owner is prosecuted. Whether the appeal will be upheld will depend on the concrete circumstances of the case and possibly on the defendant in question.

This illustrates that legalization, decriminalization, policy-based tolerance and/or other forms of regulating cannabis cultivation cannot be based on national defences. An appeal by a defendant suspected of cannabis cultivation based on for example on defence of necessity on the grounds that the obligation pursuant to the Convention and/or the criminal prohibition should be outweighed by the interests of public welfare, health and or crime control cannot be successful therefore. The conflict of interests in such a case is not

---

146 United Nations, *Commentary on the Single Convention on Narcotic Drugs, 1961*, New York: 1973, p. 111 (no. 12).

147 See Article 26 and Article 31(1) of the Vienna Convention on the Law of Treaties.

acute, concrete and specific enough for the justification of necessity to be applicable.[148]

2.2.4. DECLARATIONS AND RESERVATIONS WITH REGARD TO THE SINGLE CONVENTION

The Netherlands did not formulate any relevant reservations or make any declarations in relation to the Single Convention of 1961, the Protocol amending the Single Convention on Narcotic Drugs from 1972 or the subsequent combined version.[149] Pursuant to its Articles 49 and 50, the formulation of reservations to the Single Convention is only permitted at the time of signature, ratification or accession, so this is now no longer possible. It could have been done at the time. After all, the Convention permits the formulation of reservations in the Articles 49 and 50 of the Single Convention, although it severely restricts the possibilities for it. In the context of these possibilities, it is significant that Article 49(1)(d) of the Single Convention permits the parties to 'reserve the right to permit temporarily in any one of its territories' the 'use of cannabis, cannabis resin, extracts and tinctures of cannabis for non-medical purposes', at any rate if certain additional conditions are met. For example, there is the requirement that the consumption was traditional and permitted on 1 January 1961. In addition to this, the aforementioned cannabis use pursuant to Article 49(2)(f) 'must be discontinued as soon as possible but in any case within twenty-five years from the coming into force of this Convention'. Moreover, the production, manufacture and trade for cannabis use 'must be reduced and finally abolished simultaneously with the reduction and abolition' of that use.

As we said before, the Netherlands never used this opportunity to make a reservation. Nonetheless, it is clear that any reservations with regard to cannabis cultivation, delivery and trafficking for supplying coffee shops and the sale of cannabis to consumers by coffee shops would not have been acceptable. Even if the phenomenon of the Dutch coffee shops could have been covered by the reservation, there would have been no place for them by now in accordance with Article 41(1) of the Single Convention, seeing that the twenty-five-year grace period after the Convention came into force ended[150] in 1989. And if all that

---

148 See for example Jaap de Hullu, *Materieel strafrecht. Over algemene leerstukken van strafrechtelijke aansprakelijkheid naar Nederlands recht*, Deventer: Wolters Kluwer, 2018, pp. 309–313 (i.e. Jaap de Hullu, *Substantive Criminal Law. On general principles of criminal responsibility in Dutch Law*, Deventer: Wolters Kluwer, 2018, pp. 309–313).

149 See: http://treaties.un.org/ (Chapter VI, nos. 15, 17 and 18). Incidentally, the Netherlands did not object to the reservations or declarations of other parties to the Convention either.

150 Article 41(1) of the Single Convention says: 'This Convention shall come into force on the thirtieth day following the date on which the fortieth instrument of ratification or accession is deposited in accordance with article 40.'

was not enough, the Netherlands actually could not have used this opportunity for reservation. After all, in the case of the Netherlands the aforementioned cannabis activities as well as cannabis possession and cannabis use could hardly be labelled as traditional. This was true then even more than it is now. To merit the use of the word traditional, the UN Commentary requires that a significant part of the population has been using cannabis for a considerable period of time.[151] That was certainly not the case at the time. According to a recognized definition of tradition, this refers to something which is handed down from one generation to another, usually in an informal way, with little or no change occurring to what is being handed down.[152] It is difficult to maintain that cannabis use at the time – and perhaps this still applies for the use in this day and age – can be considered traditional in the Netherlands. Besides, these acts cannot be qualified as 'permitted' either, as they have been punishable in the Netherlands to date. The UN Commentary also reveals that in the event of a legal prohibition, such use does not qualify as permitted.[153] It is exactly the very limited room the Convention allows for reservations that underlines once again that everything outside those reservations is seen as a breach of the provisions of the Convention. Incidentally, we would like to point out already that the Netherlands did formulate a reservation to the Illicit Trafficking Convention,[154] although of course this has no significance at all for the obligations that the Netherlands assumed by signing the Single Convention.

2.2.5. INTERNATIONAL SUPERVISION OF THE SINGLE CONVENTION: IN PARTICULAR INCB AND CND

As we observed before, the implementation of the Single Convention also resulted in a reduction of the number of international treaty bodies concerned with the control of narcotic drugs. This happened by concentrating the supervision under the auspices of the United Nations. To that effect, the Convention created a new body: the *International Narcotics Control Board* (INCB).[155] Furthermore, the Single Convention also assigned a supervisory role to the *Commission on Narcotic Drugs* (CND) of the *Economic and Social*

---

151 United Nations, *Commentary on the Single Convention on Narcotic Drugs, 1961*, New York: 1973, p. 470 (no. 3).

152 Edward Shils, *Tradition*, Chicago: University of Nottingham 1981, pp. 12–21, in particular p. 9, 16, 18; Thomas A. Green (ed.), *Folklore: An Encyclopedia of Beliefs, Customs, Tales, Music, and Art*, Volume 1, Santa Barbara: ABC-CLIO, 1997, p. 800.

153 United Nations, *Commentary on the Single Convention on Narcotic Drugs, 1961*, New York: 1973, p. 470 (no. 3).

154 See for information on that section 2.3.4.

155 See Article 5 of the Single Convention.

Council (ECOSOC) of the United Nations and to ECOSOC itself.[156] Article 5 of the Single Convention recognizes the INCB and CND as international control organs. The views, judgments and decisions of the INCB, CND and ECOSOC will be discussed in more detail in section 2.4; the following is merely a brief description of their functions within the Single Convention.

The INCB is the international body responsible for monitoring the implementation of the Convention by the states parties. It acts as an independent and quasi-judicial[157] control and regulatory body responsible for the supervision of the implementation of the Single Convention. The functions of the INCB with regard to this Convention are set out in Article 9. Among other things, the INCB, in cooperation with governments, and subject to the terms of the Convention, is tasked with preventing the 'illicit cultivation, production and manufacture of, and illicit trafficking in and use of, drugs.' The Board also takes measures that are consistent with the intention to further the cooperation and dialogue with governments so as to support and facilitate national action to attain the aims of this Convention. The INCB is also the body that exercises primary control of the so-called 'estimate system' in the Articles 12 to 21bis of the Single Convention.[158] If the Board has reason to believe that the objectives of the Convention are seriously jeopardized because a party fails to carry out the provisions of this Convention, the INCB has several instruments at its disposal pursuant to Article 14 of the Single Convention. For example, the Board has the right to request that state to furnish explanations and to take necessary measures. If the party does not comply with the aforementioned requests, the INCB is authorized to inform the other states parties, the ECOSOC and the CND about this. The INCB can also compile a report. Decisions of the INCB under Article 14 are taken by a two-thirds majority of the total number of members. Pursuant to Article 15 of the Single Convention, the Board will publish an annual report. The INCB is therefore the internationally designated body to monitor compliance with the Single Convention. The states parties acknowledge this authority by their accession to the Convention.[159] The CND exists in the annual meeting of ministers and government representatives of all UN member states during which they debate, make decisions and adopt resolutions about all sort of questions regarding the worldwide drug control system, the working programme of the United Nations Office on Drugs and Crime (UNODC) and the INCB. Where the Single Convention is concerned, Article 8 shows that the CND is 'authorized to consider all matters pertaining

156 Ibid.

157 United Nations, *Commentary on the Single Convention on Narcotic Drugs, 1961*, New York: 1973, p. 135 (no. 1) and 136 (no. 6). See also: http://www.incb.org/incb/en/about/mandate-functions.html.

158 See section 2.2.2.ii.a.II.

159 See section 2.4 for more information.

to the aims' of the Convention. Among other things, its function is to draw the attention of the INCB to all matters which may be relevant to the work of the INCB, make recommendations for the implementation of the aims and provisions of the Convention and to call the attention of states that are not parties to the Convention to decisions and recommendations adopted by the INCB under the Convention.

An important function of the ECOSOC within the Single Convention is that it can confirm, modify or revoke resolutions of the CND or changes concerning the Schedules. Such resolutions by the ECOSOC are final and to that extent binding in any case.[160]

Finally, there can also be a role for the International Court of Justice (ICJ). Article 48 of the Single Convention stipulates that a dispute between two or more states parties about the interpretation or implementation of the Convention that cannot be settled by themselves will be brought before the ICJ.

2.2.6. INTERMEDIATE CONCLUSION FOR THE SINGLE CONVENTION

This intermediate conclusion is the result of the foregoing discussion of the contents, the nature and the system of the Single Convention, the preparatory history that preceded its creation and the UN Commentary about it. The conclusions at this point are preliminary in the sense that they are not based on what will be discussed later in this chapter, such as the Illicit Traffic Convention, the monitoring organs of this Convention, state practice, and generally accepted interpretations of the Convention. The final conclusion – also with regard to the Single Convention – will not be formulated until the last section of this chapter.[161]

The first relevant observation to be made in the discussion about cannabis cultivation for recreational use is that the object and purpose of the Single Convention is to ban completely the circulation of narcotic drugs for anything other than medical or scientific purposes. Permitting cannabis cultivation aimed at recreational use cannot easily be reconciled with that objective. This rationale of eradication is reflected in the following. The Preamble of the Single Convention sees drugs outside the aforementioned medical or scientific framework as abuse or even as an evil. The wording of the exception 'medical and scientific purposes' is limited from a linguistic point of view and this is deliberate. The Single Convention also imposes general obligations to restrict acts involving cannabis exclusively to these objectives, to combat cannabis cultivation for recreational purposes and fight recreational

160 Article 3(8) and (9) of the Single Convention.

161 See section 2.6.

drug use (Article 4 and Article 38 of the Single Convention). The Convention also sets out an estimate system, the purpose of which is to make sure that narcotic drugs are only available for medical and scientific purposes and in sufficient quantities (Articles 12–21 of the Single Convention). In addition to this, the Convention provides a total prohibition via criminalizations of acts – including cannabis cultivation – which are aimed at or are related to recreational use of cannabis (Article 36 of the Single Convention). Furthermore, the Convention also implies obligations to prosecute, which in principle apply to cannabis cultivation that is not small-scale and not intended for personal use. The Single Convention also imposes a complete ban on the possession of narcotic drugs including cannabis for recreational use (Article 33 of the Single Convention), imposes obligations to seize cannabis for recreational use as well (Article 33 of the Single Convention and Article 37 of the Single Convention) and provides a system of international cooperation in criminal matters.

Through the required criminalizations, enforcement through criminal law and cooperation in criminal matters, the Convention aims to provide further reinforcement to the complete elimination of, among other things, the circulation of illegal cannabis. Implementation of all these provisions would have to lead to a situation where there are no narcotic drugs in circulation or that the states parties permit *de jure* and/or *de facto* that illegal drugs are entering the market or are circulating. For this study, it is of importance that in addition to coca and poppy products, cannabis products are the main object of this Convention, since these are mentioned explicitly not only in the Schedules of the Convention, but in the Convention itself as well. This objective of eradication, which also explicitly targets cannabis, cannot be reconciled with permitting cannabis cultivation for recreational use by legalization, decriminalization, policy-based tolerance and/or other forms of regulation of such cultivation.

2.3. UN CONVENTION AGAINST ILLICIT TRAFFIC IN NARCOTIC DRUGS AND PSYCHOTROPIC SUBSTANCES 1988

The United Nations Convention Against Illicit Traffic in Narcotic Drugs and Psychotropic Substances, 1988 (Illicit Traffic Convention) constitutes a strengthening of international anti-drug regulations. Also because of the above-mentioned discourses, it must be noted that the Illicit Traffic Convention by virtue of Article 25 does not diminish the obligations that the states parties entered into pursuant to the Single Convention as amended by Protocol, nor the rights that they enjoy under the Convention for that matter. The Illicit Traffic Convention has a complementary effect in that respect, partly by supporting the cooperation between the states parties in criminal matters. Among other things, Article 1 of the Illicit Traffic Convention stipulates that: 'The purpose of this Convention is to promote cooperation among the Parties so that they may address more effectively the various aspects of illicit traffic in narcotic drugs and psychotropic substances having an international dimension.' So it is essentially an international criminal law instrument[162] that is primarily aimed at combating illicit trafficking of narcotic drugs with instruments of criminal law.

The Convention came about within the United Nations over mounting concerns about the extent and rise in the clandestine production of, trade in and demand for narcotic drugs and psychotropic substances. In principle, the Convention sets out to offer protection against the serious threat posed by drugs to the health and welfare of people and also to the economic, cultural and political foundations of society.[163] This protection is particularly needed for children who are used worldwide as drug consumers and for the production and distribution of and traffic in narcotic drugs.[164] More specifically, that protection is needed against organized criminal activities that undermine the legitimate economies and pose a threat to the stability, safety and sovereignty of states.

In order to achieve these principal goals, the Illicit Traffic Convention of 1988 aims to make it easier to deprive persons of drug profits, to reinforce the monitoring of certain substances that are used in the manufacture of narcotic drugs and psychotropic substances and to improve international cooperation in fighting illicit traffic by sea. To this purpose, the Convention contains a fair number of obligations to criminalize acts that are directly or indirectly related to the illicit trafficking of narcotic drugs. Below, we will concentrate on those obligations that pertain to the discussion about legalization, decriminalization, policy-based tolerance and/or other forms of regulating of the currently illegal cannabis market.

2.3.1. THE STATUS OF CANNABIS IN ILLICIT TRAFFIC CONVENTION

The Convention only mentions the word cannabis four times. In all four cases, it is the cannabis plant, which Article 1(b) of the Illicit Traffic Convention,

---

162 Jay Sinha, *The History and Development of the Leading International Drug Control Conventions*, Ottawa: Library of Parliament, Parliamentary Research Branch, 2001, p. 33.

163 See the preamble to the Illicit Traffic Convention 1988.

164 See Article 33 of the Convention on the Rights of the Child: 'States Parties shall take all appropriate measures [...] to prevent the use of children in the illicit production and trafficking of such substances.' See for example Rachel Hodgkin & Peter Newell, *Implementation Handbook for the Convention on the Rights of the Child*, Geneva: UNICEF, 2007, pp. 503–512; Damon Barrett, *Drugs and the Convention on the Rights of the Child*, Stockholm: Stockholm University, 2018.

in full accordance with the Single Convention, defines as: 'any plant of the genus Cannabis'. Otherwise, it is important that Article 1(n) of the Illicit Traffic Convention treats as a 'narcotic drug' 'any of the substances, natural or synthetic, in Schedules I and II of the Single Convention on Narcotic Drugs'. So under the Illicit Traffic Convention as well, cannabis – in the sense of flowering or fruiting tops of the cannabis plant and cannabis resin – is seen as a narcotic drug, whereas this is not the case for cannabis leaves.[165] Unless the opposite is evident and explicitly stated, when we refer to cannabis in general terms, we mean cannabis plants, cannabis resin and the flowering or fruiting tops of the cannabis plant.

2.3.2. THE CONVENTION'S OBLIGATIONS REGARDING CANNABIS

i. General

The Illicit Traffic Convention imposes obligations that are relevant in connection with cannabis in two different ways. First, there are the obligations with regard to flowering and fruiting tops of the cannabis plant and cannabis resin, because of their inclusion in the Schedules to the Single Convention (see section below (2.3.2.i.a.)) and also there are some obligations explicitly and directly dealing with the cultivation of cannabis plants (see below 2.3.2.i.b.). For both categories, Article 3 of the Illicit Traffic Convention is of particular importance. This lengthy provision is the core of the Convention and forms an extensive addition to, amongst others, Article 36 of the Single Convention. In fact, the Illicit Traffic Convention, particularly through Article 3, aims to introduce a modern Criminal Code with respect to drugs.[166] States parties must take into account international law and human rights in this context.[167]

ii. Obligations

a. Obligations Regarding Flowering and Fruiting Tops of the Cannabis Plant and Cannabis Resin because of the Inclusion in the Schedules to the Single Convention

It follows from the above that every time an obligation in the Illicit Traffic Convention 1988 applies to narcotic drugs, that obligation also applies to

165 See section 2.2.1 for a further explanation of the terms.

166 United Nations, *Commentary on the United Nations Convention Against Illicit Traffic in Narcotic Drugs and Psychotropic Substances*, Vienna: 1988, p. 48 (no. 3.1).

167 United Nations, *Commentary on the United Nations Convention Against Illicit Traffic in Narcotic Drugs and Psychotropic Substances*, Vienna: 1988, p. 49 (no. 3.3).

flowering and fruiting tops of the cannabis plant and cannabis resin, because of their inclusion in the Schedules of the Single Convention. The result of this is that all the obligations that will be discussed now would no longer apply if flowering and fruiting tops of the cannabis plant and cannabis resin were deleted from those Schedules. These obligations are the lion's share of the obligations that are relevant here. Our attention will now turn to the obligations in respect of criminalization, penalization, prosecution and the application of the expediency principle and seizure and also the need for implementation of the Convention. Additionally, the Illicit Traffic Convention carries various other obligations in Articles 3 to 19, which we will not go into below.[168]

I. Obligations to Criminalize and Punish: Article 3 of the Illicit Traffic Convention

The Convention aims to force the states parties to criminalize as many acts as possible that are either directly or indirectly related to the traffic in narcotic drugs. In principle, Article 3 of the Illicit Traffic Convention covers all obligations of criminalization that already ensue from Article 36 of the Single Convention. Article 3(1) of the Illicit Traffic Convention deals with, among other things, intentionally committed offences such as production, manufacture, extraction, preparation, offering, distribution, sale, delivery on any terms whatsoever, brokerage, dispatch, dispatch in transit, transport or importation or exportation of any narcotic drug and therefore also of flowering and fruiting tops of the cannabis plant and cannabis resin. Already at this point, the Illicit Traffic Convention entails that legalization or decriminalization of cannabis cultivation, delivery and trafficking with the objective of supplying retail shops is ruled out. Furthermore, Article 3 of the Illicit Traffic Convention adds a considerable number of obligations. The most important ones of these are:

- *Conduct regarding personal consumption of cannabis: Article 3(2) of the Illicit Traffic Convention.* Whereas the Single Convention still leaves room for

[168] They involve obligations concerning, among other things, periods of statutes of limitations (Article 3(8) of the Illicit Traffic Convention), the presence of person charged with an offence at the criminal proceedings (Article 3(9) of the Illicit Traffic Convention), grounds to refuse legal assistance (Article 3(10) of the Illicit Traffic Convention), jurisdiction (Article 4 of the Illicit Traffic Convention), confiscation of proceeds gained illegally (Article 5 of the Illicit Traffic Convention), extradition (Article 6 of the Illicit Traffic Convention), mutual legal assistance (Article 7 of the Illicit Traffic Convention), transfer of proceedings (Article 8 of the Illicit Traffic Convention), other forms of cooperation (Article 9 and 10 of the Illicit Traffic Convention), controlled delivery (Article 11 of the Illicit Traffic Convention), substances, materials and equipment used in the manufacture of narcotic drugs (Article 12 and 13 of the Illicit Traffic Convention) and illicit traffic by commercial carriers, by sea and by mail (Articles 15–19 of the Illicit Traffic Convention).

discussion about this,[169] the Illicit Traffic Convention[170] through Article 3(2) explicitly intends to make it clear that parties are obliged to criminalize intentional possession, intentional purchase and intentional cultivation of cannabis (that is to say: flowering and fruiting cannabis tops and cannabis resin) for personal use other than for medical or scientific purposes. In this respect, among others, the Illicit Traffic Convention focuses more explicitly on the demand side of the cannabis market, more so than the Single Convention does.[171] Nonetheless, the foregoing illustrates that cannabis use as such does not have to be criminalized.[172]

The separate inclusion of the obligations in the second paragraph mentioned above instead of including them in the first paragraph is more appropriate, given the less serious nature of the acts with regard to personal cannabis use than that of the acts referred to in the first paragraph.[173] The Dutch government observed that it had taken quite some effort to get the importance of the distinction between the 'real' traffic and small-scale use, serious crime and subcultures recognized and qualified the second paragraph in this respect as a hard-fought compromise.[174] It seems though as if the government is saying this is stretching the scope of Article 3(2) of the Illicit Traffic Convention somewhat. This provision is about possession, purchase and cultivation 'for personal consumption'. Ultimately, all drug consumption by people is 'personal'. In this sense, one can maintain that commercial and large-scale possession, purchase and cultivation for recreational use by consumers is aimed at 'personal consumption'. It is evident that this is not the purport of the provision and that the grounds for the distinction between the first and second paragraph would be removed in that interpretation. So it must be assumed that the provision only applies to possession, purchase and cannabis for one's 'own' personal use.[175] Strictly speaking, even the

169 See section 2.2.2.ii.a.VI for this.

170 United Nations, *Commentary on the United Nations Convention Against Illicit Traffic in Narcotic Drugs and Psychotropic Substances*, Vienna: 1988, p. 81 (no. 3.92). See for example Jay Sinha, *The History and Development of the Leading International Drug Control Conventions*, Ottawa: Library of Parliament, Parliamentary Research Branch, 2001, p. 35.

171 Also see the preamble: 'eliminate the root causes of the problem of abuse of narcotic drugs [...] including the illicit demand for such drugs'. See also Krzysztof Krajewski, 'How flexible are the United Nations drug conventions?', 10 *International Journal of Drug Policy* 4 (1999), pp. 329–338 on p. 331.

172 United Nations, *Commentary on the United Nations Convention Against Illicit Traffic in Narcotic Drugs and Psychotropic Substances*, Vienna: 1988, p. 75 (no. 3.74) and p. 82 (no. 3.95).

173 United Nations, *Commentary on the United Nations Convention Against Illicit Traffic in Narcotic Drugs and Psychotropic Substances*, Vienna: 1988, pp. 81–82 (nos. 3.93–94).

174 *Kamerstukken II* 1991–1992, 22 080 (R 1406), nr. 6, p. 3 (MvA) (i.e., *Dutch Parliamentary Documents II* 1991–1992, 22 080 (R 1406), no. 6, p. 3 (Memorandum of Reply)); see also p. 7.

175 See for example Krzysztof Krajewski, 'How flexible are the United Nations drug conventions?', 10 *International Journal of Drug Policy* 4 (1999), pp. 329–338 on p. 337.

possession, purchase and cultivation on a very small scale for the benefit of others are not covered by it.

The obligation in Article 3(2) of the Illicit Traffic Convention is connected with the clause regarding compliance with 'constitutional principles' of the party and 'the basic concepts of its legal system'.[176] This clause aims to have a narrower scope than the clause 'the constitutional limitations of a Party, its legal system and domestic law' in Article 36(2) of the Single Convention.[177] It would appear that a party may only refrain from criminalizing acts for the sake of personal cannabis use if such criminalization would cause a genuine breach of fundamental principles.[178] The consequence of this is that in fact most parties have no room at all to even decriminalize, let alone legalize the personal possession, purchase by consumers (in a coffee shop for example) and personal cultivation of cannabis. The provision thereby also rules out the decriminalization and legalization of so-called 'cannabis social clubs' and other structures that are aimed at shared consumption. Such phenomena are based on the reasoning that if cannabis cultivation is allowed for personal use in the private domain, cannabis cultivation should also be possible on a collective basis.[179]

- *Acts involving equipment, materials and substances.* Unlike the Single Convention, the Illicit Traffic Convention does not limit itself to acts that relate directly to narcotic drugs. The obligation of criminalization also applies to the manufacture, transport or distribution of equipment, materials or substances mentioned in Table I and Table II that belong to the Convention, 'knowing that they are to be used in or for the illicit cultivation, production or manufacture of narcotic drugs or psychotropic substances' (Article 3(1)(a) under iv of the Illicit Traffic Convention. Therefore, in principle the trade of grow shops and other companies that knowingly supply to hemp nurseries the equipment, materials and/or substances referred to are within the scope of this obligation of criminalization.
- *Organizing, managing and financing.* Criminalization is also required for the organisation, managing and financing of the criminal offences mentioned in

---

176 The authentic English text reveals that the crux of the matter is 'to establish as a criminal offence under its domestic law'. In short: the clause merely aims to define an obligation of transposition.

177 United Nations, *Commentary on the United Nations Convention Against Illicit Traffic in Narcotic Drugs and Psychotropic Substances*, Vienna: 1988, p. 72 (no. 3.65).

178 One could think of a situation where cannabis is used for religious purposes, and that the constitution of a country protects such religious drug use. Incidentally, investigation, prosecution, conviction and punishment will and must be in accordance with fundamental rights and principles, such as for example the right to privacy and the right to a fair trial. See for example Grazia Zuffa, 'How to determine personal use in drug legislation. The "threshold controversy" in the light of the Italian experience', *Series on Legislative Reform of Drug Policies*, No. 15, August 2011, p. 9.

179 Beau Kilmer et al., *Multinational overview of cannabis production regimes*, RAND Europe/WODC, 2013, pp. 8–9.

Article 3(1)(a) of the Illicit Traffic Convention (see Article 3(1)(a) under v of the Illicit Traffic Convention.

- *Receiving and handling and money laundering.* Among other things, the Convention requires criminalization of intentional money laundering (see Article 3(1)(b) of the Illicit Traffic Convention) and receiving and handling (see Article 3(1)(c) of the Illicit Traffic Convention).[180]
- *Incitement and inducement, participation and inchoate offences.* The Illicit Traffic Convention also explicitly requires the criminalization of public incitement or inducement of other people, in whatever way, to commit one or more of the offences in accordance with Article 3 of the Illicit Traffic Convention or to use narcotic drugs or psychotropic substances illicitly (see Article 3(1)(c)iii of the Illicit Traffic Convention). The obligation therefore also applies to criminal offences for personal cannabis use.[181] The clause 'subject to its constitutional principles and the basic concepts of its legal system' that applies to this obligation aims to ensure that the parties can tailor the criminalization to the structure of their own system and also that they do not have to proceed with criminalization or at any rate prosecution if this led to a breach of a constitutional right of freedom of speech.[182] Therefore, the clause cannot be used to refrain from the required criminalization altogether.
- *Participation and inchoate offences.* Much more precisely than the Single Convention, the Illicit Traffic Convention requires the criminalisation of participation in, association or conspiracy to commit, attempts to commit and aiding, abetting, facilitating and counselling for the commission of any of the offences established in accordance with Article 3 of the Illicit Traffic Convention (see Article 3(1)(c)iv of the Illicit Traffic Convention). Here too, the clause 'subject to its constitutional principles and the basic concepts of its legal system' applies, so that parties can use their own forms of participation and inchoate offences in the transposition of this obligation under the Convention to national law.[183]

As far as punishment is concerned, Article 3 of the Illicit Trafficking Convention contains a number of extensions of the obligations that are

---

180 You can read more about this in for example, Jimmy Gurulé, 'The 1988 U.N. Convention Against Illicit Traffic in Narcotic Drugs and Psychotropic Substances – A Ten Year Perspective: Is International Cooperation Merely Illusory?', 22 *Fordham International Law Journal* 1998, pp. 74–121.

181 United Nations, *Commentary on the United Nations Convention Against Illicit Traffic in Narcotic Drugs and Psychotropic Substances*, Vienna: 1988, p. 75 (no. 3.76) and p. 77 (no. 3.81).

182 United Nations, *Commentary on the United Nations Convention Against Illicit Traffic in Narcotic Drugs and Psychotropic Substances*, Vienna: 1988, p. 72 (no. 3.66).

183 United Nations, *Commentary on the United Nations Convention Against Illicit Traffic in Narcotic Drugs and Psychotropic Substances*, Vienna: 1988, p. 76 (nos. 3.78–3.79).

already applicable by virtue of the Single Convention. In addition to deprivation of liberty, the Illicit Trafficking Convention provides pecuniary sanctions and confiscation and there is more attention for measures such as treatment, education, aftercare, rehabilitation or social reintegration (Article 3 (4)).[184]

Article 3(5) of the Illicit Traffic Convention shows that, with regard to the criminal offences referred to in the first paragraph, if there is participation in 'an organized criminal group to which the offender belongs' or if there is any involvement in other[185] international organized criminal activities, these circumstances make the offences 'particularly serious'.[186] This is relevant especially, because cannabis cultivation, delivery and trade for the supply of retail shops and sale by those retail shops to consumers are regarded as criminal offences from the perspective of the Single Convention, the Illicit Traffic Convention and also the Dutch Opium Act, and this can easily involve organized activities and collaborations. In those cases, in accordance with the Convention, acts involving cannabis in relation to retail shops can be qualified as organized crime and therefore as particularly serious.[187] Another example of the same level of seriousness is the use of minors or sales to minors (Article 3(7) of the Illicit Traffic Convention).

Finally, parties are required to take into account the seriousness of the criminal offences when considering early or conditional release (Article 3(7) of the Illicit Traffic Convention).

II. General Obligations to Prosecute

Our earlier comments about obligations to prosecute with regard to the Single Convention,[188] partly apply to the Illicit Traffic Convention. At any rate, in view of the purport and content of the Convention, arguing that parties would not be obliged to prosecute persons for activities which the Convention requires to be criminalized is fraught with difficulties.

It also follows from Article 3(4)(a) in conjunction with paragraph (b) and paragraph (c) of the Illicit Traffic Convention – more explicitly than from Article 36(1)(a) and (b) of the Single Convention – that parties in the case

---

184 We will go into Article 3(4) of the Illicit Traffic Convention later in this section (2.3.2.ii.a.III).

185 See United Nations, *Commentary on the United Nations Convention Against Illicit Traffic in Narcotic Drugs and Psychotropic Substances*, Vienna: 1988, p. 91 (no. 3.117).

186 This follows clearly from the provision, which refers to 'factual circumstances which make the commission of the offences established in accordance with paragraph 1 of this article particularly serious'.

187 United Nations, *Commentary on the United Nations Convention Against Illicit Traffic in Narcotic Drugs and Psychotropic Substances*, Vienna: 1988, p. 90 (no. 3.116).

188 See section 2.2.2.ii.a.IX.

of intentionally committed serious criminal offences in the sense of the first paragraph must apply 'sanctions which take into account the grave nature of these offences, such as imprisonment or other forms of deprivation of liberty, pecuniary sanctions and confiscation.' According to paragraph (b), in addition to conviction or punishment of the offender – who does not necessarily have to be an addict under the Illicit Traffic Convention[189] – other measures can be imposed such as treatment, education, aftercare, rehabilitation or social reintegration. Only in the case of less serious offences may the parties provide these measures as alternatives to conviction or punishment. By virtue of paragraph (c), this also applies to acts for personal cannabis use in the sense of Article 3(2) of the Illicit Traffic Convention. The application of measures only may in such minor cases also be achieved by making the decision not to prosecute conditional on the offender undergoing treatment for example.[190] Although the text of Article 3(4) of the Illicit Traffic Convention could give rise to the assumption that the states parties only have to implement these obligations of penalization in law and do not have to apply them in concrete cases, that interpretation of this provision does not seem to be what is intended. First, the Illicit Traffic Convention attempts to reinforce the penalties system of the Single Convention among other things.[191] Moreover, Article 3 of the Illicit Traffic Convention is intended to make sure that the prosecution authorities and the courts treat the criminal offences described in this provision as serious.[192] The provision is therefore not only aimed at the legislator but also at the Public Prosecutions Service and the judge. In addition to this, another approach would hardly be compatible with the object and purpose of the Convention and of Article 3 of the Single Convention, which after all seeks to improve the effectiveness of national criminal law systems.[193] Insofar as Article 3(4) of the Illicit Traffic Convention presupposes that persons who have committed drug-related offences are convicted and punished, these persons will have to be prosecuted first.

As far as the Illicit Traffic Convention is concerned, it is less straightforward that the provisions relating to the proper administration of justice in

189 United Nations, *Commentary on the United Nations Convention Against Illicit Traffic in Narcotic Drugs and Psychotropic Substances*, Vienna: 1988, p. 87 (no. 3.107).

190 United Nations, *Commentary on the United Nations Convention Against Illicit Traffic in Narcotic Drugs and Psychotropic Substances*, Vienna: 1988, p. 87 (no. 3.108).

191 United Nations, *Commentary on the United Nations Convention Against Illicit Traffic in Narcotic Drugs and Psychotropic Substances*, Vienna: 1988, p. 85 (no. 3.102).

192 United Nations, *Commentary on the United Nations Convention Against Illicit Traffic in Narcotic Drugs and Psychotropic Substances*, Vienna: 1988, p. 48 (no. 3.1); see also p. 97 (no. 3.132).

193 United Nations, *Commentary on the United Nations Convention Against Illicit Traffic in Narcotic Drugs and Psychotropic Substances*, Vienna: 1988, p. 48 (no. 3.2).

international law in criminal matters imply an obligation to prosecute than in the case of Article 36(2)(a)iv of the Single Convention.[194] While it is true that the Illicit Traffic Convention with Article 6(9) also implies that a party in whose territory an alleged offender is found (this can be one of its own nationals[195]) must submit the case to the prosecuting authorities, if said person is not extradited, but the obligation does not apply (in the case of paragraph (a)) if another agreement has been reached with the party requesting extradition or (in the case of paragraph (b)) if that requesting party objects to such a prosecution. In short: the *aut dedere aut judicare* obligation may cease to apply.[196] If this happens, the requested party is still at liberty – but not required! – to exercise the powers of jurisdiction by virtue of its national law.[197] This provision thereby implies two things: 1) in the context of the proper administration of justice the Convention primarily assumes there is an obligation to prosecute but 2) this obligation is not absolute. The question then is whether that obligation is absolute in a case and/or context where strictly national law applies.

III. Obligations to Prosecute and the Expediency Principle: Article 3(6) of the Illicit Traffic Convention

Particularly relevant for the obligation to prosecute in a national context is the provision in Article 3(6) of the Illicit Traffic Convention. This provision reads:

> The Parties shall endeavour to ensure that any discretionary legal powers under their domestic law relating to the prosecution of persons for offences established in accordance with this article are exercised to maximize the effectiveness of law enforcement measures in respect of those offences and with due regard to the need to deter the commission of such offences.

The background to Article 3(6) of the Illicit Traffic Convention is a proposal for a provision which required the prosecuting authorities in all states parties to realize strict enforcement of the criminalizations laid out in Article 3 of the Illicit Traffic Convention.[198] This was triggered by the dissatisfaction with, or sometimes even the lack of understanding of the American 'plea bargaining'

194 See section 2.2.2.ii.a.IX.

195 See Article 6(9)(a) in conjunction with Article 4(2)(a) of the Illicit Traffic Convention.

196 United Nations, *Commentary on the United Nations Convention Against Illicit Traffic in Narcotic Drugs and Psychotropic Substances*, Vienna: 1988, p. 169 (no. 6.39).

197 United Nations, *Commentary on the United Nations Convention Against Illicit Traffic in Narcotic Drugs and Psychotropic Substances*, Vienna: 1988, p. 169 (no. 6.39).

198 United Nations, *Commentary on the United Nations Convention Against Illicit Traffic in Narcotic Drugs and Psychotropic Substances*, Vienna: 1988, p. 94 (no. 3.124).

system among some delegations.[199] Eventually, it had to be recognized that such an absolute obligation comes with its own disadvantages. In this respect, the UN Commentary mentions that discretion for prosecuting authorities facilitates 'rational prosecution policies' and recognizes the legitimate concern for priorities in using public funds. This seems to imply that maximum efforts in active investigation and by extension prosecution are not necessarily required. However, it cannot be inferred from this that in general – and therefore even if criminal offences and the offenders are known – prosecution may be waived on the basis of policy. According to the UN Commentary, there can also be reasons in an individual case to make concessions with regard to prosecution and punishment, so that the judicial authorities can obtain cooperation from the person involved for the benefit of investigation and prosecution of others.[200] These are limited exceptions to the principle of prosecution, as they are apparently acceptable because on balance they help achieve the objective of enforcing the criminalizations pursuant to the Convention. Once more, it confirms the conclusion that normally there is no room to abstain from prosecution if criminal offences are known to have been committed and the offenders have been identified. Article 3(6) of the Illicit Traffic Convention is a reflection of the compromise between an absolute obligation to prosecute and the interests mentioned, witness the phrase 'to maximize the effectiveness of law enforcement measures'.[201]

Still, the UN Commentary does not explicitly deal with the question whether the foregoing applies with equal force to drug-related acts aimed at personal consumption as it does to more serious acts. In that respect, it would appear that the obligation ensuing from Article 3(6) applies to both cases in equal measure. The wording of the provision also hints at that because it does not imply any distinction between minor and major offences either. The UN Commentary contains a more general statement about the sixth paragraph among others that this provision seeks to ensure that especially the illicit traffic offences mentioned in the first paragraph of Article 3 of the Illicit Traffic Convention 'are treated by with appropriate seriousness by the judiciary and the prosecutorial authorities of each party'.[202] This seems to suggest that the obligation 'to maximize the effectiveness of law enforcement

---

199 For example: *Kamerstukken II* 1990–1991, 22 080 (R 1406), nr. 3, p. 10 (MvT) (i.e., *Dutch Parliamentary Documents II* 1990–1991, 22 080 (R 1406), no. 3, p. 10 (Explanatory Memorandum)).

200 United Nations, *Commentary on the United Nations Convention Against Illicit Traffic in Narcotic Drugs and Psychotropic Substances*, Vienna: 1988, p. 94 (no. 3.125).

201 United Nations, *Commentary on the United Nations Convention Against Illicit Traffic in Narcotic Drugs and Psychotropic Substances*, Vienna: 1988, p. 94 (no. 3.126).

202 United Nations, *Commentary on the United Nations Convention Against Illicit Traffic in Narcotic Drugs and Psychotropic Substances*, Vienna: 1988, p. 97 (no. 3.132); see also pp. 82–83 (nos. 3.94–3.96).

measures' with respect to offences of the second paragraph (possession, purchase or cultivation for personal consumption) is somehow less strict. Such an interpretation is corroborated further by the fact that acts aimed at personal consumption were deliberately not included in the first paragraph but rather in the second one, which comes under a lighter regime in Article 3 of the Illicit Traffic Convention. It is also important that the Illicit Traffic Convention primarily aims to prevent trade, rather than personal use, although this argument is qualified by Article 1(m) of the Illicit Traffic Convention, according to which 'illicit traffic' means the criminal offences described in the first and second paragraphs in Article 3 of the Illicit Traffic Convention. Taking everything into account, we believe that there is a case for claiming that Article 3(6) of the Illicit Traffic Convention does not apply as strictly to drug-related acts aimed at personal use (Article 3(2) of the Illicit Traffic Convention) as it does to more serious acts (Article 3(1) of the Illicit Traffic Convention).[203] However, this does not mean that the expediency principle can be applied unrestrictedly to such acts.

In our opinion, the wording of Article 3(6) of the Illicit Traffic Convention and the background to this imply a strong premise for prosecution, which may only be departed from insofar as a rational prioritization in the general prosecution policy and the availability of public funds necessitate this or if more important interests concerning the enforcement of drug-related criminal law necessitate this in individual cases. In the case of possession, purchase and cultivation for personal use, the authorities appear to have a little bit more room for manoeuvring. It is obvious that Article 3(6) of the Illicit Traffic Convention does not permit the legalization or decriminalization of acts which the Convention requires to be criminalized. This therefore also applies to cannabis cultivation, delivery and trade for the supply of retail shops. Again, on the basis of the wording and the background of Article 3(6) of the Illicit Traffic Convention and the object and purpose of the Convention, this provision does not leave any room either to base the prosecution policy on something that is diametrically opposed to what the Convention represents. In accordance with and complementary to the Single Convention, the Illicit Traffic Convention was framed on the assumption that the problems around drugs need to be combated vigorously with criminal measures, prohibitions and repression of all acts that are directly or indirectly relevant to it.[204] There was an emphatic decision not to choose a regime that leaves room for other angles in the considerations, such as the separation of the soft drugs and the hard drugs markets or the importance of simplifying control of the quality

---

203 This view is held more firmly by David R. Bewley-Taylor & Martin Jelsma, 'The Limits of Latitude. The UN drug control conventions', *Series on Legislative Reform of Drug Policies*, No. 18, March 2012, pp. 6 and 15.

204 With regards to the Single Convention, also see section 2.2.3.i.

of illegal narcotic drugs. Whatever one thinks of the choice underlying the Convention, Article 3(6) of the Illicit Traffic Convention does not allow states parties to base their prosecution policy with regard to cannabis on such angles.

The question is whether this applies to the Netherlands too. In itself, Article 3(6) of the Illicit Traffic Convention applies there as well, since the provision and as it happens the entire Convention was ratified. That does not alter the fact that the Netherlands formulated an Understanding with regards to Article 3(6) of the Illicit Traffic Convention at the time of signing and a Reservation on accepting the Convention. We will come back to this in more detail in section 2.3.4.

IV. Obligations Regarding Confiscation: Article 5 of the Illicit Traffic Convention

The Illicit Traffic Convention contains a fair number of obligations relating to confiscation and the powers to support this, such as seizure. In the Convention, confiscation means the permanent deprivation of property.[205] The term in fact covers the Dutch concepts of forfeiture, removal from use and the deprivation of illegally obtained benefits.[206] Among other things, the Convention provides for confiscation of proceeds derived from narcotic drugs and from materials and equipment used in offences committed in relation with drugs. In Article 5(1)(b), the Convention also establishes that each party must adopt measures that may be necessary to enable confiscation of' narcotic drugs and psychotropic substances, materials and equipment or other instrumentalities used in or intended for use in any manner in offences' mentioned in Article 3(1) of the Illicit Traffic Convention. The obligation in the provision concerns making confiscation possible: parties are not required to make confiscation mandatory in all or even certain cases.[207] In that respect, Article 5(1)(b) of the Illicit Traffic Convention does not add anything to the more stringent obligations of seizure ensuing from the Single Convention.[208]

V. Obligation of Transposition: Article 3(11) of the Illicit Traffic Convention

Article 3(11) of the Illicit Traffic Convention is the slightly more elaborate equivalent of Article 36(4) of the Single Convention.[209] The Article implies

205 See Article 1(f) of the Illicit Traffic Convention.

206 See *Kamerstukken II* 1990–1991, 22 080 (R 1406), nr. 3, p. 7 (MvT) (i.e., *Dutch Parliamentary Documents II* 1990–1991, 22 080 (R 1406), no. 3, p. 7 (Explanatory Memorandum)).

207 United Nations, *Commentary on the United Nations Convention Against Illicit Traffic in Narcotic Drugs and Psychotropic Substances*, Vienna: 1988, p. 118 (no. 5.4).

208 See section 2.2.2.ii.a.VIII.

209 See section 2.2.2.ii.a.VII.

the need to transpose and implement the law of the Convention to national law and seeks to ensure that none of the provisions in the Convention is self-executing in countries where the constitution provides for the direct operation of international law.[210] So Article 3(11) of the Illicit Traffic Convention does not contain an additional clause either which affords parties the opportunity to create their own policy.[211] With respect to Article 3 of the Illicit Traffic Convention, this not only follows from the UN Commentary about it, but it is also implied by the system of this provision. After all, the clauses to protect national law included in Article 3(1)(c), (2) and (10) would be redundant if the eleventh paragraph were intended to afford freedom of implementation to the states parties, since in that case that which is now ensured by the aforementioned clauses would then already have been covered in a wider and more general sense by the eleventh paragraph. All this does not alter the fact that the transposition required by Article 3(11) of the Illicit Traffic Convention will result in the incorporation of the obligations of the Convention in national law, in the usual structure and following the terminology of national law.[212]

VI. The Clause of Article 2(1) of the Illicit Traffic Convention

Several 'safeguard clauses' have already been discussed. Until now, we have kept Article 2 of the Illicit Traffic Convention out of the picture. The first paragraph of this Article stipulates that the parties in honouring their obligations pursuant to this Convention must take the necessary measures 'in conformity with the fundamental provisions of their respective domestic legislative systems'. Does this clause offer a departure point for proceeding to allow cannabis cultivation? That is not the case.

The preparatory history and the UN Commentary show that the parties did not want a clause that could be used to wriggle out of the obligations under the Convention.[213] The clause was not even intended to go further

210 United Nations, *Commentary on the United Nations Convention Against Illicit Traffic in Narcotic Drugs and Psychotropic Substances*, Vienna: 1988, p. 97 (no. 3.131).

211 The government of the Netherlands seems to overlook this, when it maintains that the second paragraph [of Article 3 of the Illicit Traffic Convention] must also be read in connection with the eleventh paragraph [...]. In other words, that the Article does not affect the prosecution and sentencing policy conducted in the Netherlands; see *Kamerstukken II* 1990–1991, 22 080 (R 1406), no. 3, pp. 9–10 (MvT) (i.e., *Dutch Parliamentary Documents II* 1990–1991, 22 080 (R 1406), nr. 3, pp. 9–10 (Explanatory Memorandum)); see also *Kamerstukken II* 1991–1992, 22 080 (R 1406), nr. 6, p. 7 (MvA) (i.e., *Dutch Parliamentary Documents II* 1990–1991, 22 080 (R 1406), no. 6, p. 7 (Memorandum of Reply)), where reference is made to the eleventh paragraph.

212 See also *Kamerstukken II* 1990–1991, 22 080 (R 1406), nr. 3, p. 8 (MvT) (i.e., *Dutch Parliamentary Documents II* 1990–1991, 22 080 (R 1406), no. 3, p. 8 (Explanatory Memorandum)).

213 See United Nations, *Commentary on the United Nations Convention Against Illicit Traffic in Narcotic Drugs and Psychotropic Substances*, Vienna: 1988, pp. 40–42 (nos. 2.1–2.5), with

than the principles of international law that are clearly established and universally recognized. This seems to imply that the clause is all about international cooperation. This conclusion is corroborated by Article 2 of the Illicit Traffic Convention itself. The clause is part of the first paragraph and follows the sentence that the purpose of the Convention is the promotion of cooperation among the parties; and the remainder of Article 2 of the Illicit Traffic Convention – paragraphs two and three – relates to that cooperation. At this stage already, the clause does not appear to have any bearing on the obligations in the Convention that do not directly concern that international cooperation. To that extent, it does not appear to be relevant for the discussion about allowing cannabis cultivation.

Be that as it may, the UN Commentary notes that Article 2 of the Illicit Traffic Convention is not intended as a clause covering all other provisions under the Convention.[214] The fact that this is not the case also follows systematically from the Convention, because if it were the case, the 'safeguard clauses' in the other provisions would be superfluous. From the preparatory history, it also transpires that the clause in Article 2(1) of the Illicit Traffic Convention does not intend to tie the obligations under the Convention to the national law systems of the parties and that the clause must not in any way be construed that parties can derogate from their obligations under the Convention.[215] None of the obligations arising from the Conventions is therefore qualified as such by Article 2(1) of the Illicit Traffic Convention. It is only meant to ensure that the parties can implement those obligations within the structures and the terminologies of their systems using their familiar legal instruments (such as statutes and other (lower) legislation and regulations). For that reason, the wording of the clause in Article 2(1) of the Illicit Traffic Convention uses 'in conformity with' and not 'subject to'[216] the fundamental provisions of the domestic legislative systems.

In short: it follows from the preparatory history, the system of the Convention and the wording of the clause in Article 2(1) of the Illicit Traffic Convention that its aim is not to give the parties additional freedom of policy in implementing and fulfilling their obligations arising from the Conventions. Nor can the clause be used to legitimize the legalization, decriminalization, policy-based tolerance and/or other forms of regulating cannabis cultivation.

---

reference to United Nations, 'Conference for the Adoption of a Convention against Illicit Traffic in Narcotic Drugs and Psychotropic Substances, Vienna, 25 November–20 December 1988, Official Records, Volume II', *UN Doc.* E/CONF. 82/16/Add.1, e.g. para 86–93.

214 United Nations, *Commentary on the United Nations Convention Against Illicit Traffic in Narcotic Drugs and Psychotropic Substances*, Vienna: 1988, p. 42 (no. 2.5).

215 United Nations, *Commentary on the United Nations Convention Against Illicit Traffic in Narcotic Drugs and Psychotropic Substances*, Vienna: 1988, pp. 43–44 (nos. 2.8–2.11).

216 However, that wording does appear in Article 36(1) and (2) of the Single Convention and Article 3(1)(c) and (2) of the Illicit Traffic Convention.

b. Obligations Regarding Cannabis Plants: Articles 3 and 14 of the Illicit Traffic Convention

As we said before, the Illicit Traffic Convention also has some obligations that specifically concern cannabis – in addition to the obligations that ensue from the inclusion of cannabis in the Schedules of the Single Convention. These are to be found in Articles 3 and 14 of the Illicit Traffic Convention, and they both deal with cultivation of cannabis plants among other things. These obligations can only be avoided by amending or denouncing the Convention; modifying the Schedules would have no effect therefore.

I. Criminalization of Cannabis Cultivation: Article 3(1) and (a)ii of the Illicit Traffic Convention

This provision imposes on the parties the obligation to criminalize the intentional cultivation of cannabis which does not fall under the exception of 'medical or scientific purposes'. This obligation directly applies to the cultivation of the cannabis plant with a view to producing narcotic drugs (and these include the flowering and fruiting tops of the cannabis plant and cannabis resin). Unlike Article 36 of the Single Convention, which only deals with criminalization of cultivation of flowering and fruiting cannabis tops and cannabis resin – this Article also makes the cultivation of cannabis plants that have not yet produced flowering and fruiting tops or cannabis resin already a completed offence which is punishable according to the Convention. Seeing that possession, sale and cultivation for personal use are already covered by Article 3(2) of the Illicit Traffic Convention, it must be assumed that the first paragraph of that Article does not cover that, as is confirmed by the UN Commentary.[217] So in principle, Article 3(1) and (a)ii of the Illicit Traffic Convention is limited to commercial cultivation, which is not small-scale. That means that, among other things, cannabis cultivation for retail shops, but also other cultivation that is not restricted to one's personal consumption – or at any rate not very small-scale[218] – will have to be criminalized. To that extent, decriminalization and legalization of such cannabis cultivation is ruled out under the Illicit Traffic Convention.

II. Obligation to Take Measures Against Cultivation of Cannabis: Article 14(2) of the Illicit Traffic Convention

Because of this provision, each party is obliged to take ('appropriate measures') to prevent illicit cultivation of cannabis plants and to 'eradicate' them in

217 See, amongst others, United Nations, *Commentary on the United Nations Convention Against Illicit Traffic in Narcotic Drugs and Psychotropic Substances*, Vienna: 1988, p. 56 (no. 3.29).

218 See the comments about 'personal consumption' in section 2.3.2.i.a.I (see: Behaviours for personal cannabis use).

its territory. While it is true that Article 14(2) of the Illicit Traffic Convention does not force parties to criminalize or to take action in criminal matters, the provision does form an obstacle towards allowing (non-medical or non-scientific) cannabis cultivation. After all, it is that very cultivation that the parties are required to take measures against. In this way, the provision – for which the Netherlands did not formulate a declaration or reservation by the way – also precludes the legalization, policy-based tolerance or other forms of regulating cannabis cultivation for recreational use. Criminal prosecution is not required by the provision per se, but other measures are: to this extent, the provision (unlike other Articles in the Convention) does leave some room for penal tolerance (i.e., non-prosecution), but not for administrative tolerance as well (for example by issuing permits). Because Article 14(2) of the Illicit Traffic Convention makes no specific exception for personal consumption, strictly speaking it also applies to this particular use as long as cannabis is included in the Schedules. That is why cultivation in the framework of so-called 'Cannabis Social Clubs' and other structures aimed at shared consumption are also within the scope of this provision. This is also something that the party must take measures against to prevent and eradicate it. Since the provision does not specify the particulars, the parties have a fair amount of leeway in choosing their own approach with respect to fulfilling this obligation. Nevertheless, these measures will at least have to be effective and the party must act in good faith in this respect. The least the authorities would have to do, so it seems, would be to seize illegal stocks that the authorities are aware of. According to Article 14(2) of the Illicit Traffic Convention, these measures must of course be compatible with human rights. So in this case too, it is not simply a question of barging in somewhere to put a nursery out of business:[219] the government must adhere to the procedural conditions and safeguards that apply. Incidentally, the measures have to take into account historical and traditional use of the drug, but we will not discuss this further as this is not relevant for states like the Netherlands.[220]

2.3.3. 'MEDICAL OR SCIENTIFIC PURPOSES' AND OTHER EXCEPTIONS

With regard to the exception of medical or scientific purposes, the Illicit Traffic Convention is also fully based on the system of the Single Convention.

219 Let alone that authorities, in the name of the fight against drugs, could resort to arbitrary detention, torture, capital punishment or extra-judicial executions, which we can see all over the world; for further references see Rick Lines, '"Deliver us from evil"? – The Single Convention on Narcotic Drugs, 50 years on', 1 *International Journal on Human Rights and Drug Policy* 2010, pp. 1–13.

220 See section 2.2.4.

The actual terms or similar terminology cannot be found in the Illicit Traffic Convention, but that obviously does not mean that the exception does not apply for this Convention. This Convention is aimed, among other things, at narcotic drugs that are contrary to the provisions in the Single Convention, and these are all the substances that are within the scope of this Convention which are used for purposes other than 'medical or scientific' (see Article 3 of the Illicit Traffic Convention.[221] This means that the observations in section 2.2.3 about the exception for the Single Convention also apply here.

This also applies to national defences. These are therefore also applicable under the Illicit Traffic Convention for offences with an underlying obligation for criminalization pursuant to the Convention, provided of course that this application does not contravene the obligation to interpret and implement the Convention in good faith. In contrast to the Single Convention, this is a little more explicit in the Illicit Traffic Convention itself. After all, Article 3(11) of the Illicit Traffic Convention states that 'the description [...] of legal defences [...] is reserved to the domestic law [...]'.

2.3.4. DECLARATIONS AND RESERVATIONS WITH REGARD TO THE ILLICIT TRAFFIC CONVENTION

The Netherlands accepted by law the entire Illicit Traffic Convention without any exception. The approval therefore also applies to Article 3(6) of the Illicit Traffic Convention.[222] However, the Netherlands did formulate a so-called 'Understanding' with respect to the functioning of Article 3(6) of the Illicit Traffic Convention at the time of signature of the Illicit Traffic Convention and a 'Reservation' in connection with that functioning on the acceptance of the Convention.[223]

i. *The 'Understanding' Made by the Netherlands*

First, a few comments about the 'Understanding' from the Netherlands. It says:

> With respect of article 3, paragraph 6, [the Government of the Netherlands] notes that its provisions cover offences established both under paragraph 1 and paragraph 2. In view of the provisions of paragraph 4 (d) and paragraph 11 of the same article, [the Government of the Netherlands] understands that the measure of discretionary

221 See also United Nations, *Commentary on the United Nations Convention Against Illicit Traffic in Narcotic Drugs and Psychotropic Substances*, Vienna: 1988, p. 53 (no. 3.11); in connection with cultivation, see also pp. 56–57 (no. 3.29).

222 The full English text is included in section 2.3.2.i.a.III.

223 See: http://treaties.un.org/ (Chapter VI, no. 19).

> legal powers relating to the prosecution for offences established in accordance with paragraph 2 may in practice be wider than for offences established in accordance with paragraph 1.

This essentially means that the Netherlands interprets Article 3(6) of the Illicit Traffic Convention in the sense that there is more freedom for considerations of expediency in the case of criminal offences aimed at personal use in the sense of Article 3(2) of the Illicit Traffic Convention than for criminal offences referred to by Article 3(1) of the Illicit Traffic Convention. This makes the expediency principle in relation to the second paragraph the main theme of the 'Understanding'. Implicitly, the Netherlands is also saying that there is less room for considerations of expediency with respect to criminal offences that are not aimed at personal consumption. At any rate, that limited room concerns the supply side of the drug economy and in that context also applies to cannabis cultivation, delivery and trade and consumer sales. Such conduct aimed at supplying third parties by definition is not intended for consumption by the perpetrator.

The Dutch government was of the opinion that Article 3(6) of the Illicit Traffic Convention was formulated in a way that revealed some lack of understanding of the importance and the function of the expediency principle.[224] It is unclear what this view is based on. On the one hand, the Convention does not force the abolition of the expediency principle, it merely requires that its application is such that the investigation and law enforcement for the criminal drug-related offences defined in the Convention are as effective as possible, while on the other hand the expediency principle in itself does not form an obstacle to prosecution in all cases involving acts that are required to be criminalized by the Convention. Even if one argues that there should be room for expediency considerations in each concrete case,[225] no conflict with the expediency principle needs to arise, so long as one assumes that in principle, the expediency of the prosecution is a given, in the light of international obligations. It is exactly because the Netherlands endorses the content of the Convention that such a supposition is quite possible. Therefore, Article 3(6) of the Illicit Traffic Convention does not seem to pose any legal problems for the Netherlands. The question is whether there is a problem from the perspective of the Dutch culture of politics and policy on crime, where the expediency principle plays a fundamental role. At any rate, it is not evident that this is the case. Also in this context it is true that the Convention does not force parties to relinquish the expediency principle as such, and that the obligations

---

224 *Kamerstukken II* 1990–1991, 22 080 (R 1406), nr 3, p. 10 (MvT) (i.e., *Dutch Parliamentary Documents II* 1990–1991, 22 080 (R 1406), no. 3, p. 10 (Explanatory Memorandum)).

225 In the Netherlands on the grounds of Article 167 Criminal Code.

arising from the Conventions can be fulfilled perfectly well while applying this principle. Of course, it must be borne in mind that the considerable freedom with which the Netherlands Public Prosecutions Service can apply the expediency principle in certain cases does not exist for offences covered by the UN narcotic drugs conventions.

ii. The Reservation Made by the Netherlands

Although the Netherlands approved Article 3(6) of the Illicit Traffic Convention and the entire Convention for that matter, it is partly because of that provision that eventually a reservation was formulated with regard to the functioning of that provision on the ratification of the Illicit Traffic Convention:

> The Government of the Kingdom of the Netherlands accepts the provisions of article 3, paragraphs 6, 7, and 8, only in so far as the obligations under these provisions are in accordance with Dutch criminal legislation and Dutch policy on criminal matters.

The question arises what exactly the Dutch government had in mind with this reservation. At any rate, there is no intention of going against the object and purpose of the Convention, as it says that the government shares the view that the Netherlands cannot really afford to go against the letter and the spirit of the Convention and implement a policy that runs counter to that of the countries surrounding Netherlands.[226] So what is it about then? According to the government, the reservation basically means that Dutch applicable law will continue to apply in full to the areas covered by these three paragraphs.[227] With the phrase 'will continue to apply' the government implies that the reservation aims to preserve the law existing at the time and not to safeguard room for future legislation as well. With 'Dutch law' and in those places where the reservation refers to 'Dutch criminal legislation and Dutch policy on criminal matters', the government obviously refers to the expediency principle as far as the sixth paragraph is concerned. That is after all the only thing that it mentions explicitly – insofar as it is relevant at this point – as a reason for the reservation. The expediency principle is indeed one of the general principles

---

226 *Kamerstukken II* 1991–1992, 22 080 (R 1406), nr. 6, p. 3 (MvA) (i.e., *Dutch Parliamentary Documents II* 1991–1992, 22 080 (R 1406), no. 6, p. 3 (Memorandum of Reply)). In Parliament, a few members of a governing party observed that even with the greatest sympathy for pleas for further liberalization of the policies, they failed to see how the Netherlands could be the only country to go against the letter and spirit of the United Nations Convention; see *Kamerstukken II* 1991–1992, 22 080 (R 1406), nr. 4, p. 3 (Voorlopig verslag) (i.e., *Dutch Parliamentary Documents II* 1991–1992, 22 080 (R 1406), no. 4, p. 3 (Preliminary report)).

227 *Kamerstukken II* 1990–1991, 22 080 (R 1406), nr. 3, p. 10 (MvT) (i.e., *Dutch Parliamentary Documents II* 1990–1991, 22 080 (R 1406), no. 3, p. 10 (Explanatory Memorandum)).

of the Dutch legal system[228] and the government does not see why it should be reviewed because of the Convention.[229] It is not clear though whether that comment applies to the functioning of the expediency principle in general or to the application of this principle in relation to drug-related offences, and if the latter is the case, whether cannabis is implied as well.

Let us first turn to the expediency principle in general. There is no reason to assume that the government wanted to safeguard this principle as such. After all, the Conventions do not suggest that the Netherlands should abolish it, so a reservation that protects against this possibility would be groundless. Is the objective of the reservation then to ensure that the Public Prosecutions Service can apply the expediency principle in full at all times to criminal offences within the scope of the Illicit Traffic Convention? Or does the reservation have a more limited objective, namely that the Netherlands can continue to apply the prosecution policy that was applicable at the time and was based on the expediency principle? These are no simple questions. After all, the Explanatory Memorandum does not refer at all to the Netherlands policy on cannabis and coffee shops, and therefore not to the reservation either. Yet, the drug policy is the unmistakable background of the reservation as far as the expediency principle is concerned. For example, the government states that the proposed reservation regarding Article 3(6) Illicit Traffic Convention ensures that the existing Dutch prosecution policy will not need to be changed as a consequence of the Convention.[230] This comment indicates that the reservation intends to preserve the prosecution policy with respect to drugs that applied at the time. In this light, the reservation does not aim to guarantee that the expediency principle can be applied to all criminal drug-related offences in full at all times or also to safeguard room for future legislative or policy initiatives. After all, none of that is part of the existing Dutch prosecution policy. Also, if one takes into account the previously mentioned 'Understanding', it looks as if the reservation is meant to protect the prosecution policy on drugs that applied at the time. After all, that 'Understanding' was also about ensuring room for considerations of expediency – also as a general policy – in the case of criminal behaviour aimed at personal consumption in the sense of Article 3(2) of the Illicit Traffic Convention. Without the reservation, the Netherlands

228 See for example Pim Geelhoed, *Het opportuniteitsbeginsel en het recht van de Europese Unie* (diss. Leiden), Deventer: Kluwer, 2013, p. 1: 'Het opportuniteitsbeginsel is een systeemkenmerk van het Nederlandse strafrecht.' (i.e., Pim Geelhoed, *The expediency principle and European Union law* (dissertation Leiden), Deventer: Kluwer, 2013, p. 1, where he says that the expediency principle is a characteristic of the Dutch criminal law system.).

229 *Kamerstukken II* 1990–1991, 22 080 (R 1406), nr. 3, p. 28 (MvT) (i.e., *Dutch Parliamentary Documents II* 1990–1991, 22 080 (R 1406), no. 3, p. 28 (Explanatory Memorandum)).

230 *Kamerstukken II* 1991–1992, 22 080 (R 1406), nr. 6, p. 7 (MvA) (i.e., *Dutch Parliamentary Documents II* 1991–1992, 22 080 (R 1406), no. 6, p. 7 (Memorandum of Reply)).

would have less room for a general policy of tolerance towards the personal consumption of soft drugs, instead of basing non-prosecution on special circumstances in concrete cases. The reservation therefore undoubtedly covers, for example, the applicable policy[231] not to prosecute someone if he has no more than 5 grams of cannabis in his possession or when an adult cultivates no more than 5 cannabis plants for such use, but instead to dismiss the case by police and confiscate the cannabis or plants.

The foregoing means that the reservation did not a priori intend to create extra room for any future application of the expediency principle to the supply side of the drug economy, nor to cannabis cultivation, delivery and trade for the supply of coffee shops. In any event, there is nothing that specifically points to the possibility. But even if the Netherlands had such a broad reservation in mind, this was not communicated to the other states parties, while a reservation is actually typically directed at them. Also in view of this, it seems to us that is hard to see how the reservation was intended to justify a general policy to refrain from prosecution with respect to cannabis cultivation, delivery and trade for recreational use and the supply of coffee shops.

iii. Later Extension of the Application of the Reservation

The question is whether the Netherlands could presently invoke the reservation – therefore without regard to the focus on personal consumption at that time – for regulating cannabis cultivation, delivery, trade and sales for recreational use. First, it must be noted that the reservation to the Illicit Traffic Convention cannot derogate from the obligations of criminalization and prosecution (among other things) which ensue from the Single Convention. This is because the reservation has no bearing on that Convention, and it could not possibly apply to it anyway. See also Guideline 4.4.1 of the Guide to Practice on Reservations to Treaties of the International Law Commission (hereinafter: ILC Guide to Reservations).[232] Insofar as the Single Convention requires states to prosecute, these obligations still apply in full for the Netherlands too.[233]

Furthermore, the reservation is in any case not usable for decriminalization or legalization of behaviour which the Conventions require to be criminalized,

---

231 College van procureurs-generaal openbaar ministerie, 'Aanwijzing Opiumwet (2015A003)', *Stcrt.* 2015/5391 (i.e., Board of Procurators General of the Dutch Public Prosecutions Service, 'Instruction regarding the Opium Act (2015A003)', Dutch Government Gazette, 2015/5391), with effect from 1 March 2015.

232 Included in Report of the ILC on the Work of its 63rd session, General Assembly, Official Records, 66th Session, Supplement n° 10, Addendum 1, *UN Doc.* A/66/10/Add.1. (2011); see also the comments on that provision on p. 498 (also: Commentaries to the ILC Guide to Reservations). For an explanation of the use of ILC guidelines here and commentaries see section 2.1.2.

233 See section 2.2.2.ii.a.IX for information about the obligations to prosecute.

since the reservation only seeks to protect the expediency principle. This follows not only from the fact that the principle was the reason for making the reservation in the first place, but also from the fact that the reservation applies to Article 3(6) of the Illicit Traffic Convention, which provision deals with 'discretionary legal powers under [...] domestic law relating to the prosecution of persons'.

Does the reservation offer the possibility for the Netherlands to refrain from prosecution in connection with cannabis cultivation, delivery and trade for the supply of coffee shops as a matter of general policy? As seen above, the reservation was formulated to protect the prosecution policy which was based on the expediency principle and in force at the time when the Convention was approved, and not to safeguard room for future legislative or policy initiatives. In addition to this, pursuant to Article 19 of the Vienna Convention on the Law of Treaties, parties can formulate a reservation 'when signing, ratifying, accepting, approving or acceding to a treaty'. That is also the assumption of Guideline 1.1 ILC Guide to Reservations. Moreover, the principle of good faith (*pacta sunt servanda*) implies that a party bound by the obligations in the Convention is not allowed to modify those obligations unilaterally to the disadvantage of other parties or to shirk these obligations.[234] Late reservations are therefore problematic.[235] In principle, there is no place for such reservations,[236] witness Guideline 1.1 as well as the Commentaries to the ILC Guide to Reservations.[237] The same goes for modifying a reservation with a view to increasing its scope. This should meet the same conditions that apply in the case of late reservations.[238] Late reservations or modifications are not permitted, unless the Convention states that this is allowed (this is not the case in the Illicit Traffic Convention, while the Single Convention absolutely excludes this) or none of the parties object to this (only the Illicit Traffic Convention still allows this option).[239] Against this background, it is also problematic to use the reservation to the Illicit Traffic Convention not only to offer protection

234 See Commentaries to the ILC Guide to Reservations, p. 39 (no. 7) and p. 177 (no. 7); see also Daniel Müller, 'Reservations and Time: Is There Only One Right Moment to Formulate and to React to Reservations?', 24 *Eur. J. Int. Law* 4 (2013), p. 1115.

235 See Daniel Müller, 'Reservations and Time: Is There Only One Right Moment to Formulate and to React to Reservations?', 24 *Eur. J. Int. Law* 4 (2013), pp. 1120–1121; see also Robin Room & Sarah McKay, *Roadmaps for Reforming the UN Drug Conventions*, Oxford: Beckley Foundation Press 2012, p. 14 and 55.

236 In principle, see Guideline 2.3 ILC Guide to Reservations.

237 'Text of the guidelines with commentaries thereto', in: Report of the ILC on the Work of its 63rd session, General Assembly, Official Records, 66th Session, Supplement n° 10, Addendum 1, *UN Doc.* A/66/10/Add.1, p. 34 (no. 11), p. 174 (no. 2) and pp. 176–177 (nos. 5 and 7) (also: Commentaries to the ILC Guide to Reservations).

238 Guideline 2.3.4 ILC Guide to Reservations.

239 Guideline 2.3 ILC Guide to Reservations; see also Guideline 2.7.4.

to 'Dutch criminal legislation and Dutch policy on criminal matters' that was in force at the time of the reservation, but also to use it to implement new legislation and/or policy measures later to derogate from the Convention. This conclusion gains even more traction if one considers the Guidelines in the ILC Guide to Reservations and the Commentaries on it. These deal more specifically with reservations in connection with national law. And this is exactly what the reservation by the Netherlands is all about. The Commentaries to the ILC Guide to Reservations illustrate that reservations in order to protect national law are not free from objections but they are not banned either. Insofar as this is relevant at the moment, Guideline 3.1.5.5 applies to reservations that are formulated to preserve 'the integrity of specific rules of the internal law of that State' that are 'in force at the time of the formulation of the reservation'. Neither this provision, nor the Guide as a whole or Commentaries recognize the opportunity to formulate a reservation to leave room for future legislative or policy initiatives. On the contrary: the Commentaries make it clear that the prohibition on formulating vague or general reservations (Guideline 3.1.5.2) implies, among other things, that countries with reservations to preserve national law must specify the legal provisions which are to be protected[240] – and these will by definition be existing provisions. If reservations applying to future law or policy were permitted, it would be impossible for the other parties to establish whether the reservation is acceptable or not.[241] Also for that reason it is completely understandable that the possibility of reservations to leave room for future law or policy is not recognized anywhere.

If from now on the Netherlands were to refrain from prosecution with regard to cannabis cultivation, delivery and trade for the supply of coffee shops as a matter of policy, this would bring about an essential change in policy in respect of the approach to cannabis-related offences. In that case, the Public Prosecutions Service will tolerate not only consumer sales, but also all preceding operations up to and including cannabis cultivation, in other words an entire domestic cannabis economy from organized cultivation to consumer sales aimed at recreational use. Seen against that background, the foregoing leads to the conclusion that the Dutch reservation to Article 3(6) of the Illicit Traffic Convention can hardly leave room for such penal tolerance. For this conclusion, it is therefore particularly important that the Netherlands formulated the reservation to preserve the applicable law at the time of approval of the Convention and not with a view to leaving room for future initiatives, while this latter scenario is hardly feasible, in view of international public law, as reflected in the ILC Guide to Reservations and the Commentaries thereon.

---

240 Commentaries to the ILC Guide to Reservations, pp. 364–365 (no. 4).

241 Commentaries to the ILC Guide to Reservations, pp. 364–367 (nos. 3–8).

iv. Compatibility with the Object and Purpose of the Convention

It also is worth noting here that it is not allowed to make reservations that are not compatible with the object and purpose of the Convention.[242] In that respect, the Dutch reservation seems acceptable. At any rate, other parties have not raised any official objections to it.[243] However, a reservation will not only have to be acceptable in its own right, but the manner in which parties make use of a reservation must equally be acceptable, because otherwise the prohibition regarding object and purpose would be of very little use. According to Guideline 3.1.5 ILC Guide to Reservations, a reservation is not compatible with the object and purpose of the Convention or treaty 'if it affects an essential element of the treaty that is necessary to its general tenour, in such a way that the reservation impairs the raison d'être of the treaty'. Guideline 3.1.5.1[244] adds to this that the object and purpose of the Convention must be determined in good faith, which implies that the terms in the Convention and the context in which they are used must be taken into account, in particular those in the title of the Convention and the preamble; recourse may be had to the preparatory work of the Convention, the circumstances of its conclusion and in some cases the later practice of the parties. At any rate, parties are not allowed to misuse a reservation that was designed to protect national law for covering up the fact that the obligations assumed have not actually been accepted.[245] Moreover, it is also significant in this respect that Conventions are actually meant to adapt and harmonize law and practice in the states parties.

Seen against that background, it is hard to argue that any use of the reservation by the Netherlands to tolerate cannabis cultivation, delivery and trade for the supply of coffee shops or to regulate it otherwise is acceptable, in the light of the object and purpose of the convention. With respect to that object and purpose, the Illicit Traffic Convention aims to build on and reinforce the system of the Single Convention. The fight against illegal coca, poppy products and cannabis products is at the heart of both Conventions, since these substances are mentioned not only in the Schedules, but also in the Conventions themselves. Additionally, by means of the required criminalizations, enforcement through criminal law and cooperation in criminal matters, the Illicit Traffic Convention seeks to provide further reinforcement of the complete prohibition of the circulation of illegal cannabis among other things, and in the context of the Convention this means: all flowering and fruiting tops of cannabis plants, cannabis resin and cannabis

---

242 See Article 19 Vienna Convention on the Law of Treaties and Guideline 3.1 ILC Guide to Reservations.

243 See: http://treaties.un.org/ (Chapter VI, no. 19, under: 'Objections').

244 Of course, see also Article 31(1) of the Vienna Convention on the Law of Treaties.

245 Commentaries to the ILC Guide to Reservations, pp. 382–383 (nos. 5, 7).

plants for non-medical and non-scientific purposes. The preamble shows that in order to achieve this reinforcement, the Convention focuses in particular on clandestine production, demand for and trade in narcotic drugs and on the 'eradication of illicit traffic'. In accordance with Article 1(m) of the Illicit Traffic Convention, illicit traffic means all the offences described in Article 3(1) and (2) of the Illicit Traffic Convention, including cultivation, delivery of and trade in cannabis for the supply of retail shops for consumer sales.

Taking all this into account, it is dubious whether the current state of affairs in the Netherlands, where the sale of cannabis to consumers by coffee shops is tolerated on the basis of a general policy, is permissible given the object and purpose of the Convention.[246,247] The fact that the other states parties raised no objection to the reservation as such does not detract in any way from this, if only because it is not the reservation that is the problem here, but the practice based on it. It would be yet one step further to tolerate the cultivation and delivery of, and trade in cannabis (which is not intended for medical or scientific purposes) via permissive constructions or the general application of the expediency principle. After all, that would give rise to a situation where, on the one hand, the Convention seeks to combat all behaviours that are directly or indirectly important in connection with the illegal cannabis economy, while the Dutch authorities, on the other hand, would actually tolerate an entire domestic cannabis economy from cultivation to consumer sales for recreational use on the basis of general policy. Furthermore, there would be no individual considerations of expediency regarding the decision to prosecute or not. It is hard to imagine anyone defending the view that this would not be diametrically opposed to the purpose, content and the system of the Illicit Traffic Convention and, for that matter, Article 3(6) of the Illicit Traffic Convention.

2.3.5. INTERNATIONAL SUPERVISION OF THE ILLICIT TRAFFIC CONVENTION: IN PARTICULAR INCB AND CND

The International Narcotics Control Board (INCB) has a more limited role in the Illicit Traffic Convention than in the Single Convention.[248,249] Pursuant to

---

246 See for example, Jay Sinha, *The History and Development of the Leading International Drug Control Conventions*, Ottawa: Library of Parliament, Parliamentary Research Branch, 2001, p. 35; David R. Bewley-Taylor & Martin Jelsma, 'The Limits of Latitude. The UN drug control conventions', *Series on Legislative Reform of Drug Policies*, No. 18, March 2012, p. 15.

247 At any rate, the International Narcotics Control Board (INCB) rules that the Dutch coffee shop policy (tolerate sales via the front door as opposed to illegal production for supply and delivery at the back door) is a breach of the UN Narcotic Drugs Conventions; see section 2.4 below.

248 For information on that more limited role, see Neil Brett Boister, *The Suppression of Illicit Drugs Through International Law*, Nottingham: University of Nottingham, 1998, pp. 506–510.

249 With regards to the Single Convention, see section 2.2.5.

Article 22 of the Illicit Traffic Convention, the main duty of the Board is to monitor Article 12 of the Illicit Traffic Convention (regarding substances frequently used in the illicit manufacture of narcotic drugs or psychotropic substances), Article 13 of the Illicit Traffic Convention (regarding materials and equipment) and Article 16 of the Illicit Traffic Convention (regarding commercial documents and labelling of exports). In accordance with Article 23, this body issues an annual report about this. With respect to the Illicit Traffic Convention, the INCB therefore has a less obvious and at any rate more limited quasi-judicial[250] function to ensure that the states parties fulfil their obligations in accordance with the Convention.[251] For example, the Illicit Traffic Convention does not bestow an explicit authority on the INCB to attempt to prevent clandestine cultivation, production and manufacture of, illicit traffic in and clandestine use of narcotic drugs.[252] In contrast to the situation with the Single Convention, the Board does not function as a supervisory body for the Convention as a whole.[253] The more restricted mandate for the INCB under this Convention was a deliberate decision. According to the UN Commentary, this choice was undoubtedly informed by the character of the Illicit Traffic Convention, which touches more explicitly and emphatically on criminal law and its enforcement and therefore on the sovereignty and jurisdiction of states parties.[254] Incidentally, the more limited mandate under the Illicit Traffic Convention does not detract from the functions and powers the INCB has in connection with the Single Convention.[255]

The Commission on Narcotic Drugs (CND) is entrusted with the general supervision of the implementation of the Illicit Traffic Convention, and reports its findings at the annual meeting of the international drug control system for ministers and government representatives. Pursuant to Article 21 of the Illicit Traffic Convention, the Commission is required to supervise the implementation of the Convention based on information furnished by the parties. Based on that information, the CND can make proposals and

---

250 United Nations, *Commentary on the Single Convention on Narcotic Drugs, 1961*, New York: 1973, pp. 135 (no. 1) and 136 (no. 6). See also: http://www.incb.org/incb/en/about/mandate-functions.html.

251 For more information see International Drug Policy Consortium, *The International Narcotics Control Board: Current Tensions and Options for Reform*, IDPC Briefing Paper 7, 2008, pp. 1–4, which also contains a great deal of criticism on the methods of the INCB.

252 See Article 9(4) of the Single Convention, in which this power has been granted to the INCB for the Single Convention.

253 United Nations, *Commentary on the United Nations Convention Against Illicit Traffic in Narcotic Drugs and Psychotropic Substances*, Vienna: 1988, pp. 374 (no. 22.2(a)).

254 United Nations, *Commentary on the United Nations Convention Against Illicit Traffic in Narcotic Drugs and Psychotropic Substances*, Vienna: 1988, pp. 374 (no. 22.2).

255 See Article 22(1) of the Illicit Traffic Convention.

general recommendations. This is done in resolutions for example. This gives the Commission far-reaching powers.[256]

ECOSOC has a fairly limited brief under the Illicit Traffic Convention. None of these merit particular attention here.

Any disputes between two or more parties to the Convention relating to the interpretation or implementation of the Illicit Traffic Convention will also be dealt with by the International Court of Justice if those parties are unable to settle the dispute amongst themselves.[257]

2.3.6. INTERMEDIATE CONCLUSION FOR THE ILLICIT TRAFFIC CONVENTION

This intermediate conclusion too is the result of the foregoing discussion of the contents, the nature and the system of the Illicit Traffic Convention, the history of deliberations that preceded its creation and the UN Commentary about it. As this conclusion does not take into account what will be discussed later in this chapter, such as the control organs, state practice and generally accepted interpretations of the Convention, we refer you to the final section of this chapter for the final conclusion – also as far as the Illicit Traffic Convention is concerned.

In accordance with and complementary to the Single Convention, the Illicit Traffic Convention was created on the assumption that the problems around drugs need to be combated vigorously with criminal measures, prohibitions and repression of all acts that are directly or indirectly relevant to it. To supplement the Single Convention, the Illicit Traffic Convention contains obligations to combat cannabis cultivation for recreational purposes and to fight recreational drug use (Article 14(2) of the Illicit Traffic Convention), a total prohibition via criminalizations of acts – including cannabis cultivation – which are aimed at or are related to recreational use of cannabis (Article 3(1) and (2) of the Illicit Traffic Convention), obligations to prosecute persons for cannabis cultivation that is not small-scale and not intended for personal use, which obligations result both explicitly and implicitly from the Conventions, and a system of international cooperation in criminal matters. The Illicit Traffic Convention focuses on the demand side of the cannabis market, more explicitly than the Single Convention does. This is done for example,

256 United Nations, *Commentary on the United Nations Convention Against Illicit Traffic in Narcotic Drugs and Psychotropic Substances*, Vienna: 1988, pp. 370 (no. 21.6).

257 See Article 32 of the Illicit Traffic Convention, see the similar Article 48 of the Single Convention. For the possible significance of the ICJ for the Illicit Traffic Convention see Jimmy Gurulé, 'The 1988 U.N. Convention Against Illicit Traffic in Narcotic Drugs and Psychotropic Substances – A Ten Year Perspective: Is International Cooperation Merely Illusory?', 22 *Fordham International Law Journal* 1998, pp. 74–121 on pp. 112–118.

by explicitly making it clear that parties are obliged to criminalize possession, purchase and cultivation of cannabis for personal use other than for medical or scientific purposes if these acts are intentional (Article 3(2) of the Illicit Traffic Convention). This means that the Convention does not permit the legalization or decriminalization of any form of intentional cannabis cultivation for recreational use.

Article 3(6) of the Illicit Traffic conveys a fairly strong principle of prosecution. This obligation to prosecute applies to cannabis cultivation, delivery and trade for the supply of retail shops, among other things. In the case of possession, purchase and cultivation for personal use, the authorities appear to have a little bit more room for manoeuvring than for more serious offences. The reservation concerning Article 3(6) of the Illicit Traffic Convention that was formulated by the Netherlands can hardly create extra room for any future application of the expediency principle to the supply side of the drug economy, nor to cannabis cultivation, delivery and trade for the supply of retail shops. In view of the content and background of the reservation, and the object and purpose of the Convention, this does not leave sufficient room for adopting a policy of permitting cannabis cultivation. So far, the conclusion must be that the Illicit Traffic Convention does not permit legalization, decriminalization, policy-based tolerance and/or other forms of regulating cannabis cultivation for recreational use.

2.4. OPINIONS AND JUDGMENTS OF THE INCB, CND AND ECOSOC

The International Narcotics Control Board (INCB), as we said before, is the international body responsible for monitoring the implementation of the Single Convention and to a lesser extent also the Illicit Traffic Convention by the states parties.[258] It acts as an independent and quasi-judicial[259] control and regulatory body responsible for the supervision of the implementation of the UN Conventions pertaining to the fight against drugs. To this end, the Board publishes a report each year on the functioning of the international drug control system (the three UN narcotic drugs conventions) and developments in the international fight against drugs.[260] On the basis of its

258 See section 2.2.5 and section 2.3.5 respectively for this; see these sections for more information about the functions of the INCB under the conventions mentioned.

259 United Nations, *Commentary on the Single Convention on Narcotic Drugs, 1961*, New York: 1973, pp. 135 (no. 1) and 136 (no. 6). See also: http://www.incb.org/incb/en/about/ mandate-functions.html.

260 For the most recent version see: INCB, *Report of the International Narcotics Control Board for 2012*, New York: United Nations, 2013, pp. v–vi. From this point onwards, the reports will be listed as: INCB Report [year that the report refers to].

findings, the INCB makes recommendations to governments and regional and international organizations to improve the various aspects of the fight against drugs.

This raises the question what the status of the findings of the Board is. First of all, the INCB is a so-called 'expert body', not a 'political' body. This means that the organization is expected to draw conclusions based on the consideration of facts and not on political considerations.[261] However, the INCB is not a judicial body and does not necessarily consist, and at any rate not exclusively, of lawyers. That is why it is not comparable to the European Court of Human Rights (ECHR) or the Court of Justice of the European Union (CJEU). The INCB does not pass judgment on complaints in concrete cases either, unlike the equally non-judicial UN committees that monitor human rights treaties. To that extent, the quasi-judicial nature of the INCB is not as strong as that of these UN committees. Therefore, the judgments of the INCB on the compliance by states with the UN narcotic drugs conventions are not legally binding,[262] in contrast with the rulings by the EHRM and the ECJ. So the INCB cannot engage in binding law-making independently, which is not to say that its judgments lack authority. In this respect, INCB is comparable to UN human rights committees. That also applies to the fact that none of these bodies have a legal mechanism to enforce compliance with its judgments, although the INCB can draw the attention of the states parties, ECOSOC and the Commission on Narcotic Drugs to failures to heed its findings.[263]

However, the INCB happens to be the designated international body to monitor compliance with the Single Convention and to a lesser extent also the Illicit Traffic Convention. The states parties acknowledged this authority by their accession to the Convention.[264] The responsibilities assigned to the INCB entail that it will have to interpret and implement the Convention in order to assess whether each of the parties fulfils its obligations under the Convention with its laws, policies and practice. The Board being the primary supervisor, its judgments must in any case be deemed to represent the Convention, at any rate insofar as they stay close to the text of the Convention, its system, title and preamble.[265] In that case, the judgments actually convey the binding

261 See Article 9 of the Single Convention, which describes the composition and functions of the INCB and includes safeguards for the impartiality and competence of its members.

262 See also Damon Barrett, *'Unique in International Relations'? A Comparison of the International Narcotics Control Board and the UN Human Rights Treaty Bodies*, London: International Harm Reduction Association, 2008, pp. 26–28.

263 See Article 14(1)(d) of the Single Convention.

264 This and also what we will note below is overlooked in the discussion about the legal weight of the judgments by the INCB, by Daniel Dupras, *Canada's International Obligations under the Leading International Conventions on the Control of Narcotic Drugs*, Ottawa: Library of Parliament, 1988, pp. 30–31.

265 See Article 31 Vienna Convention on the Law of Treaties and Guideline 3.1.5.1 of the Guide to Practice on Reservations to Treaties by the International Law Commission (included

contents of the Convention. In the light of this and given the function of the INCB, a party will not be allowed to ignore one of this body's judgments which is based on the Single Convention without compelling reasons.

Against this background, it is appropriate to dwell on opinions and judgments of the International Narcotics Control Board. We will address the following questions:

- How does the INCB assess cultivation, trade and use of cannabis in a more general way?
- How does the INCB judge the Dutch cannabis policy, including the policy-based tolerance of the sale of cannabis to consumers by coffee shops (which are allowed to have a stock of up to 500 grams and sell up to 5 gram in each transaction) and the low investigation priority for cultivation and possession of up to five plants and 5 gram for personal consumption?[266]
- How does the INCB interpret the exception of 'medical or scientific purposes'?
- What is the INCB's view on obligations to prosecute and to what extent does it recognize that parties have room for considerations of expediency?
- How does the INCB judge developments in certain countries regarding toleration or otherwise regulation of narcotic drugs, particularly cannabis, outside the exception of medical or scientific purposes?

As far as this is relevant, in addition to the judgments and interpretations of the INCB, we will pay some attention to insights and resolutions of the Commission on Narcotic Drugs (the annual meeting of ministers and government representatives from all UN member states, where they discuss and adopt resolutions on a wide range of subjects with respect to the international drug control system) and the General Assembly of the United Nations.

---

in Report of the ILC on the Work of its 63rd session, General Assembly, Official Records, 66th Session, Supplement n° 10, Addendum 1, *UN Doc.* A/66/10/Add.1). See criticism on the interpretations of the INCB: International Drug Policy Consortium, *The International Narcotics Control Board: Current Tensions and Options for Reform*, IDPC Briefing Paper 7, 2008, 22 pp.

266 For the current prosecution policy and the associated policy of tolerance with regard to coffee shops and cultivation and possession of cannabis for personal use: College van procureurs-generaal openbaar ministerie, 'Aanwijzing Opiumwet (2015A003)', *Stcrt.* 2015/5391 (i.e., Board of Procurators General of the Dutch Public Prosecutions Service, 'Instruction regarding the Opium Act (2015A003)', Dutch Government Gazette, 2015/5391), with effect from 1 March 2015. For detailed prosecution guidelines see College van procureurs-peneraal openbaar ministerie, Richtlijn voor strafvordering Opiumwet, softdrugs (2016R007), *Stcrt.* 2016/23647 (i.e., Board of Procurators General of the Dutch Public Prosecutions Service, 'Guideline for prosecution Opium Act', (2016R007), Dutch Government Gazette, 2016/23647), with effect from 1 June 2016.

2.4.1. GENERAL JUDGMENTS ON CANNABIS CULTIVATION, TRADE AND CONSUMPTION

The views of the INCB on the discussion about legalization, decriminalization, policy-based tolerance or other regulation of cannabis cultivation, distribution, trade, consumer sales and/or consumption are illustrated more generally in the preamble to the *Report of the International Narcotics Control Board for 2012*, which contains the following passage:

> We note with concern [...] that [...] some declarations and initiatives have included proposals for the legalization of the possession of drugs for non-medical and non-scientific use, that is, for 'recreational' use, that would allow the cultivation and consumption of cannabis for non-medical purposes. Any such initiatives, if implemented, would violate the international drug control conventions and could undermine the noble objectives of the entire drug control system, which are to ensure the availability of drugs for medical purposes while preventing their abuse. Proponents of such initiatives ignore the commitment that all Governments have made to promote the health and well-being of their communities, and such initiatives run counter to the growing body of scientific evidence documenting the harm associated with drug abuse, including occasional use, particularly among young people during their formative years. Furthermore, such initiatives would create a false sense of security and would send a false message to the public, in particular children, regarding the health impact of abuse of drugs. Some have argued that these proposals would eliminate the illicit markets and organized crime associated with drugs of abuse. Yet, even if such initiatives were implemented, organized criminal groups would get even more deeply involved, for instance by creating a black market for the illicit supply of newly legalized drugs to young people. To target the organized crime and violence associated with the illicit trade in drugs, the most effective tool is primary prevention of drug abuse, coupled with treatment and *rehabilitation*, and complemented by supply reduction measures, as provided for in the conventions.[267]

Moreover, the INCB made it clear in 2008 for example that it sees no reason to relax the regime for cannabis. On the contrary, they observed:

> The international community may wish to review the issue of cannabis. Over the years, cannabis has become more potent and is associated with an increasing number of emergency room admissions. Cannabis is often the first illicit drug that young people take. It is frequently called a gateway drug. In spite of all these facts, the use of cannabis is often trivialized and, in some countries, controls over the cultivation, possession and use of cannabis are less strict than for other drugs.[268]

---

267 INCB Report 2012, pp. v–vi.

268 INCB Report 2008, p. iv; see also pp. 7–8 (nos. 33–34). Also in recent Annual Reports the INCB has paid attention to cannabis and States' intended or adopted measures to regulate

The Commission on Narcotic Drugs also pays regular attention to cannabis. It is worth mentioning the 'Political Declaration and Plan of Action on International Cooperation towards an Integrated and Balanced Strategy to counter the World Drug Problem', which was adopted by the CND in 2009[269] and later that year by the General Assembly of the United Nations.[270] The General Assembly calls for the parties to take measures that are necessary for a full implementation of the actions agreed.[271] The 'Political Declaration' entails among other things:

> We, the States Members of the United Nations, [...]
>
> 36. Decide to establish 2019 as a target date for States to eliminate or reduce significantly and measurably: (a) The illicit cultivation of opium poppy, coca bush and cannabis plant [...].[272]

Among other things, the 'Plan of Action' states the following:

> 43. Member States should: [...] (c) Provide the necessary financial and political support, to the extent possible, to survey, monitor and verify the extent of coca bush, opium poppy and cannabis cultivation, both in indoor and outdoor cultivation sites, consistent with international drug control conventions, and share this information with relevant international agencies and other Governments with a view to increasing cooperation on drug crop eradication and on alternative development, including, where appropriate, on preventive alternative development, in accordance with the specificities of each country or region; [...].[273]

---

non-medical use of cannabis. The INCB repeatedly emphasizes that such regulation contravenes the UN drugs conventions and notices that 'While it is difficult to predict the effects of the legislative measures making cannabis available for non- medical use, it is certain that the abuse of cannabis potentially carries serious health consequences, as acknowledged by WHO.' See INCB Annual Report 2016, pp. 42–43, para. 319–326, at 324. The INCB pays special attention to the 'therapeutic' use of cannabinoids in the INCB Annual Report 2017, pp. 49–50, para. 287–302.

For an earlier similar message see INCB Report 2001, pp. 36–37 (nos. 228–230), where the INCB asserts, among other things, that the inclusion of cannabis in the category of tobacco and alcohol would be a 'historical mistake'.

269 CND, Report on the fifty-second session (14 March 2008 and 11–20 March 2009), *UN Doc.* E/2009/28, E/CN.7/2009/12, p. 5 (para 3). The 'Political Declaration and Plan of Action' were adopted on 12 March 2009 by the ministers and government representatives in the CND; see p. 119, para 154. For a more recent confirmation see CND Resolution 56/10, *UN Doc.* E/2013/28, E/CN.7/2013/14, pp. 38–41 on p. 39.

270 UN General Assembly Resolution 64/182, 'International cooperation against the world drug problem', adopted 65th plenary meeting on 18 December 2009, *UN Doc.* A/RES/ 64/182, 30 March 2010.

271 Ibid, p. 2, para 1.

272 *UN Doc.* E/2009/28, E/CN.7/2009/12, pp. 37–44 on p. 37 and p. 44.

273 *UN Doc.* E/2009/28, E/CN.7/2009/12, pp. 45–70 on p. 65.

Several other CND Resolutions insist that states must take measures against the illegal cultivation of cannabis plants, against the trade in and use of cannabis and also cannabis seeds and against cannabis consumption.[274] That does not alter the fact that the formulations are fairly general. Concrete obligations to criminalize, prosecute and penalize under criminal law are absent. The discussion between 'zero-tolerant' states and states advocating less stringent strategies led to compromises in the wording and prevented the resolutions from calling for criminalization of the *use* of narcotic drugs, which is something that the Single Convention and the Illicit Traffic Convention do not require.[275] However, the resolutions generally clearly oppose legalization, policy-based tolerance and other regulation of cannabis cultivation, distribution, trade and use for recreational consumption. Incidentally, it is pointed out consistently that measures must be in accordance with the Single Convention and the other UN narcotic drugs conventions, which are confirmed as the cornerstones of the international drug control system time and again.[276] Among other sources, the aforementioned 'Political Declaration and Plan of Action' confirms the important role of the CND and the INCB as the bodies of the United Nations with final responsibility with regard to drug control.

2.4.2. THE NETHERLANDS CANNABIS POLICY

In the light of the above-mentioned, it is hardly surprising that the INCB consistently deems The Netherlands coffee shop policy to be a breach of the UN narcotic drugs conventions.[277] This implies that the Board must be of the

---

274 CND Resolution 52/5, *UN Doc.* E/2009/28, E/CN.7/2009/12, pp. 15–17 on p. 16 (para 1); CND Resolution 56/2, *UN Doc.* E/2013/28, E/CN.7/2013/14, pp. 15–20 on p. 16, which insists on taking appropriate measures in accordance with the Accra Declaration to combat narcotic drugs. The Accra Declaration contains additional measures (not explicitly provided in the UN narcotic drugs conventions) to fight the illegal cultivation of and the trade in cannabis (see Annex to CND Resolution 56/2). See also CND Resolution 53/15, *UN Doc.* E/2010/28, E/CN.7/2010/18, pp. 38–42 on p. 39, and UN General Assembly Resolution 67/193, *UN Doc.* A/RES/67/193, 23 April 2013, which points out the problem of 'the increasing illicit production of and trafficking in cannabis'. See also CND Resolution 59/1, adopted by the General Assembly on 19 April 2016 at the thirtieth special session, 'Our joint commitment to effectively addressing and countering the world drug problem', A/RES/A-30/1, 4 May 2016, p. 9.

275 See for more information David R. Bewley-Taylor, 'The Contemporary International Drug Control System: A History of the UNGASS Decade', in: John Collins (ed.), *Governing the Global Drug Wars*, London: London School of Economics, 2012, pp. 49–55, in particular p. 53.

276 See the 'Political Declaration and Plan of Action', *UN Doc.* E/2009/28, E/CN.7/2009/12, pp. 37–77 on p. 38 (para 3) and p. 46 (para 2f and 4), and additionally, for example.: CND Resolution 55/9, *UN Doc.* E/2012/28, E/CN.7/2012/18, pp. 23–25 on p. 23; CND Resolution 52/5, *UN Doc.* E/2009/28, E/CN.7/2009/12, pp. 15–17 on p. 16 (para 1).

277 See the recent INCB Report 2017, p. 36 (no. 186). ('... the Board reiterates that the operation of "coffee shops" is inconsistent with the 1961 Convention as amended.') See also INCB

opinion that the Dutch reservation with regard to the expediency principle in connection with Article 3(6) of the Illicit Traffic Convention, which incidentally does not have any bearing on the Single Convention, does not intend to cover or cannot cover the sale of cannabis to consumers on a commercial scale, such as by coffee shops. That is an important conclusion. The implication of this after all is that the INCB then must hold the view *a fortiori* that tolerating cannabis cultivation in order to supply coffee shops cannot be justified as an extension of the current policy of tolerance under the conventions. More generally, the Board notes that certain 'harm reduction' measures are not compatible with the UN narcotic drugs conventions.[278] They explicitly refer to so-called coffee shops where the sale, possession and use of small quantities of cannabis is tolerated.

The INCB deems such phenomena not only problematic because they are a breach of the Convention, but also because they encourage the social acceptance of drug abuse[279] and also discourage other states – in particular developing countries – from combating cannabis.[280] It is understandable that from this perspective the INCB emphasizes the importance of universal implementation of the UN narcotic drugs conventions by all states parties.[281] This does not alter the fact that there may be various problems in various regions. For example, the countries in Europe have recently been strongly reminded about the necessity of addressing systematically the illegal cultivation of cannabis (other than for 'medical or scientific purposes') and of preventing the abuse of cannabis.[282] The indoor cultivation of cannabis is also a cause of concern for the INCB and it points out that tolerating this is prohibited, on an industrial scale as well as for personal use.[283]

The INCB takes the view that parties cannot avoid the obligations under the Convention with an appeal to the constitutional organization of their state or on the grounds of their national legal system: a state signing up to a Convention must ensure that national and/or provincial policies and the associated measures

Report 2012, p. 100 (no. 757); INCB Report 2004, p. 36 (no. 220); INCB Report 2008, p. 32 (nos. 178, 180, 182); INCB Report 2009, p. 49 (no. 278); INCB Report 2010, p. 104 (no. 709); INCB Report 2011, p. 94 (no. 718). In INCB Report 1997, p. 7 (no. 28), the Board still described the deliberate tolerance of cannabis sales in coffee shops as 'an activity that might be described as indirect incitement'.

278 INCB Report 2008, pp. 6–7 (no. 29).

279 INCB Report 2016, p. 42 (no. 324). See also INCB Report 2011, p. 38 (no. 283).

280 INCB Report 2008, pp. 7–8 (no. 34).

281 See for example INCB Report 2016, p. 105 (no. 815) and (Recommendation 11); INCB Report 2012, p. 12 (no. 83) and p. 116 (Recommendation 5).

282 INCB Report 2012, p. 118 (Recommendation 21); see previously for example INCB Report 2009, p. 126 (Recommendation 29).

283 INCB Report 2011, p. 91 (no. 699); see also p. 95 (no. 730) and p. 110 (Recommendation 26); INCB Report 2009, p. 18 (no. 74).

do not undermine the fight against drug abuse and traffic.[284] By implication, according to the Board, the Netherlands will therefore also be unable in this respect to invoke the expediency principle – which, incidentally, does not entail an obligation to tolerate cannabis cultivation, distribution, trade and/or sale – as a justification of a policy of tolerance. Additionally, the Board is of the opinion that it is misleading and not really possible to make a distinction between so-called 'soft drugs' and 'hard drugs'.[285] This also applies to the coffee shop policy.[286] In that respect too, the fact that states attempt to legitimize the policy of tolerance based on the distinction between various markets does not go down very well with the INCB.

2.4.3. EXCEPTIONS TO THE CONVENTION: MEDICAL OR SCIENTIFIC PURPOSES

The INCB interprets the Convention system with regard to the exception of 'medical and or scientific purposes' as mandatory: states parties must ensure that the use of internationally controlled narcotic drugs are 'solely' used for those purposes.[287] The Board applies a literal and therefore obviously limited reading of the Convention and its terminology. In view of its supervisory role, the INCB defines a medicine as a substance that has been designed or approved for the following medical applications: to improve health and welfare; to prevent and treat diseases (including the alleviation of symptoms of the disease); as a diagnostic tool; to promote conception or anti-conception; and as general anaesthetics.[288] A 'medical use' for the substance is then taken to mean its use for the above-mentioned medical purposes. Such use must be approved by the competent regulatory body in that country and its efficacy must have been recognized by the medical community.

From this, it follows that the exception does not cover legislation or policies allowing cultivation and distribution of, trade in and sales of cannabis to consumers and/or consumption of cannabis on account of considerations of public health. In all those cases, – contrary to what the INCB and the Single Convention require – cannabis is not the medicine itself, but it is the regulation of the cannabis market which is presented as a medicine. It is understandable from a legal perspective that the Board expressly opposes the cultivation,

---

284 INCB Report 2011, pp. 38–39 (no. 287).

285 INCB Report 1992, p. 5 (no. 18); see also INCB Report 2008, p. 115 (Recommendation 21). See also Article 27 of the Vienna Convention on the Law of Treaties.

286 INCB Report 2001, p. 35 (no. 217).

287 See recently INCB Report 2016, p. iii; and furthermore, for example: INCB Report 2012, on p. 8 (no. 53 sub c) and p. 11 (no. 80).

288 INCB Report 2003, p. 38 (no. 233) see also no. 237.

trade, sale and use of cannabis under the exception of 'medical or scientific purposes' when in actual fact it involves recreational use.[289]

Cannabis as such cannot simply be branded as a medicine. The fact is, there is no room to allow the medical use of cannabis, unless there are convincing research results available to that effect.[290] The INCB has on several occasions expressed its concern that states allow the use of cannabis on medical grounds, when they do not actually have adequate scientific proof of its efficacy.[291] The Board itself has doubts about that efficacy.[292] Even narcotic drugs prescribed by physicians do not fall within the exception when this is not 'medically appropriate'.[293] The Board insists that states must take the necessary measures in accordance with their obligations arising from the Conventions, to guarantee that cannabis is not used for anything but medical or scientific purposes and to prevent abuse and the spread of cannabis use beyond this specific context.[294]

Finally, a few comments about 'scientific purposes'. Earlier on, we concluded that the exception 'scientific purposes' is also meant to be interpreted in a rather narrow way that (in principle) it is restricted to science regarding medicine, i.e., medical science.[295] This is also the interpretation by the INCB. According to the Board, this exception is applicable if a narcotic drug is used as a substance for research into health or disease or in research with respect to a product as a potential medicine. If patients are involved, the research can be done as part of a clinical trial, which requires prior approval from an ethical review body.[296]

2.4.4. OBLIGATIONS TO PROSECUTE AND ROOM FOR EXPEDIENCY

The INCB also has pertinent views with regard to policies of prosecution and/or considerations of expediency. The Board reiterates that states parties

289 INCB Report 2012, for example on p. vi, p. 10 (no. 68), p. 31 (no. 221) and p. 58 (no. 428); INCB Report 2009, p. 49 (no. 278); INCB Report 2003, p. 24 (no. 141). See also the older INCB Report 1992, for example nos. 13–23, where the Board rejects the arguments for the legalization of non-medical use of narcotic drugs.

290 INCB Report 2003, p. 24 (no. 141); INCB Report 2004, p. 28 (no. 166).

291 INCB Report 2017, p. iii. See also INCB Report 2009, p. 17 (no. 62). For an earlier similar message see for example INCB Report 2008, p. 66 (no. 432).

292 See also David R. Bewley-Taylor & Martin Jelsma, 'The Limits of Latitude. The UN drug control conventions', *Series on Legislative Reform of Drug Policies*, No. 18, March 2012, p. 13, who incidentally dispute that the INCB has the authority to pass judgment on the efficacy. We believe that while the Board as such does not have that authority, but they can rely on convincing scientific research representing the latest scientific evidence available.

293 INCB Report 2012, p. 43 (no. 307).

294 INCB Report 2012, e.g. p. vi, p. 10 (no. 68), p. 31 (no. 221), p. 66 (no. 471).

295 See section 2.2.3.i.

296 INCB Report 2003, p. 38 (no. 236).

must first and foremost meet their obligations arising from the Conventions in all their dealings with drug-related offences and that their responses must not lead to a weakening of the implementation of the Conventions. The Board does not formulate an absolute obligation to prosecute. Having said that, the room for prosecuting authorities to refrain from prosecution proves to be restricted. According to the INCB, a proportional reaction from the perspective of the Drug Conventions implies that in general prosecution takes place in the event of serious criminal offences that can be prosecuted, unless the circumstances demonstrate that the case is only of minor importance.[297] So the INCB appears to leave some room for considerations of expediency *in concreto* for serious criminal drug related offences, but not for a general policy intended to refrain from prosecution for a certain category of such offences. This also applies to criminal offences such as cultivation, delivery and traffic of cannabis for retail shops, as well as sales of weed/marijuana and hashish by coffee shops, since these offences in principle must be treated as serious.[298] The INCB even goes so far as to say that governments must ensure that the police and judicial authorities give a high priority to investigating, prosecuting and sentencing of those heading large drug organizations or supply produce to them.[299] Furthermore, due attention must be given to dealing on the streets and drug possession. That does not alter the fact that there is more room to refrain from prosecution in the case of cannabis related offences involving personal consumption.[300] This is also possible on the basis of general policy:

> While the practice of exempting small quantities of drugs from criminal prosecution is consistent with the international drug control treaties, the Board emphasizes that the objective of the treaties is to prevent drug abuse and to limit the use of controlled substances to medical and scientific purposes.[301]

This consideration also illustrates, though, that the absence of an obligation to prosecute offenders for possession, purchase and cultivation involving small quantities does not mean that there is no obligation to act at all, let alone that states parties are allowed to decriminalize or legalize those offences. In short: room for tolerance from a criminal law point of view does not imply that there is also room for tolerance in other ways – in particular from an administrative point of view. In that respect, the Board is consistent with the Single Convention and the Illicit Traffic Convention, as both Conventions

297 INCB Report 2007, p. 8 (no. 30). See also INCB Report 1997, p. 7 (no. 28).

298 See section 2.2.2.ii.a.IX.

299 INCB Report 2007, p. 13 (no. 60a); see also p. 14 (no. 60g) regarding necessary financial means.

300 INCB Report 2007, p. 8 (no. 30).

301 INCB Report 2004, p. 80 (no. 538). See more recently INCB Report 2016, p. iii.

feature various obligations that do not pertain to criminal law which are an obstacle to full legalization or a general policy of tolerance, either explicitly or intentionally implicitly.[302] Moreover, the INCB is afraid that to refrain from prosecution or to apply only light sentences for relatively small-scale cultivation or possession for personal consumption will foster the notion that cannabis is a harmless substance.[303] The Board requires that every decision to prosecute or not is based on legal grounds in order to ensure a fair and consistent application of the discretion.

2.4.5. INITIATIVES IN OTHER COUNTRIES

In its 2016 report, the INCB paid special attention to the adoption or consideration by some states of measures aimed at regulated non-medical use of cannabis and 'has reaffirmed the incompatibility of such measures with the legal obligations incumbent upon States to the 1961 Convention with a view to promoting compliance.'[304] The INCB has categorically rejected the initiatives for regulating the cultivation, trade, sale and/or possession of cannabis in federal states of the United States (Colorado and Washington)[305] and in Uruguay.[306] The INCB also clearly opposes the initiatives and plans concerning regulation of cannabis for recreational use in Canada and Spain, for example.[307]

---

302 See among other things, the Articles 33, 37 and 38 of the Single Convention and 14(2) of the Illicit Traffic Convention discussed above.

303 See for example INCB Report 2003, p. 49 (no. 320).

304 INCB Report 2016, p. 42 (nos. 319–322). See also INCB Report 2017, pp. 33–34 (nos. 162–164).

305 INCB Report 2012, p. 11 (no. 80), p. 63 (no. 451) and p. 116 (Recommendation 5). See more recently INCB Report 2016, p. 29 (no. 198) ('In its discussions with the Government of the United States, the Board has continued to reiterate that the legislative and administrative measures taken by several states in the country to legalize and regulate the sale of cannabis for non-medical purposes cannot be recon-ciled with the legal obligation contained in article 4, paragraph *(c)*, of the 1961 Convention to limit exclusively to medical and scientific purposes the production, manufacture, export, import and distribution of, trade in and use and possession of drugs.'). See also INCB Report 2014, p. 25 (no. 142).

306 INCB Report 2012, p. 36 (nos. 257–258). See also the INCB press release 'Uruguay is breaking the International Conventions on Drug Control with the Cannabis Legislation approved by its Congress', UNIS/NAR/1190, 11 December 2013. See more recently INCB Report 2016, p. 29 (no. 202) ('The Board notes the continued implementation by the Government of Uruguay of measures aimed at creating a regulated market for the non-medical use of cannabis. While this policy has not yet been fully implemented, the Board wishes to reiterate its position that such legislation is contrary to the provisions of the international drug control conventions'. See also INCB Report 2014, p. 26 (no. 149).

307 INCB Report 2016, p. 31 (no. 223) (Canada) and the Press Release of INCB of 21 June 2018 (*International Narcotics Control Board expresses deep concern about the legalization of cannabis for non-medical use in Canada)*, UNIS/NAR/1353; INCB Report 2016, p. 28 (no. 187) (Spain).

It is also worth mentioning that the INCB strongly criticized the withdrawal from the Single Convention by Bolivia and its re-accession to the Convention with a reservation regarding the coca leaf.[308] The INCB stresses that in spite of Bolivia's conduct, the coca leaf remains a narcotic drug in the sense of the Single Convention and 'all aspects of national and international control upon its cultivation, production, import, export and use will continue to remain in force'.[309] Not only is the reservation by Bolivia at odds with the 'fundamental object and spirit' of the Single Convention, but the INCB also underlines that Bolivia's action can set a dangerous precedent with unpredictable consequences that can jeopardize the international system of control of narcotic drugs in the long term.[310] In view of the fact that cannabis and coca have a similar status in the Single Convention and that roughly the same obligations apply to both substances, it is plausible that the Board would reach the same conclusion if a state were to take a leaf out of Bolivia's book and follow the Bolivian reservation rigmarole in the case of cannabis. Because Bolivia's reservation is based on traditional cultural use of narcotic drugs (i.e., coca leaf), a reservation for non-traditional recreational use of narcotic drugs (such as cannabis) would be even more problematic. Where the Convention leaves at least some room for a reservation in the context of 'traditional' consumption in Article 49 of the Single Convention, it does not do so for any other, recreational, use. To that extent, the Bolivian reservation is of only marginal relevance for the discussion around regulating cannabis cultivation in the Netherlands. Seeing that there was not at least one third of the states parties that had objected to the reservation by 10 January 2013, the re-accession of Bolivia is formally valid.[311]

2.5. AMENDMENT OF CONVENTION LAW THROUGH STATE PRACTICE OR ACCEPTED EVOLVED INTERPRETATION OF THE CONVENTION?

The foregoing shows that the Single Convention and the Illicit Traffic Convention contain various barriers to legalization, decriminalization, policy-based

308 The reservation reads as follows: 'The Plurinational State of Bolivia reserves the right to allow in its territory: traditional coca leaf chewing; the consumption and use of the coca leaf in its natural state for cultural and medicinal purposes, such as its use in infusions; and also the cultivation, trade and possession of the coca leaf to the extent necessary for these licit purposes.'

309 INCB Report 2012, p. 13 (no. 92).

310 INCB Report 2012, p. 12 (no. 93); see also p. 71 (no. 512). See for a more recent evaluation of the Bolivian approach to coca INCB Report 2017, pp. 31–32 (nos. 138–147).

311 In total, 15 states parties, including the Netherlands, objected to the reservation; see C.N.94.2013.TREATIES-VI.18 (Depositary Notification).

tolerance and/or other forms of regulating cannabis cultivation for recreational use. It is also clear that there are governments (of countries, federal states and municipalities) that would like to allow cannabis cultivation for recreational use in one form or another.[312] They could make a formal attempt to amend the provisions of the convention, but in principle this is not possible without unanimity among the states parties. That is why one could ask oneself the question whether creating customary law via 'state practice' is perhaps an option to achieve a de facto amendment of a convention. It is interesting that this is also possible – though not uncontroversial – in a way that is not in line with the convention but goes against its rationale, contents and system.[313] It is exactly because of the conflict with the convention as such that even more stringent requirements will have to be placed on the creation of such customary law than normally. Can one therefore argue that the Single Convention and the Illicit Traffic Convention have by now been modified by 'states practice' to such an extent that the cultivation of cannabis for recreational use is now permissible under the conventions (in other words, state practice that de facto renders the prohibitive provisions of the convention a dead letter)?

2.5.1. AMENDMENT OF CONVENTION LAW THROUGH STATE PRACTICE?

The answer to the last question is negative in any case. The number of states parties is the first relevant factor in the conclusion that it cannot be assumed that the cultivation of cannabis for recreational use is now considered permissible because of' state practice'. The number of states that are party to the Single Convention currently stands at 186 and at 190 for the Illicit Traffic Convention.[314] The number of countries that openly came out in favour of or began legalization, decriminalization, policy-based tolerance and/or other forms of regulating cannabis cultivation for recreational use makes up only a small part, both in absolute terms and in relative terms. Moreover, violations of clauses in the convention as such cannot render the obligations in question invalid or obsolete.[315] Besides, the Commission on Narcotic Drugs (CND) and the General Assembly of the United Nations – in which all parties are directly represented – have recently reconfirmed the conventions and also adopted a

---

312 See Chapter 4.

313 See Arthur M. Weisburd, 'Customary International Law: The Problem of Treaties', 21 *Vanderbilt Journal of Transnational Law* 1988 (1), pp. 1–46 on pp. 20–23; the fact that this is not without controversy is illustrated on p. 20 in footnote 86 and on pp. 29–45.

314 See: http://treaties.un.org/ (Chapter VI, numbers 18 and 19) (status on 1 January 2019).

315 See for example Arthur M. Weisburd, 'Customary International Law: The Problem of Treaties', 21 *Vanderbilt Journal of Transnational Law* 1988 (1), pp. 1–46 on pp. 30–31.

resolution to the effect that the cultivation of cannabis must be eradicated in 2019 or at least reduced significantly.[316]

This is not to say, as we saw before, that all parties see eye to eye with each other with regards to cannabis and fully endorse the conventions in that respect,[317] but the opposite is even further removed from reality. In order to adopt customary law on the basis of 'state practice', it is certainly necessary that there is a consistent practice which is extensive and virtually uniform. In other words, there are not meant to be significant inconsistencies, ambiguities and variations. It is of overriding importance that all or the majority of parties that can contribute to the creation of the rule or those whose interests are at stake in particular apply the rule in practice.[318] It is therefore obvious that there is no 'state practice' that cultivation of cannabis for recreational use is permissible. Incidentally, the same is true for stretching the exception of medical purposes so as to include general public health policies as well as the notion that states are free to decide whether or not to prosecute persons for acts that have to be criminalized pursuant to the UN narcotic drugs conventions. If one takes into account that the development of customary law on the basis of state practice also requires *opinio juris*, in other words that states recognize the rule which is applied in practice, in the firm belief that they are obliged to do so, then it is even harder to assert that there is a state practice concerning the above-mentioned subjects that is contrary to the UN narcotic drugs conventions. After all, there is no reason to assume that there is *opinio juris* that cannabis cultivation is permissible, that the medical exception by now can include public health policy as well or that there is complete or considerable freedom of choice around prosecution policy.

It is also relevant in this context that the Single Convention expressly provides a procedure for amending the Schedules, so it is possible to transfer narcotic drugs to another Schedule and to delete them altogether from the Schedules.[319] Seeing that various provisions in the Convention specifically

---

316 See section 2.4.

317 See for example 'Leaked paper reveals UN split over war on drugs', *The Guardian*, 30 November 2013, available on: http://www.undrugcontrol.info/en/newsroom/latest-news/item/5152-leaked-paper-reveals-un-split-over-war-on-drugs; 'CND informal consensus rule tested in decriminalization standoff', *IDPC*, 6 November 2013, available on:http://idpc.net/blog/2013/11/cnd-informal-consensus-rule-tested-in-decriminalization-standoff; 'Why are so many countries now saying cannabis is OK?', *BBC News*, 11 December 2018, available on: https://www.bbc.com/news/world-46374191.

318 More on identification of customary international law (general practice and acceptance of that practice as law (*opinion juris*) see International Law Commission, *Draft Conclusions on Identification of Customary International Law, with Commentaries*, adopted on 17th session in 2018, A/73/10, *Yearbook of the International Law Commission*, 2018, vol. II, Part. Two. See also e.g. James Crawford, *Brownlie's Principles of Public International Law*, Oxford: Oxford University Press, 2012, pp. 23–30; M. Bossuyt & J. Wouters, *Grondlijnen van internationaal recht*, Antwerpen/Oxford: Intersentia, 2005, pp. 105–111.

319 See section 2.2.1.

apply to the cultivation of cannabis, deleting cannabis from the Schedules would not mean that cannabis cultivation is no longer covered by the regime of the Conventions. Nevertheless, the Conventions would then be meaningless with regards to cannabis cultivation and possession, and this would make it clear that the parties have come to regard cannabis as less serious. As far as we could see, not a single country has yet even tried to transfer cannabis to another Schedule or to have it deleted from the Schedules by means of this procedure.[320] The availability of this procedure, when it has not even been used once to achieve declassification, is a contraindication that the parties in general would be of the opinion that the distribution, trade, sale and use of cannabis should be possible outside the exception of medical or scientific purposes. After all, this seems to indicate that none of the parties considers that possibility desirable or that none of the parties considers it realistic to think that other parties would back this move.

2.5.2. AMENDMENT OF CONVENTION LAW THROUGH ACCEPTED EVOLVED INTERPRETATION OF THE CONVENTION?

In addition to customary law that goes against the convention, the meaning of a convention can change over time by generally accepted interpretations of the provisions in the convention.[321] In that case, the convention itself remains the source of law. In this respect too, we believe that it cannot be claimed that cultivation of cannabis for recreational use under the UN narcotic drugs conventions is now considered to be permissible. First and foremost, the judgments of the International Narcotics Control Board (INCB) merit attention for this conclusion. This body points out consistently and repeatedly that the cultivation of cannabis for recreational use runs counter to the UN narcotic drugs conventions and that there is no room for allowing it.[322] The same is true for stretching the exception of medical purposes so as to include general public health policies as well as the notion that states are at liberty to decide whether or not to prosecute persons for acts that have to be criminalized pursuant to the UN narcotic drugs conventions. The INCB is designated in the conventions as the primary supervisor of the implementation of the Single Convention and to a lesser extent also the Illicit Traffic Convention and therefore has been accepted as such by the states parties. Even if we only look

[320] Also UNODC, *A Century of International Drug Control*, Vienna: United Nations, 2008, p. 82.

[321] The same view is expressed by David R. Bewley-Taylor & Martin Jelsma, 'The Limits of Latitude. The UN drug control conventions', *Series on Legislative Reform of Drug Policies*, No. 18, March 2012, p. 3.

[322] See for more information section 2.4.

at this fact, it is hard to argue that divergent interpretations of the previously mentioned subjects are now generally accepted. In addition to this, the states parties generally do not follow different interpretations regarding those subjects. Admittedly, there are places in the world where this is happening, for example in various federal states of the United States.[323] However, this does not apply to the United States as a state party, where federal law does not even recognize that cannabis can have a medical application, so that according to that law, every use is prohibited,[324] and globally, this phenomenon is not widespread enough to justify calling it a generally accepted interpretation of the Convention.[325]

Another matter is the significance of Article 36 of the Single Convention for cultivation, possession and purchase of cannabis for personal recreational use. Does this provision at this moment (still) carry an obligation to criminalize these acts?[326] Before we address this question briefly, we observe that it is only of limited importance. First, this is because Article 33 of the Single Convention is one of the obstacles to allowing the possession of drugs for personal recreational use and thereby to legalizing or tolerating it in general.[327] Also, Article 3(2) of the Illicit Traffic Convention entails an obligation to criminalize these acts one way or another.[328] To answer the question itself, it is important to remember that already at the time that the convention was drawn up, some parties were of the opinion that Article 36(1) of the Single Convention does not require criminalization of growing, possessing and buying small amounts of cannabis for personal recreational use.[329] By the way, at the time of the acceptance of the Illicit Traffic Convention, the Netherlands was of the opinion that possession, purchase and cultivation of cannabis for personal recreational use as incorporated in Article 3(2) of the Illicit Traffic Convention is already embodied in the Single Convention.[330] There is a case for arguing that the question must by now be considered as having been settled

323 For an overview, see 'Medical cannabis in the United States' on: https://en.wikipedia.org/wiki/Medical_cannabis_in_the_United_States.

324 See for example Beau Kilmer et al., *Multinational overview of cannabis production regimes*, RAND Europe/WODC, 2013, p. 22.

325 For more information on stretching the exception of 'medical and scientific purposes' and the rejection of that notion David R. Bewley-Taylor & Martin Jelsma, 'The Limits of Latitude. The UN drug control conventions', *Series on Legislative Reform of Drug Policies*, No. 18, March 2012, p. 15.

326 See also section 2.2.2.ii.a.VI for this.

327 See section 2.2.2.ii.a.V for more information.

328 See section 2.3.2.i (Obligations to criminalize and punish). See for more information section 2.4.ii and iv.

329 United Nations, *Commentary on the Single Convention on Narcotic Drugs, 1961*, New York: 1973, p. 112 (no. 18), pp. 402–403 (nos. 1–3) and p. 428 (no. 8).

330 *Kamerstukken II* 1990–1991, 22 080 (R 1406), nr. 3, p. 9 (MvT) (i.e., *Dutch Parliamentary Documents II* 1990–1991, 22 080 (R 1406), no. 3, p. 9 (Explanatory Memorandum)).

by the INCB, in view of the function of this body. At any rate, it is clear that the Board assumes that there is an obligation to criminalize cultivation, purchase and possession of cannabis for personal recreational use.[331] Given the limited function that this body has with regard to the Illicit Traffic Convention, formally the assumption can only be based on Article 36(1) of the Single Convention. Since the Board often bases itself on the UN drugs system as a whole (the three drug conventions), it cannot be ruled out that Article 3(2) of the Illicit Traffic Convention does play a part in this judgment. The UN Commentary also seems to suggest that Article 36(1) of the Single Convention can be – and by implication may be? – interpreted that it does not extend to drug-related acts for personal use.[332] At any rate, in the literature it is generally assumed that this interpretation is acceptable.[333,334]

We come to the conclusion that, although the wording of Article 36(1) of the Single Convention, the rationale of the Convention and its system justify the conclusion that this provision contains an obligation to criminalize acts of personal recreational drug use, it can now be argued that there is a generally accepted interpretation that Article 36(1) of the Single Convention, unlike Article 3(2) of the Illicit Traffic Convention, does not require that criminalization.[335] Nevertheless, we firmly believe that there is no ground for the claim that by now there is a generally accepted interpretation of the Convention according to which the cultivation of cannabis for recreational use is permissible when it is commercial, not done on a small scale or not for personal consumption. Nor can interpretations be accepted which stretch

---

331 See for a recent example INCB Report 2017, p. 43 (no. 326). See also INCB Report 2007, p. 8 (no. 30).

332 United Nations, *Commentary on the Single Convention on Narcotic Drugs, 1961*, New York: 1973, pp. 112–113 (nos. 18–22).

333 The following authors, among others, assume that Article 36(1) of the Illicit Traffic Convention does not entail an obligation to criminalize the possession and cultivation of drugs (and therefore also cannabis) for personal consumption: Jos Silvis, 'De internationale juridische speelruimte voor Nederlands drugbeleid', in: Tom Blom, Hans de Doelder & Dick J. Hessing (eds.), *Naar een consistent drugbeleid. Een congresverslag*, Deventer: Gouda Quint, 1996, pp. 221–222 (i.e., Jos Silvis, 'The room for Dutch drug policy under international law', in: T. Blom, Hans de Doelder & Dick J. Hessing (eds.), *Towards a consistent drug policy. A conference report*, Deventer: Gouda Quint, 1996, pp. 221–222); Neil Brett Boister, *The Suppression of Illicit Drugs Through International Law*, Nottingham: University of Nottingham, 1998, pp. 86–89 and 143; Krzysztof Krajewski, 'How flexible are the United Nations drug conventions?', 10 *International Journal of Drug Policy* 4 (1999), pp. 329–338 on pp. 332–333; Daniel Dupras, *Canada's International Obligations under the Leading International Conventions on the Control of Narcotic Drugs*, Ottawa: Library of Parliament, 1988, pp. 22–24.

334 However, for another view see Gérald Le Dain-Commission, *Cannabis. A Report of the Commission of Inquiry into the Non-Medical Use of Drugs*, Ottawa 1972, p. 212.

335 In the same vein, see David R. Bewley-Taylor & Martin Jelsma, 'The Limits of Latitude. The UN drug control conventions', *Series on Legislative Reform of Drug Policies*, No. 18, March 2012, p. 12.

the exception of medical purposes to include general public health policies, or interpretations that states are free to decide whether or not to prosecute persons for acts that are required to be criminalized pursuant to Article 36(1) of the Single Convention and Article 3(1) of the Illicit Traffic Convention.

As stated above, this is a strictly legal study. The legal policy question whether a state should play a pioneering role internationally in breach of the conventions with regard to permitting cannabis cultivation, in the hope that this would eventually lead to a generally accepted interpretation of the Conventions or even to state practice, is therefore beyond the scope of this legal study. The question whether it is desirable for a state to leave the conventions or to initiate a process of amendment thereof and/or of the Schedules[336] – which would be the appropriate route under international law – is also well outside this scope.

2.6. CONCLUSION

The UN drug control system has two fundamental goals. It aims to ensure that narcotic drugs are available for medical use and for scientific purposes. At the same time, it aims to guarantee that the use of narcotic drugs is exclusively restricted to those medical and scientific purposes.

The first relevant observation to be made in the discussion about cannabis cultivation for recreational use is that the object and purpose of the conventions is to ban completely the circulation of narcotic drugs for anything other than medical or scientific purposes. Permitting cannabis cultivation aimed at recreational use is not easily compatible with that objective. This rationale of eradication is reflected in the following:

- The Preamble to the Single Convention (among other things: limiting the use of narcotic drugs to medical and scientific purposes, where measures are taken to ensure that those objectives are reached) and the Preamble to the Illicit Traffic Convention (among other things: the eradication of illicit traffic is a joint responsibility of all states);
- The estimate system (Articles 12–21 of the Single Convention);
- General obligations to restrict acts involving cannabis exclusively to 'medical and scientific purposes', to combat cannabis cultivation for recreational purposes and fight recreational drug use (Article 4 of the Single Convention, Article 14(2) of the Illicit Traffic Convention and Article 38 of the Single Convention);

336 Whether this is possible in the first place and whether such attempts have any chance of success will be dealt with in sections 4.2.1, 4.2.2 and 4.2.3.

- A total prohibition via criminalizations of acts – including cannabis cultivation – which are aimed at or are related to recreational use of cannabis (particularly: Article 36 of the Single Convention and Article 3(1) and (2) of the Illicit Traffic Convention);
- Obligations to prosecute which ensue from the Conventions explicitly and implicitly and which apply to cannabis cultivation that is not small-scale and not intended for personal use;
- A complete ban of the possession of narcotic drugs including cannabis for recreational use (Article 33 of the Single Convention);
- Obligations to seize cannabis for recreational use as well (Article 33 of the Single Convention and Article 37 of the Single Convention);
- The system of international cooperation in criminal matters (in the Single Convention and particularly the Illicit Traffic Convention).

Complying with all these requirements should lead to the end of the circulation of narcotic drugs. For this book, it is of importance that in addition to coca and poppy products, cannabis products are the main object of this Convention, since these are mentioned explicitly not only in the Schedules of the Convention, but also in the Convention itself. This objective of eradication, which also explicitly targets cannabis, cannot be reconciled with permitting cannabis cultivation for recreational use by legalization, decriminalization, policy-based tolerance and/or other forms of regulation of such cultivation.

The overview given above also shows that the UN narcotic drugs conventions comprise a prohibitive, repressive and multi-layered system. If one managed to neutralize one of those obligations with a view to regulating the cultivation of cannabis, one would immediately find oneself facing all sorts of other obstacles.

The most serious provisions in the Conventions are those about the obligations to criminalize specific acts. These obligations to criminalize cover both small-scale cultivation for personal use (see Article 36(1) of the Single Convention (which is not entirely clear), and the indisputable Article 3(2) of the Illicit Traffic Convention) and cultivation that is not small-scale and/or is not intended for personal use (see Article 36(1) of the Single Convention and Article 3(1) of the Single Convention). Given these obligations, legalization or decriminalization of the cultivation of cannabis for recreational use is not a legal option.

The question then is whether it is possible to adopt a general policy of refraining from prosecution for these punishable offences (penal tolerance). There are obligations to prosecute persons for essentially serious offences, ensuing implicitly in particular from the Single Convention. One can hardly argue that tolerating cannabis cultivation in order to supply retail shops in general or as a matter of policy is permissible on the grounds of the expediency principle under the Single Convention. More specifically, such a policy of penal tolerance would contravene Article 3(6) of the Illicit Traffic Convention. It is only for this provision – not with reference to the Single Convention nor to other provisions pertaining to cannabis in the Illicit Traffic Convention – that the Netherlands formulated a reservation insofar as this is relevant here. In view of the content and background of the reservation, and the object and purpose of the Convention, this does not leave sufficient room for adopting a policy of permitting cannabis cultivation. The INCB, too, takes the view that general policy-based penal tolerance of cannabis cultivation for recreational consumption – not designated for personal use – is contrary to the drugs conventions.

However, even if the Public Prosecutions Service were able to refrain from prosecution for cannabis cultivation intended for the supply of coffee shops, with an appeal to the expediency principle and the reservation, this still would not clear the path to regulating this cultivation. After all, the expediency principle – also by virtue of Article 167(2) of the Dutch Code of Criminal Procedures and Article 3(6) of the Illicit Traffic Convention – is only a principle with regard to prosecution for criminal offences: it does not derogate from obligations under the Convention to criminalize nor does it touch on obligations under the Convention imposed on the state with regard to other law than criminal law. Therefore, the following obligations simply remain in force in the case of policy-based non-prosecution:

- the general obligation to pursue actively the limitation of the production, distribution, trade, use and possession of cannabis for medical and scientific purposes (Article 4 of the Single Convention);
- obligations to prohibit and seize cannabis (Article 33 of the Single Convention and possibly Article 37 of the Single Convention);
- the obligation to take measures against cannabis use (Article 38 of the Single Convention); and the obligation to fight the cultivation of cannabis (Article 14(2) of the Illicit Traffic Convention).

However, a policy of tolerating and actually permitting cannabis cultivation would imply that these obligations are not fulfilled, whereas the Netherlands is also legally bound to do so (as are all the government bodies in the Netherlands). Many of these obligations rest with the government, and also apply to municipalities.

This above-mentioned multi-layered system of diverse criminal law, administrative and other obligations would be incompatible with legalizing, decriminalizing, policy-based tolerance and/or otherwise regulating the cultivation of cannabis for recreational use for the benefit of retail shops. This concerns cannabis cultivation aimed at recreational users.

One final question that arises is whether it is possible to avoid all these obligations simultaneously by allowing cannabis cultivation for recreational use via the exception of 'medical and scientific purposes'. There are those who argue that this is possible (or should be possible), because regulating such cannabis cultivation would serve the interests of public health and that the Single Convention in particular refers to the protection of those interests. The plea that the regulation of cannabis cultivation for personal use can be covered by the exception for that reason cannot be successful though.

It is undeniably true that the UN narcotic drugs conventions intend to meet the interests of public health. These conventions do so in three ways: 1. Availability of narcotic drugs as meaningful and/or effective medicine or research into this; 2. Treatment of and care for drug users so as to wean them off these drugs; 3. Protecting society against narcotic drugs by fighting and eliminating the production, trade, possession and use of these drugs for recreational purposes by means of criminal law and many other social prohibitions and measures. Public health in a general sense therefore is not an interest recognized or pursued by the convention. Arguments aimed at legalization, decriminalization or regulation of the cannabis market which attempt to ride piggyback on public health interests in general but are not compatible with one of the three recognized interests, or even conflict with these, must be deemed to be contrary to the Single Convention and the Illicit Traffic Convention. This is also the view of the INCB, which resolutely rejects stretching the exception of medical purposes in order to enable access to cannabis for recreational use.

In fact, the UN narcotic drugs conventions reveal a limited, one-sided and rigid view of public health interests.[337] With regard to the latter point, it is important that nowhere under the Conventions is the interest of general public health recognized as a ground to trump or alleviate the repression of narcotic drugs required by the Conventions, whereas conversely that same interest can very well necessitate an even more forceful repression of narcotic drugs than is already required by default. This latter point is emphatically made in Article 22 of the Single Convention: this provision contains the requirement to prohibit cultivation of plants yielding drugs that in itself is permitted (i.e. for medical or scientific purposes) if that is necessary 'for protecting the public health and welfare and preventing the diversion of drugs into the illicit traffic'. A similar obligation also applies to narcotic drugs in Schedule IV – such as cannabis – by virtue of Article 2(5)(b) of the Single Convention.[338] In this context, it is also worth mentioning Article 12(4)(b) of the Illicit Traffic Convention: this provision gives the INCB monitoring duties and – powers 'if the volume and

---

[337] See for example Senate Canada, *Cannabis: Our Position for a Canadian Public Policy. Report of the Senate Special Committee on Illegal Drugs*, 2002, p. 439: 'This chapter could begin and end with the same words: The international drug control conventions are, at least with respect to cannabis, an utterly irrational restraint that has nothing to do with scientific or public health considerations.'

[338] Incidentally, for narcotic drugs under the lighter regime of Schedule II – which therefore does not apply to cannabis – see a similar obligation in Article 39 of the Single Convention.

extent of the illicit manufacture of a narcotic drug or psychotropic substance creates serious public health or social problems'. Here too, there is no mention anywhere that conversely the INCB has a duty to reduce the repression of narcotic drugs if this were in the interest of public health.

The foregoing leads to the conclusion that subject to the UN narcotic drugs conventions, it is not possible to legalize, decriminalize, tolerate by virtue of a policy and/or otherwise regulate the cultivation of cannabis for recreational use to supply retail shops.[339] However, there is more to it than that. We will again look at the question whether there are possibilities for regulation of such cultivation in Chapter 4 on the basis of arguments in favour of such regulation, which have been put forward by Dutch municipalities and in other countries. We will also dwell in more detail on the question whether the joint cultivation and consumption of cannabis is permissible in the context of so-called Cannabis Social Clubs.

---

339 See also for example Krzysztof Krajewski, 'How flexible are the United Nations drug conventions?', 10 *International Journal of Drug Policy* 4 (1999), pp. 329–338 on p. 329; David R. Bewley-Taylor, 'The Contemporary International Drug Control System: A History of the UNGASS Decade', in: John Collins (ed.), *Governing the Global Drug Wars*, London: London School of Economics, 2012, pp. 49–55 on p. 50; David R. Bewley-Taylor & Martin Jelsma, 'The Limits of Latitude. The UN drug control conventions', *Series on Legislative Reform of Drug Policies*, No. 18, March 2012, p. 16.

CHAPTER 3

OBLIGATIONS UNDER EUROPEAN LAW REGARDING CANNABIS

EU Laws on Drugs

3.1. INTRODUCTION

Although the UN narcotic drugs conventions already constitute a strict and detailed drug control system that applies to the entire European Union, the fight against drugs is also the subject of legislation in the Union. This chapter provides an elaborate account and analysis of the EU laws on drugs insofar as these are relevant for cannabis cultivation for recreational use. Please note that the EU-framework is closely connected to the Single Convention and the Illicit Traffic Convention. In the case of the latter convention, the European Union itself is a party, with respect to the areas within the competence of the Union.[1] The instruments of the Union only aim to supplement the UN narcotic drugs conventions. The reason for adopting additional instruments is that the member states (initially the signatories to the Schengen Agreement and eventually the entire Union) deem the measures in these instruments to be necessary to compensate for the negative effects of the abolition of checks at the internal borders within the Union. Therefore, the key question in this chapter is twofold. First: what is the extent of the obligations under the EU laws on drugs regarding cannabis cultivation? Secondly: to what extent and in what manner does European law supplement the obligations that ensue from the UN narcotic drugs conventions? In a European context, there are three important instruments:

1. *Schengen acquis* (1985 and 1990)[2]

---

[1] 90/611/EEC: Council Decision of 22 October 1990 concerning the conclusion, on behalf of the European Economic Community, of the United Nations Convention against Illicit Traffic in Narcotic Drugs and Psychotropic Substances, *OJ* 1990 L 326/56.

[2] An agreement between the Kingdom of the Netherlands, the Kingdom of Belgium, the Federal Republic of Germany, the French Republic and the Grand Duchy of Luxembourg regarding the gradual abolition of checks at the common borders, Schengen 14 June 1985 (Schengen Agreement), *OJ* 2000 L 239/13, and the Convention implementing the Schengen Agreement of 14 June 1985, 19 June 1990, *OJ* 2000 L 239/19 (Schengen Implementation Agreement).

2. *Joint Action of the European Union to combat drug addiction and to prevent and combat illegal drug trafficking* (1996)[3]
3. *Council Framework Decision laying down minimum provisions on the constituent elements of criminal acts and penalties in the field of illicit drug trafficking* (2004).[4]

The Schengen acquis, under which checks at the internal borders of the states parties are abolished with a view to completing the internal market, forms the first common framework for transnational cooperation in the area of combating the illicit trade in narcotic drugs, cannabis included. As a consequence of the creation of the European Union,[5] the legal basis for the Union's action in the field of criminalizing and sanctioning illicit drug trafficking is found in Article 83[6] of the Treaty on the Functioning of the European Union (TFEU).[7] In the context of judicial cooperation in criminal matters (Chapter 4 TFEU), the European Parliament and the Council can adopt 'minimum rules concerning the definition of criminal offences and sanctions in the areas of particularly serious crime [including illicit drug trafficking] with a cross-border dimension resulting from the nature or impact of such offences or from a special need to combat them on a common basis.' (Article 83(1) of the TFEU). For this purpose, two other instruments were created, namely the 1996 Joint Action on Illegal Drug Trafficking and the 2004 Framework Decision on Illegal Drug Trafficking. As we noted earlier in respect of the UN narcotic drugs conventions, one must keep in mind with respect to EU laws on drugs that social and political views on the use of drugs and the fight against drugs vary considerably among member states.[8]

---

3 96/750/JHA: Joint Action of 17 December 1996 adopted by the Council on the basis of Article K.3 of the Treaty on European Union concerning the approximation of the laws and practices of the Member States of the European Union to combat drug addiction and to prevent and combat illegal drug trafficking, *OJ* 1996 L 342/6.

4 Council Framework Decision 2004/757/JHA of 25 October 2004 laying down minimum provisions on the constituent elements of criminal acts and penalties in the field of illicit drug trafficking, *OJ* 2004 L 335/8. The Framework Decision has been amended by Directive (EU) 2017/2103, with a view to reducing the availability of new psychoactive substances. This amendment is, however, not relevant for the following discussion on cannabis so we will continue referring to the original Framework Decision.

5 Maastricht Treaty of 1993, the Amsterdam Treaty of 1999, and the Lisbon Treaty of 2007.

6 See ex Article 31 and ex Article K.3.

7 Consolidated version of the Treaty on the Functioning of the European Union; the most recent consolidated versions were published in *OJ* 2012 C 326 and C 327.

8 See for example Tom Blom, *Opiumwetgeving en drugsbeleid*, Deventer: Kluwer, 2008, p. 106 (i.e., Tom Blom, *Opium legislation and drug policy*, Deventer: Kluwer, 2008, p. 106), who explains why the Dutch coffee shop policy in 2005 at any rate would hardly induce the EU member states to be enthusiastic about a more generous policy on soft drugs, and to that effect refers to *Kamerstukken II* 2005–2006, 24 077, nr. 168 (Drugsbeleid; Brief van de Minister van Justitie) (i.e., *Dutch Parliamentary Documents II* 2005–2006, 24 077, no. 168 (Drug policy; Letter from the Dutch Minister for Justice)).

3.2. THE SCHENGEN ACQUIS

The so-called Schengen acquis is based on the Schengen Agreement and the Schengen Implementation Agreement. The following must be pointed out.

3.2.1. SCHENGEN AGREEMENT 1985

With the Agreement reached in Schengen between the Netherlands, Belgium, Germany, France and Luxembourg about the gradual abolition of checks at the common borders (hereinafter to be referred to as: Schengen Agreement), the member states undertook to 'combat vigorously illicit drug trafficking on their territories and to coordinate their action effectively in this area' (Article 8 Schengen Agreement). The states involved accepted this commitment so as to relax the border checks and because of major differences between the laws of the member states.[9] With regard to combating illicit drug trafficking, the member states agreed to reinforce cooperation between their customs and police authorities.[10] Ultimately, the aim was to achieve harmonization of the laws and regulations, in particular, among other things, on narcotic drugs (Article 19 of the Schengen Agreement). The Agreement creates a wide and general framework with respect to narcotic drugs in which the fight against illicit drug trafficking on their own territories, potentially through transnational cooperation plays a pivotal role. It was foreseen that the abolition of border checks would lead to an intensification of the import and export of narcotic drugs. To counteract this consequence, the Schengen Agreement is the first step towards a common approach to address (international) drug trafficking. However, the Agreement neither contains a definition of 'narcotic drugs' nor a reference to cultivation or other acts involving cannabis. This is largely because the problems surrounding the cultivation of cannabis were not yet a significant topic of discussion at the time. The Schengen Implementation Agreement is important for the more specific implementation of the arrangements.

---

9 Article 8 of the Schengen Agreement.

10 Article 9 of the Schengen Agreement: 'The Parties shall reinforce cooperation between their customs and police authorities, notably in combating crime, particularly illicit trafficking in narcotic drugs and arms, the unauthorised entry and residence of persons, customs and tax fraud and smuggling. To that end and in accordance with their national laws, the Parties shall endeavour to improve the exchange of information and to reinforce that exchange where information which could be useful to the other Parties in combating crime is concerned.'

3.2.2. SCHENGEN IMPLEMENTATION AGREEMENT 1990

Chapter six of the Convention implementing the Schengen Agreement of 14 June 1985 (Schengen Implementation Agreement)[11] pays specific attention to narcotic drugs, including cannabis. The fact that the UN drug control system plays a decisive role becomes clear in Article 71(1) of the Schengen Implementation Agreement. In this provision, the member states undertake 'to adopt in accordance with the existing *United Nations Conventions*, all necessary measures to prevent and punish the illicit trafficking in narcotic drugs and psychotropic substances' (emphasis added).[12] For the definition and the status of cannabis, one must therefore fall back on the UN narcotic drugs conventions.[13]

It is remarkable that the Implementation Agreement does not contain an independent definition of 'narcotic drugs' nor an explicit reference to the Schedules of the Single Convention, but assigns special importance to cannabis by explicitly mentioning it: 'narcotic drugs and psychotropic substances of whatever type, including cannabis'. Given the status of cannabis in the UN narcotic drugs conventions, the addition of 'including cannabis' seems superfluous. Nonetheless, this explicit reference identifies cannabis as one of the narcotic drugs to which the obligations that ensue from the Implementation Agreement apply.

The Implementation Agreement contains explicit references to cannabis in the first, second, third and fifth paragraphs of the aforementioned Article 71(1) of the Schengen Implementation Agreement. It does not define cannabis more specifically. Bearing in mind that the Implementation Agreement refers to the UN narcotic drugs conventions, it is obvious that in any case, 'cannabis' is taken to mean that which is forbidden under those conventions. This concerns flowering or fruiting tops of the cannabis plant and cannabis resin (on account of the entry in the Schedules included with the Single Convention) and cannabis plants (because they are mentioned in the actual UN narcotic drugs conventions).[14]

i. General Obligations: Article 71(1) of the Schengen Implementation Agreement

The general obligation in Article 71(1) of the Schengen Implementation Agreement to 'adopt [...] all necessary measures' 'to prevent [...] the illicit

---

11 Regarding the points below, it is relevant that the original languages of the Implementation Agreement are German, French and Dutch; so the English version is merely an official translation.

12 By UN Conventions we mean: 'The Single Convention on Narcotic Drugs, 1961, as amended by the Protocol [of 1972] amending the Single Convention on Narcotic Drugs, 1961, the Convention on Psychotropic Substances, 1971 and the United Nations Convention against illicit traffic in narcotic drugs and psychotropic substances, 20 December 1988.'

13 See Chapter 2 of this volume.

14 See for more information section 2.2.1.

trafficking in narcotic drugs' explicitly refers to the following acts: the direct and indirect sale and possession for sale or export of cannabis.[15] Regarding the term 'preventing' (in the German version: 'Unterbindung'), it is important to note that this is rather generic in nature, and consequently it is not clear which measures the member states need to take and whether these should pertain to administrative or criminal law. The French version is a bit clearer about this, witness the words 'à la prévention et à la répression', since the term 'répression' already has a stronger association with criminal law. The English version of the Implementation Agreement (which, we stress, is not an original language version) ties in with that French approach where it mentions 'all necessary measures to prevent and punish the illicit trafficking in narcotic drugs and psychotropic substances'. So what is meant in this language version is: measures to prevent and punish the illicit trafficking in cannabis. This English version in fact builds on the French one, in that the former version has a more specific counterpart of the French term 'répression', namely the term 'punish'. Moreover, Article 71(1) of the Schengen Implementation Agreement carries an obligation for the signatories to adopt 'all [....] measures' that are 'necessary' to prevent illicit trafficking (German: 'alle notwendigen Maßnahmen'; French: 'toutes mesures nécessaires'). As criminal law measures absolutely come under 'all measures' also, and it seems to us that it is hard to argue that preventing the illicit trafficking in narcotic drugs can be effective without any criminal proceedings, it must be assumed that states are also bound by Article 71(1) of the Schengen Implementation Agreement to apply criminal law where the efforts to combat illicit trafficking require this.

The question then is what exactly 'measures' refer to: does it mean only legislative measures (criminal law) or operational measures too (investigation and prosecution)? Taking into account the wording, context and system of the Implementation Agreement, there is little ground to assume that the latter would not be included. Not only does the word 'all' that precedes measures imply a broad interpretation, but it is important that the Implementation Agreement also contains operational obligations[16] and that sometimes the term measures is used there in that sense as well.[17] Apart from that, the purpose of the Implementation

15 Article 71(1) of the Schengen Implementation Agreement says: 'The Contracting Parties undertake as regards the direct or indirect sale of narcotic drugs and psychotropic substances of whatever type, including cannabis, and the possession of such products and substances for sale or export, to adopt in accordance with the existing United Nations Conventions, all necessary measures to prevent and punish the illicit trafficking in narcotic drugs and psychotropic substances.' (footnote reference omitted).

16 For example, see Article 40 of the Schengen Implementation Agreement regarding the surveillance of persons presumed to have committed criminal offences (suspects), and Article 41 of the Schengen Implementation Agreement regarding the hot pursuit of such suspects across borders.

17 For example, see the obligation to take measures in connection with communications as set forth in Article 44 of the Schengen Implementation Agreement.

Agreement is to implement the Schengen Agreement. As mentioned above, in Article 8 of that Agreement the member states undertake to combat illicit drug trafficking 'vigorously' and to 'coordinate their action' effectively 'in this area'. This points clearly at operational action, not just legislative measures.

Meanwhile, it is important that cultivation of cannabis or other related production activities are not specifically mentioned in the Implementation Agreement. Here too, this is probably because cultivation did not feature prominently in the discussion at the time. To the extent that cultivation takes place for the purpose of sale or export of cannabis, at some point in time this cultivation implies the possession of cannabis for the purpose of these actions. The consequence of all this is that the authorities must then initiate criminal proceedings regarding such cultivation if that is necessary in connection with combating illicit trafficking.

ii. Obligation to Criminalize and Punish: Article 71(2) of the Schengen Implementation Agreement

A more specific obligation to take criminal law measures can be read in paragraph 2 of Article 71 of the Schengen Implementation Agreement, on the basis of which the Schengen states undertake to 'prevent [...] by administrative and penal measures the illegal export of narcotic drugs [...], including cannabis, as well as the sale, supply and handing over of such products and substances'[18] (German: 'mit verwaltungsrechtlichen und strafrechtlichen Mitteln zu unterbinden'). In any case, this means that the member states are obliged to criminalize these acts. The French text of this provision says 'à prévenir et à réprimer par des mesures administratives et pénales'. This version of the provision can be interpreted more clearly as an obligation to prevent and suppress the acts mentioned. This is the case even more so in the non-original English version: 'to prevent and punish by administrative and penal measures'. Punishment via penal measures must be preceded by prosecution. Of course, this English text cannot be regarded as decisive, certainly not when compared to the authentic language versions. However, as this is an official EU document, and the English version does not contradict the German and the Dutch version, and even matches the French one fairly well, it may perhaps play an authoritative part in the interpretation of the authentic texts. Moreover, criminal law in itself would not make enough of a contribution to the actual fight against the illegal export, sale, supply and handing over of cannabis. In this respect too, Article 71(2) of the Schengen Implementation

[18] Article 71(2) of the Schengen Implementation Agreement says: 'The Contracting Parties undertake to prevent and punish by administrative and penal measures the illegal export of narcotic drugs and psychotropic substances, including cannabis, as well as the sale, supply and handing over of such products and substances, without prejudice to the relevant provisions of Articles 74, 75 and 76.'

Agreement seems to presuppose actively combating crime, which fits in with the German and Dutch wording and follows the French text a little more explicitly. That conclusion is corroborated even more by the Statement in the next paragraph, as little meaning would attach to that Statement if Article 71(2) of the Schengen Implementation Agreement only constituted obligations to take legislative measures. We therefore draw the conclusion that in those situations in which the fight preventing the illegal acts requires action in criminal matters, it is hard to maintain that the authorities are not obliged to do so on the grounds of this provision. This conclusion also matters with respect to cannabis cultivation, although in a limited way. As we observed above, the Implementation Agreement does not contain specific provisions about the cultivation of cannabis, and Article 71(2) of the Schengen Implementation Agreement does not carry an obligation to criminalize the possession of cannabis as such: that obligation only applies to the possession of cannabis for sale (Article 71(1) of the Schengen Implementation Agreement). The framework of the UN Conventions therefore continues to determine all other cases of cannabis possession.

iii. The Exception to Article 71(2) of the Schengen Implementation Agreement, Created with the Joint Declaration

The Schengen states created some room to deviate from the obligations ensuing from Article 71(2) of the Schengen Implementation Agreement. In fact, this concerns an exception. The Joint Declaration included in the Final Act of the Schengen Implementation Agreement (for Article 71(2) of the Schengen Implementation Agreement) states that:

> In so far as a Contracting Party departs from the principle referred to in Article 71(2) in connection with its national policy on the prevention and treatment of addiction to narcotic drugs and psychotropic substances, all Contracting Parties shall adopt the necessary administrative measures and penal measures to prevent and punish the illicit import and export of such products and substances, particularly towards the territories of the other Contracting Parties.[19]

So if a state refrains from administrative and criminal enforcement as regards the prevention and treatment of addiction, that state is also bound to adopt all necessary administrative measures and penal measures to combat the illicit import and export of cannabis. The leeway in national policy to depart from Article 71(2) of the Schengen Implementation Agreement only exists for the 'prevention and treatment' of addiction to narcotic drugs. Is the exception then applicable to protect a national policy that is aimed at keeping the cannabis

---

[19] *OJ* 2000 L 239/55, under 3.

market and hard drugs market separate, where the sale of cannabis is explicitly tolerated so as to deter users from turning to hard drugs? Treatment of addiction in a medical or therapeutic sense does not enter into this. However, supposing that certain forms of policies of tolerance or non-prosecution help prevent addiction to certain narcotic drugs, one can argue perfectly well that this is within the scope of the declaration.

It is interesting that the report by the Asser Institute appears to give pride of place to preventing the illegal import and export of cannabis as the limit of the scope of the exception in the Joint Declaration. The report says: 'In concrete terms, it is defensible to claim that the Netherlands would be in breach of the Schengen obligations if an experiment with the supply of coffee shops led to an escalation in drugs tourism and consequently meant a significant shift at the expense of the partner countries, the effects of which could not be countered or remedied.'[20] The Asser Institute seems to imply that there is only room for a national policy on the prevention and treatment of addiction so long as this does not result in a significant deterioration of the fight against illegal import and export. In other words: the possibility to apply the exception is made conditional on the importance of combating illegal import and export. This approach is the opposite of that in the Declaration, which puts the possibility of discretion in the policy first, but imposes an obligation to take the required measures to prevent the harmful consequence involved with the import and export of drugs. That does not, however, mean that it should then be possible to achieve the same result as when the addiction policy was not implemented. It does mean, though, that the policy's consequences that are harmful for foreign countries must be prevented as much as possible through countervailing measures.

It can be argued that the Netherlands with its coffee shop policy acts in agreement with the Joint Declaration, so long as all reasonably possible measures are taken to stop cannabis that is purchased, supplied or handed over in the context of the prevention or treatment of addiction from finding its way across the border into other states parties. Since the Declaration only permits an exception to the obligations ensuing from Article 71(2) of the Schengen Implementation Agreement with respect to prevention and treatment of addiction, in principle it is only because of that policy that there will be room to refrain from applying the administrative and penal measures required by this provision. As noted above, this Declaration at the same time implies that the aforementioned provision requires its enforcement through criminal law in addition to criminalizations. Indeed, if this were not the case, the states would

---

20 T.M.C. Asser Instituut, *Experimenteren met het Gedogen van de Teelt van Cannabis ten Behoeve van de Bevoorrading van Coffeeshops – Internationaal rechtelijke en Europees rechtelijke aspecten*, Den Haag: 2005, p. 19 (i.e., Asser Institute – Centre for International & European Law; *Experimenting with tolerating the cultivation of cannabis for the supply of coffee shops – aspects of international and European law*, The Hague: 2005).

have room to implement their own policies in respect of the prevention and treatment of addiction to narcotic drugs without the Declaration.

iv. Obligations to Prosecute

The Schengen Implementation Agreement contains no explicit provisions about obligations of prosecution that may fall to states. As shown by the foregoing, the obligation in Article 71(2) of the Schengen Implementation Agreement to prevent illegal drug trafficking (sale, supply, handing over and import and export) 'by administrative and penal measures' is first and foremost an obligation to criminalize these actions. It is also true that in those situations in which the fight to prevent the illegal acts requires action in criminal matters, it is hard to maintain that the authorities are not obliged to do so on the grounds of this provision. Article 71(2) of the Schengen Implementation Agreement does not imply though that there must be a prosecution in each specific case. However, one can hardly maintain that a member state that never takes action in criminal matters – through investigation, prosecution and punishment – still fulfils the obligation under this provision. There should at least be a cannabis control policy that effectively combines administrative and penal measures and sanctions. This, however, then also implies that the member state has considerable freedom in determining what that combination looks like and which of its components are applied in concrete cases.

This is consistent with the provision in Article 71(5) of the Schengen Implementation Agreement. After all, this provision says that the member states 'shall do their utmost to prevent and combat the negative effects arising from the illicit demand' for cannabis among other things. The member states enjoy a fair amount of discretion in this respect. Indeed, Article 71(5) of the Schengen Implementation Agreement also says that each 'Contracting Party shall be responsible for the measures' adopted to meet the obligation under this provision. Nonetheless, it is hard to insist that a party does 'its utmost' to prevent those negative effects if its authorities seldom or never proceed to prosecution for the acts of export, sale, supply and handing over of cannabis for recreational use as mentioned in Article 71(2) of the Schengen Implementation Agreement.

The same holds true for cannabis cultivation. Admittedly, there is not a single provision in the Implementation Agreement that refers explicitly to this activity, but one must assume that the efforts to fight and control it are part and parcel of the general obligation of Article 71(5) of the Schengen Implementation Agreement. Can a state really maintain that it does its 'utmost' to prevent the negative effects of the illegal demand for cannabis, if the cultivation of cannabis is not combated through prosecution as well? It seems to us that it is even hard to claim that one acts in accordance with this obligation if, on the grounds of a general policy on prosecution, the prosecuting authorities refrain from prosecution for concrete serious offences – such as the cultivation of cannabis that is not small-scale – that meet or generate that illegal demand, at least where that policy is not based on the exception of the aforementioned Joint Declaration.[21] In our opinion, that exception applies here insofar as the obligation to prosecute ensuing from Article 71(5) of the Schengen Implementation Agreement is tied in with the obligations related to criminal law arising from Article 71(2) of the Schengen Implementation Agreement. After all, it is the latter provision that the Declaration refers to. However, it is precisely cannabis cultivation that Article 71(2) of the Schengen Implementation Agreement does not apply to, while the fight against such cultivation implicitly seems to be covered by the obligation ensuing from Article 71(5) of the Schengen Implementation Agreement. Since the exception of the Joint Declaration does not apply to Article 71(5), it would appear that because of this provision, the member states have a general duty to combat cannabis cultivation, in the form of prosecutions if necessary.

v. Obligations Regarding Seizure and Confiscation

By virtue of Article 72 of the Schengen Implementation Agreement, the states 'in accordance with their constitutions and their national legal systems' undertake to 'ensure that legislation is enacted to enable the seizure and confiscation of the proceeds of the illicit trafficking in narcotic drugs and psychotropic substances'. In this respect, the Implementation Agreement reflects the similar obligation laid down in the Illicit Traffic Convention. Incidentally, the Implementation Agreement does not contain a provision that explicitly applies to the seizure of narcotic drugs.

However, Article 73(1) of the Schengen Implementation Agreement states that controlled deliveries of illegal narcotic drugs must be possible. The underlying assumption of this provision is that usually, the substances will be seized. This does not, however, mean per se that the Implementation Agreement itself requires seizure as a matter of principle. Because the provision emphasizes that states should have the option of controlled delivery, it seems to be intended primarily to ensure that even in states where seizure of drugs is required, it is still possible to effect a controlled delivery. In this light, it would appear that the raison d'être for the provision is not so much a supposed obligation to seize cannabis under the Implementation Agreement as the existence of obligations to that effect in member states.

A certain obligation to seize cannabis seems to ensue from Article 71(5) of the Schengen Implementation Agreement that was mentioned earlier. In general, it seems a tall order to claim that one does one's 'utmost' in accordance with this

21 See this section (3.2.2.iii).

provision to prevent the negative effects of the illegal demand for cannabis if the authorities do not proceed to seize the supplies of cannabis for recreational use that they are aware of. However, there is room for the member states to make their own decisions: Article 71(5) of the Schengen Implementation Agreement also says that each 'Contracting Party shall be responsible for the measures' adopted to meet the obligation under this provision. The question that remains is whether the exception of the aforementioned Joint Declaration[22] still applies to this obligation. In our view, that is the case insofar as the seizure is treated as an administrative or a penal measure for the purpose of preventing the sale, supply and handing over of cannabis. This is because in that case measures in the sense of Article 71(2) of the Schengen Implementation Agreement are involved, to which this exception applies. However, the case is more complicated if the offences lead to the illegal import and export of cannabis. As the Joint Declaration requires measures to counteract this, it would appear that cannabis that is to be imported or exported must be seized. After all, it is difficult to argue in principle that allowing that export or import serves a policy intended to ensure the care for or prevention of addiction. Seeing that Article 71(2) of the Schengen Implementation Agreement has no bearing on cannabis cultivation, whereas fighting such cultivation seems to be implied by the obligation of Article 71(5) of the Schengen Implementation Agreement, it looks as if the obligation to seize cannabis also extends to cannabis plantations.

vi. Obligations that in Principle do not Pertain to Criminal Law

Furthermore, the abolition of controls on individuals at internal borders also entails that the Schengen states undertake to step up the fight against the illicit trade in cannabis among other drugs at the external borders (Article 71(3) of the Schengen Implementation Agreement). With a view to compliance with the provisions under Article 71 of the Schengen Implementation Agreement, the state parties must also 'carry out surveillance of places known to be used for drug trafficking', according to Article 71(4) of the Schengen Implementation Agreement. Undoubtedly, retail shops are within the scope of this provision. This cannot possibly include supervision of a licensing system, though, as this contravenes the UN narcotic drugs conventions.[23] It is also important that the states parties should not jeopardise the efficiency of more rigorous national controls of narcotic drugs by other states parties and that they therefore must, where necessary, take appropriate measures, in accordance with their medical, ethical and practical usage (Article 76(1) and Article 76(2) of the Schengen Implementation Agreement).

---

22 See this section (3.2.2.iii).

23 See for more information section 4.4.2.i.b.

3.2.3. INTERMEDIATE CONCLUSION FOR THE SCHENGEN ACQUIS

The Schengen acquis aims to complement the UN narcotic drugs conventions with respect to narcotic drugs, explicitly including cannabis. The acquis specifically concerns itself with establishing and ratifying mutual efforts to combat the illicit trafficking (the import and export, sale, supply and handing over and possession of such drugs for sale or export) and to ensure that other states parties do not experience any adverse effects of a state party's own policy on the prevention and treatment of addiction. The obligation to fight the above-mentioned acts by means of criminal law, in the sense of prevention, criminalization and enforcement through criminal law is invalidated by the member states in their Joint Declaration as they may now also abstain from these measures with regard to the national policy on the care for and prevention of drug addiction. Preventing the movement of narcotic drugs across country borders and transnational cooperation are therefore central. Neither the production of narcotic drugs nor the cultivation of cannabis is mentioned explicitly in the Schengen acquis. Nonetheless, the general Article 71(5) of the Schengen Implementation Agreement seems to imply an obligation to combat cannabis cultivation for recreational use as well, if necessary by prosecutions for such cultivation. However, this also means that the member states fall back on the UN narcotic drugs conventions in particular, for the more detailed obligations regarding cannabis.

3.3. JOINT ACTION ON ILLEGAL DRUG TRAFFICKING 1996

On the initiative of France, the European Council in 1996 adopted the Joint Action 96/750/JHA of 17 December 1996 concerning the approximation of the laws and practices of the Member States of the European Union to combat drug addiction and to prevent and combat illegal drug trafficking (hereinafter also referred to as: Joint Action). This instrument expresses the need for an integrated approach in the fight against drugs (addiction and trafficking). The key point is that 'Member States fulfil their obligations under the United Nations Conventions of 1961, 1971 and 1988' and that they will 'examine ways of making *strict compliance* with those Conventions *more effective*, in particular by helping third countries to fulfil their obligations' (emphasis added).[24] This is also

[24] The English version of the Joint Action states that the aim is to make that strict compliance with the Conventions is to be 'more effective', the French one says 'plus effectif' and the German 'besser gewährleistet'. Notably, the Dutch version refers to 'efficiëntere' ('more

reflected in the provision of the Joint Action itself. Pursuant to Article 7 of the Joint Action, the member states must make sure that their obligations under the United Nations Conventions on narcotic drugs and psychotropic substances are applied 'strictly and effectively'. In this way, the Joint Action stresses and confirms the UN framework for combating drugs and the obligations that the states took upon themselves in this context. The fact that the instrument plays a subsidiary role in relation to the national policy of the member states is clear from both the Preamble[25] and Article 10 of the Joint Action. This provision entails that nothing in this instrument prevents 'a Member State, with due regard for its international commitments, from maintaining or introducing in its territory any additional measure it deems appropriate to fight drug addiction and to prevent and combat illicit drug trafficking.'

3.3.1. THE OBLIGATIONS REGARDING CANNABIS

None of the provisions in the Joint Action refers explicitly to cannabis. Nor does it contain a definition thereof. There are provisions that apply to 'drugs', 'narcotic drugs and psychotropic substances', 'illegal drug trafficking' and 'illicit cultivation of plants'. As the Joint Action refers explicitly to the UN narcotic drugs conventions and to strict and effective compliance therewith, it must be assumed that these terms apply to, among other things, flowering or fruiting tops of the cannabis plant and cannabis resin and cannabis plants.[26] As will be shown below, the relevance of the Joint Action in relation to the Schengen acquis lies in the fact that it contains a few commitments that go beyond those of the Schengen acquis.

i. Obligations to Fight Drug Trafficking and Cultivation

The Joint Action on Illegal Drug Trafficking aims to create commitments for the EU member states regarding the harmonization of national legislation and the practices of the police, customs services and judicial authorities so as to prevent and combat illegal drug trafficking in the European Union

efficient') in this context. In light of the other versions, and also because the objective of more effectiveness/efficacy seems to tie in better with the rationale of the Joint Action than more efficiency/expediency, we assume that the Dutch version contains a translation error in the sense that it too should be about effectiveness. Incidentally, such a term is absent from the Spanish version altogether.

25 In the Preamble, the Council considers that 'the provisions of this joint action are without prejudice to the general principle that a Member State may maintain or step up its national policy in the fight against drugs in its territory'.

26 See for more information section 2.2.1.

(Articles 1 and 2 of the Joint Action). Member states also commit to combating illicit flows of narcotic drugs and psychotropic substances within the Community, including drug tourism (Article 3 of the Joint Action). The objective of achieving compatibility of legislation and practice among member states is an addition to the obligation to combat drug trafficking as assumed in the framework of the Schengen acquis.

Of particular importance here is that the Joint Action goes further than the Schengen acquis in stating an obligation with respect to cultivation. According to Article 8 of the Joint Action, the member states are obliged 'to take the most appropriate steps to combat the illicit cultivation of plants containing active ingredients with narcotic properties'. Therefore, the cultivation of cannabis for recreational use – apart from the reference in the Joint Action to the UN narcotic drugs conventions – is definitely covered by this wording. Article 8 of the Joint Action does not specify which measures the member states should take, other than that these need to be 'the most appropriate' for the purpose of combating cultivation. This means that member states have considerable discretion in choosing the measures they will adopt, although they will have to be effective, as otherwise they could hardly be called appropriate. When criminalization and prosecution are the most appropriate, the state in principle will have to provide for this too, although the authorities still have a fair amount of freedom in deciding whether prosecution is called for in a concrete case. It will not be possible for a state, though, to permit cannabis cultivation for recreational use by, for example, legalizing or regulating it in any way or by tolerating it as a matter of policy. After all, that does not square with the obligation to adopt appropriate measures to fight that cultivation.

ii. Obligations to Criminalize and Punish

The Joint Action also goes further than the Schengen acquis in specifying the obligations to criminalize and punish. The obligation to criminalize is limited to the deliberate attempt to incite the illegal use or production of drugs: 'Member States undertake, subject to their constitutional principles and the basic concepts of their legal systems, to make it an offence publicly and intentionally to incite or induce others, by any means, to commit offences of illicit use or production of narcotic drugs' (Article 9 of the Joint Action). The Joint Action does not contain an obligation to make the use or the production of cannabis in itself an offence. This confirms that the Joint Action is primarily intended to supplement rather than repeat the prohibitive approach of the Schengen acquis and particularly the UN narcotic drugs conventions. In the area of sanctions, the member states are bound to ensure that 'under their legal systems the penalties imposed for serious drug trafficking are among the most severe penalties available for crimes of comparable gravity' pursuant to Article 4 of the Joint Action. While the wording is exceedingly general, this is a first step in the EU laws on drugs towards minimum penalties for drug related offences, which is reflected in the 2004 Framework Decision, which we will turn to later. The phrase 'available' suggests that the obligation is primarily meant for the national legislator. This is also true for the French text ('les sanctions applicables'), German ('im Rahmen ihrer Rechtsordnungen die Sanktionen [...] zu den strengsten Strafen [...] gehören') and Spanish ('las sanciones aplicables'). The wording of the English text, 'ensure that [...] the penalties imposed [...] are among the most severe' offers a slightly stronger indication that states must see to it that the heaviest penalties are actually imposed. This language version more closely matches the Joint Action's objective of effectiveness, as evidenced by the Preamble among other places, as mentioned above. In our view, however, this is not sufficient to assume, when no such evidence can be found in the Dutch, German, French and Spanish versions, that sanctions must not merely be applicable, but have to be imposed as well.

iii. Obligations to Prosecute

The Joint Action contains no explicit provisions about obligations to prosecute that may fall to states. Article 11 of the Joint Action does contain the obligation to take all 'appropriate steps' that are necessary for the implementation of the Joint Action. In addition to this, to the extent that Article 4 of the Joint Action, which we have just discussed, contains an obligation to apply the heaviest sanctions for serious drugs related offences, there will have to be a prosecution to begin with.

3.3.2. INTERMEDIATE CONCLUSION FOR THE JOINT ACTION

The aim of the Joint Action is to reinforce strict and effective adherence to the UN narcotic drugs conventions. It generally confirms the obligations that were discussed in the previous chapter. With regard to the cultivation of cannabis for recreational use, it is especially important that the Joint Action requires the member states to 'take the most appropriate steps' to combat such cultivation. At any rate, permitting such cannabis cultivation by for example, legalizing or regulating it in any way or by tolerating it as a matter of policy would be at odds with this obligation. The Joint Action is an obstacle to that.

3.4. FRAMEWORK DECISION ON ILLEGAL DRUG TRAFFICKING 2004

The most important instrument for the minimum harmonization of the laws and practices of the EU member states in respect of illegal drug trafficking is the Council Framework Decision 2004/757/JHA of 25 October 2004 laying down minimum provisions on the constituent elements of criminal acts and penalties in the field of illicit drug trafficking (hereinafter also referred to as: Framework Decision). The Framework Decision too, builds on the UN narcotic drugs conventions.[27] The Framework Decision aims to develop the Schengen acquis from the perspective of criminal law. It does not refer to preventative and administrative measures, so these are still determined by the acquis, among other instruments.[28] The Framework Decision also builds on the Joint Action of 1996, where the latter remains valid with regard to the 'numerous other aspects connected with developing cooperation between the police, the customs services and the judicial authorities with a view to combating illicit drug trafficking more effectively'.[29] The Framework Decision also replaces the resolution adopted by the Council in 1996 regarding the appropriate sanction in the case of serious forms of illegal trafficking in drugs.[30]

The rationale for the Framework Decision is the wish to reduce the demand for and supply of drugs and to fight illicit drug trafficking by a multi-disciplinary and integrated approach, and to reinforce and coordinate the international cooperation both on a national level and at the level of the European Union.[31] The fact is, illicit drug trafficking is seen as a threat to the health, safety and quality of life of the citizens in the Union, and also for the legal economy, stability and safety of the member states.[32] Common minimum requirements for criminalizing and sanctioning illicit drug trafficking are aimed at preventing problems in the cooperation among the police and judicial authorities of member states, which problems can be attributed to differences in national criminalizations. Although the primary responsibility for fighting the illicit drug trafficking lies with the member states themselves, establishing a common minimum is necessary given the nature of illegal drug trafficking, which does

27 See Article 1 of the Framework Decision.

28 Explanatory Statement, Proposal Framework Decision Illegal Drug Trafficking, Brussels: Commission of the European Communities, 23 May 2001, COM(2001) 259, 2001/0114 (CNS), p. 4.

29 Explanatory Statement, Proposal Framework Decision Illegal Drug Trafficking, Brussels: Commission of the European Communities, 23 May 2001, COM(2001) 259, 2001/0114 (CNS), p. 4.

30 Council Resolution of 20 December 1996 on sentencing for serious illicit drug-trafficking, *OJ* 1997, C 10/02. Explanatory Statement, Proposal Framework Decision Illegal Drug Trafficking, Brussels: Commission of the European Communities, 23 May 2001, COM(2001) 259, 2001/0114 (CNS), p. 5.

31 Explanatory Statement, Proposal Framework Decision Illegal Drug Trafficking, Brussels: Commission of the European Communities, 23 May 2001, COM(2001) 259, 2001/0114 (CNS), p. 2.

32 Preamble to the Framework Decision under (1).

not stop at borders.[33] At the time of the adoption of the Framework Decision, the Council made the following declaration:

> Drug trafficking is a heinous crime, which the Council is determined to fight with all possible means. The Council condemns all forms of drug trafficking and sees this Framework Decision as a first and very important step in the intensified fight against drug trafficking. The Council underlines the importance of taking a strong stance against drug trafficking at all levels and emphasises the need for a transnational and coherent approach in combating drug trafficking. In this connection, the Council also stresses the interrelation existing between legislation of all Member States and stresses the importance of dissuading the phenomenon of drug tourism.[34]

The declaration makes it clear that, as far as the Council is concerned, the rationale for the Framework Decision is to intensify the fight against all forms of drug trafficking and that this requires taking a strong stance against drug trafficking on all levels.

3.4.1. THE OBLIGATIONS REGARDING CANNABIS

The Framework Decision refers to cannabis once, namely in Article 2(1)(b), which is about the cultivation of cannabis plants. This does not mean that the Framework Decision is not relevant for cannabis otherwise. According to Article 1 of the Framework Decision, 'drugs' is understood to mean the following: all substances covered by, among other items, the 1961 Single Convention on Narcotic Drugs (as amended by the 1972 Protocol).[35] That is why flowering and fruiting tops of the cannabis plant and cannabis resin are also classified as narcotic drugs under the Framework Decision because of their inclusion in the Schedules accompanying the Single Convention, whereas this is not the case for cannabis leaves.[36] It is not entirely clear whether cannabis plants are also subsumed under 'drugs', but this is not essential, as such plants are at any rate covered by the Framework Decision in the sense of Article 2(1)(b). Unless the opposite is evident and explicitly stated, when we refer to cannabis

---

33 Explanatory Statement, Proposal Framework Decision Illegal Drug Trafficking, Brussels: Commission of the European Communities, 23 May 2001, COM(2001) 259, 2001/0114 (CNS), p. 2.

34 Declaration for entry in the Council minutes, in: Annex to Council of the European Union, Adoption of the Council Framework Decision illicit drug trafficking, Brussels: 28 September 2004, 2001/0114 (CNS), 12451/04, DROIPEN 47, CORDROGUE 63.

35 The term 'drugs' also covers substances that fall under the 1971 Vienna Convention on Psychotropic Substances and substances subject to controls under Joint Action 97/396/JHA of 16 June 1997 concerning the information exchange risk assessment and the control of new synthetic drugs.

36 See section 2.2.1 for a further explanation of the terms.

in general terms hereafter, we mean cannabis plants, cannabis resin and the flowering and fruiting tops of the cannabis plant.

It follows from the above that every time an obligation in the Framework Decision applies to narcotic drugs ('drugs'), that obligation also applies to flowering and fruiting tops of the cannabis plant and cannabis resin because of their inclusion in the Schedules of the Single Convention. The result of this is that nearly all the obligations that will be discussed now would no longer apply if flowering and fruiting tops of the cannabis plant and cannabis resin were removed from those Schedules. Only the obligation regarding cannabis cultivation in Article 2(1)(b) of the Framework Decision would remain in force. That obligation can only be avoided by amending the Framework Decision. We will now turn our attention to the obligations regarding criminalization, sanctions, prosecution and seizure. All these obligations are currently applicable to cannabis.

i. Obligations to Criminalize: General

Article 2 of the Framework Decision defines which acts in the field of illicit drug trafficking must be considered crimes. Whereas the Dutch and French versions of the Framework Decision even state that those acts 'bestraft worden' or 'soient punis' respectively, which refers to punishment of the perpetrators and therefore requires the criminalization of those acts, the German version ('unter Strafe gestellt werden') and the Spanish version ('la punibilidad') merely say that those acts must be 'punishable' (English version). On the basis of this, one would have a good case for arguing that Article 2(1) of the Framework Decision does not include an obligation to punish as such, and therefore no obligation to prosecute either, which would be its implicit consequence. However, it can be inferred from the preparatory history of the Framework Decision involving the provision of Article 2(2) that the Netherlands at any rate were of the opinion (in accordance with the Dutch version) that the first paragraph of this article comprises an obligation for prosecution and sanction.[37] We will come back to this at the end of the section in 3.4.1.ii.

Article 2(1)(a) of the Framework Decision concerns itself among other things with the intentional production, manufacture, extraction, offering, offering for sale, distribution, sale, delivery on any terms whatsoever, brokerage, dispatch in transit, transport, importation or exportation of drugs, which therefore also includes cannabis. Furthermore, Article 2(1)(c) of the Framework Decision requires the criminalization of the possession and the sale of drugs with regard to the previously mentioned conduct. Article 2 sub 1 preamble and sub b of

[37] See the *Kamerstukken II* 2005–2006, 30 339, nr. 3, p. 2 (MvT) (i.e., *Dutch Parliamentary Documents II* 2005–2006, 30 339, no. 3, p. 2 (Explanatory Memorandum)).

the Framework Decision explicitly adds to this the obligation to criminalize the cultivation of opium poppy, coca bush or cannabis plant. Consequently, the cultivation of cannabis plants that do not yet have flowering and fruiting tops or resin is already punishable as a completed offence according to the Framework Decision. Thus, the Framework Decision also confirms the obligations of criminalization that ensue from the UN Illicit Traffic Convention with respect to cannabis cultivation.[38] It also adds the harmonization of sanctions.[39] The obligations of criminalization in the Framework Decision entail that legalization or decriminalization of cannabis cultivation, supply and trafficking for recreational use is not possible. This also means that such cultivation for the supply of retail shops is ruled out by virtue of the Framework Decision.

ii. The Provisions in Respect of Behaviour for Own Personal Consumption

Because of the limitation ensuing from the principle of subsidiarity for the authority of the European Union to bring about regulations (see Article 5 of the TEU), the Preamble to the Framework Decision states that the Union must focus on the serious drug offences (Preamble under 4).[40] Although the Framework Decision does not contain any specific provision with criteria for assessing the seriousness of such crimes,[41] it draws a clear line with respect to conduct only for personal use. This is because Article 2(2) of the Framework Decision says that the conduct described in the first paragraph are not included in the Framework Decision 'when it is committed by its perpetrators *exclusively* for *their own personal consumption* as defined by national law' (emphasis added). Therefore, cannabis cultivation exclusively for one's personal consumption falls outside the

---

38 See Chapter 2.3 for an analysis of the obligations ensuing from the Illicit Traffic Convention.

39 See also Implementatiewet Kaderbesluit no. 2004/757/JBZ illegale drugshandel (*PbEU* L 335), *Kamerstukken II* 2005–2006, 30 339, no. 3, pp. 1–2 (MvT), i.e. Law implementing Framework Decision no. 2004/757/JHA illicit drug trafficking (OJ L 335), Dutch Parliamentary Documents II 2005–2006, 30 339, no. 3, pp. 1–2 (Explanatory Memorandum)).

40 This fourth point is absent from the Commission's proposal that served as the basis for the negotiations about the Framework Decision. However, in its Explanatory Memorandum accompanying the proposal for a Framework Decision the Commission notes that in accordance with the principle of subsidiarity and proportionality the objectives of the Framework Decision can be more easily achieved by the European Union, as the member states are not deemed capable of doing that on account of the transnational aspects of these offences. The explanation also states: 'This framework decision is confined to the minimum necessary to achieve these aims and does not go beyond what is required for this purpose.' Explanatory Statement, Proposal Framework Decision Illegal Drug Trafficking, Brussels: Commission of the European Communities, 23 May 2001, COM(2001) 259, 2001/0114 (CNS), p. 3.

41 T.M.C. Asser Instituut, *Experimenteren met het Gedogen van de Teelt van Cannabis ten Behoeve van de Bevoorrading van Coffeeshops – Internationaal rechtelijke en Europees rechtelijke aspecten*, Den Haag: 2005, p. 23 (i.e., Asser Institute – Centre for International & European Law; *Experimenting with tolerating the cultivation of cannabis for the supply of coffee shops – aspects of international and European law*, The Hague: 2005).

scope of the Framework Decision and such cultivation is not considered serious within the European laws on drugs either. The question is whether it follows from this that the punishability of this conduct can be ruled out by the member states.

At any rate, the Framework Decision assumes that the provision excluding from the scope of this Framework Decision the punishability of certain types of behaviour related only to personal consumption should not be seen as a 'guideline on how Member States should deal with these other cases in their national legislation'.[42] Thus, the member states retain some freedom to provide for the criminalization of 'personal use', as the Framework Decision itself does not impose an obligation for a specific criminalization.[43] However, those states are bound by the obligations ensuing from the UN narcotic drugs conventions if, like the Netherlands, they are a party to that. The Framework Decision cannot alter that in any way.[44] In the previous chapter, we saw that in any case Article 3(2) of the Illicit Traffic Convention requires the criminalization of the cultivation, possession and purchase of cannabis for personal consumption.[45] So in this respect as well, the Framework Decision cannot be said to exclude the punishability of types of behaviour that are related only to personal consumption of cannabis. This, however, is not yet decisive for the question that will be dealt with later, namely to what extent the member states have the freedom to adopt their own prosecution policies with regard to such types of behaviour.

The scope of the restriction clause has been greatly limited with the wording '*exclusively* [...] their own personal consumption'[46] (emphasis added). All acts that do not pertain 'exclusively' to personal consumption are excluded. Strictly speaking, even the possession, purchase and cultivation as well as sale on a very small scale for the benefit of oneself and others are not covered by it.[47] In this interpretation, the provision would not be applicable to joint cultivation and consumption within Cannabis Social Clubs (CSCs) either, because people there look after the plants together and therefore cultivate them together. CSCs

---

42 Preamble to the Framework Decision under (4): 'By virtue of the principle of subsidiarity, European Union action should focus on the most serious types of drug offence. The exclusion of certain types of behaviour as regards personal consumption from the scope of this Framework Decision does not constitute a Council guideline on how Member States should deal with these other cases in their national legislation.'

43 See the Report on the Proposal for the Framework Decision Illegal Drug Trafficking, Brussels: European Parliament, Committee on Citizens' Freedoms and Rights, Justice and Home Affairs, Rapporteur A.M. Oostlander, A5-0095/2004, 23 February 2004, PE 338.598, p. 6.

44 Incidentally, as we have observed before, the European Union itself is a party to the Illicit Traffic Convention too, albeit only insofar as it concerns the areas that fall under the Union's competence.

45 See section 2.3.2.i.a.I.

46 Similarly, see the following language versions: French: 'exclusivement à des fins de consommation personnelle'; German: 'ausschließlich für ihren persönlichen Konsum'; Dutch: 'uitsluitend beoogen te voorzien in hun persoonlijk gebruik'.

47 See section 2.3.2.i.a.I (see: Conduct regarding personal consumption of cannabis: Article 3(2) of the Illicit Traffic Convention).

would then also be subject to the obligations in the Framework Decision.[48] In addition, the question is whether cannabis cultivation in the context of a CSC can be considered as small-scale. Can cultivation be called small-scale in the case of a club with a hundred members, simply because each member only has one plant? Or is the number of members not relevant really, and is the only thing that matters in this example the fact that we are looking at a hundred plants? This is also relevant because it can be inferred from the system of the Framework Decision and also from the history of the negotiations[49] that the restriction clause can only refer to small quantities of narcotic drugs. After all, it is not plausible generally that greater quantities are 'exclusively' for personal use. The scale of cultivation for the benefit of retail shops alone makes it impossible to include it in the restriction clause, and apart from that also because such cultivation takes place aimed at supplying third parties and therefore is not exclusively intended for personal use. In other ways, the scope of the clause is fairly wide. After all, it covers all types of conduct that are punishable according to the Framework Decision (so that includes cultivation, possession, purchase and supply). All these actions – and therefore not merely 'consumption' of drugs in a strict sense – are therefore outside the scope of the Framework Decision.

The preparatory history of the Framework Decision shows that the Dutch coffee shop policy was one of the greatest barriers in a laborious process towards an agreement.[50] The provision in Article 2(2) of the Framework Decision – based on the principle of subsidiarity of the current Article 5 of the TEU – that drugs related activities exclusively for personal consumption do not fall within the scope of this Framework Decision, was an important addition to this instrument for the Netherlands. According to the rapporteur of the discussion in the European Parliament about the Framework Decision, it gave the Netherlands

48 However, see Explanatory Statement, Proposal Framework Decision Illegal Drug Trafficking, Brussels: Commission of the European Communities, 23 May 2001, COM(2001) 259, 2001/0114 (CNS), p. 6, from which it becomes clear that according to the Commission 'users who sell narcotics without the intention of making a profit (for example, someone who passes on narcotics to their friends without making a profit)' are excluded from the scope of the proposed Framework Decision. Because the narrow definition of Article 2(2) of the Framework Decision was not part of the proposal though, it is not clear whether this still applies to the Framework Decision that was eventually adopted. The word 'exclusively' in the aforementioned provision indicates that this is not the case.

49 See below section 3.4.1. ii.

50 Report on Proposal Framework Decision Illegal Drug Trafficking, Brussels: European Parliament, Committee on Citizens' Freedoms and Rights, Justice and Home Affairs, Rapporteur Arie M. Oostlander, A5-0095/2004, 23 February 2004, PE 338.598, p. 7: 'The Dutch determination to be able to continue to allow the possession of small quantities of soft drugs and for such drugs to be sold in "coffee shops" was one of the main problems to resolve in order to reach a final agreement.' See also Tom Blom, *Opiumwetgeving en drugsbeleid*, Deventer: Kluwer 2008, p. 104 (i.e., Tom Blom, *Opium legislation and drug policy*, Deventer: Kluwer, 2008, p. 104).

the opportunity to uphold its existing policy of tolerating such possession.[51] This is a remarkable observation. If one reads Article 2(1) of the Framework Decision in the English, German and Spanish versions, this provision only constitutes an obligation of criminalization.[52] Seeing that the possession of small quantities of cannabis for personal use has always been a criminal offence in the Netherlands and still is, the provision of the second paragraph does not provide a meaningful protection of existing policy in that reading. It is a different matter if one reads Article 2(1) of the Framework Decision in the Dutch and French versions: then this provision seems to constitute an obligation to punish actual perpetrators, preceded by prosecution therefore. According to the Explanatory Memorandum to the Dutch Implementation Act of the Framework Decision, the wording of the second paragraph has achieved that the Netherlands does not need to change its policy regarding small quantities of drugs for personal use.[53] The government of the Netherlands must have assumed here that Article 2(1) of the Framework Decision is to be interpreted as containing obligations to prosecute and to punish, next to the obligation of criminalization (which the Netherlands, as we have said before, already fulfilled). However, in a preceding part the same Explanatory Memorandum says that the Framework Decision only imposes an obligation with regard to legislative measures and does not refer to the prosecution policies of the member states.[54] Consequently, there is an implied contradiction in the Dutch Explanatory Memorandum and it is still not clear whether or not Article 2(1) of the Framework Decision also presupposes obligations to prosecute and punish.

It is obvious, however, that the cultivation of cannabis for retail shops cannot be subsumed under the restrictive provision without prejudice to the text of Article 2(2) of the Framework Decision.[55] This also holds true for the sale of cannabis by retail shops, as such a sale is by definition not intended for personal consumption and it does not involve small quantities either, given the cumulative effect. Yet, according to the history of deliberations of the European Parliament about the Framework Decision, this instrument in theory

---

51 Report on Proposal Framework Decision Illegal Drug Trafficking, Brussels: European Parliament, Committee on Citizens' Freedoms and Rights, Justice and Home Affairs, Rapporteur A.M. Oostlander, A5-0095/2004, 23 February 2004, PE 338.598, p. 7.

52 See section (3.4.1.i) for these language versions.

53 *Kamerstukken II* 2005–2006, 30 339, nr. 3, p. 2 (MvT) (i.e., *Dutch Parliamentary Documents II* 2005–2006, 30 339, no. 3, p. 2 (Explanatory Memorandum)).

54 *Kamerstukken II* 2005–2006, 30 339, nr. 3, p. 1 (MvT) ('dat het kaderbesluit uitsluitend verplicht tot wetgevende maatregelen en niet ziet op het vervolgingsbeleid van de lidstaten') (i.e., *Dutch Parliamentary Documents II* 2005–2006, 30 339, no. 3, p. 2 (Explanatory Memorandum)).

55 This also follows from Court of Justice EU, Judgment of 16 December 2010, case C-137/09, ECLI:EU:C:2010:774 (*Josemans*), para. 39–42.

'does not ask any Member State to change its drug policy and the Netherlands could continue to tolerate the coffee shops.'[56,57] Because this policy of tolerance cannot find protection under the provision of Article 2(2) of the Framework Decision, only two options remain. The first one is that the Netherlands has actually managed to stipulate and obtain room to uphold its coffee shop policy. This room follows from the history of negotiations, not from the Framework Decision itself. In fact, this would constitute some kind of reservation of a political nature. That room has then in no case been stipulated for cannabis cultivation for recreational use by third parties, so that the Netherlands cannot occupy an exceptional position under the Framework Decision. The other option is that the government of the Netherlands is right in its view that the Framework Decision does not refer to the prosecution policy of the member states. In that case, the provision in Article 2(2) of the Framework Decision is of little importance to the Netherlands. Moreover, this would also apply insofar as it concerns cannabis cultivation for coffee shops: this will have to be punishable, but the Framework Decision would be without importance to policy to prosecute for this act. Below, we will demonstrate that if this point of view was ever tenable at all, it is now under pressure because of the obligations of prosecution as laid down by the European Court of Justice.[58]

iii. Incitement, Participation, Inchoate Offences and Legal Persons

The Framework Decision also explicitly requires the criminalization of incitement to commit, aiding and abetting, or attempting to commit the offence referred to in Article 2(1) (Article 3(1) of the Framework Decision). However, Article 3(2) of the Framework Decision stipulates that a member state 'may exempt from criminal liability the attempt to offer or prepare drugs referred to in Article 2(1)(a) and the attempt to possess drugs referred to in Article 2(1)(c).' This second paragraph was not part of the Commission's proposal.[59] It was added by the Council afterwards. In the explanatory statement accompanying the legislative resolution of the European Parliament about the Council's proposal, a comment is made in the brief discussion of Article 3(2):

---

56 Report on Proposal Framework Decision Illegal Drug Trafficking, Brussels: European Parliament, Committee on Citizens' Freedoms and Rights, Justice and Home Affairs, Rapporteur A.M. Oostlander, A5-0095/2004, 23 February 2004, PE 338.598, p. 7.

57 It is unclear what this conclusion is based on. Incidentally, this observation is primarily of informative value here, as the European Parliament only had an advisory right regard to Framework Decisions in what was the third pillar at the time.

58 See below in this section (3.4.1.vii).

59 Commission proposal for a Council Framework Decision laying down minimum provisions on the constituent elements of criminal acts and penalties in the field of illicit drug trafficking, Brussels: Commission of the European Communities, 2001/C 304 E/03, *OJ* C 304 E/171, 30 October 2001, Article 3.

'It is said that this formulation helped to facilitate the agreement with the Netherlands'.[60] It is not entirely clear why the second paragraph was added to Article 3, but it would appear that it is because of the offering of drugs by coffee shops.[61] Finally, Articles 6 and 7 of the Framework Decision deal specifically with the criminal liability of legal persons as well as the sanctions that member states can impose on legal persons that are held criminally liable.

iv. Obligations Regarding Minimum Limits for Maximum Penalties

Article 4 of the Framework Decision contains the maximum penalties that must at least be defined by the member states in the context of harmonization. It is about the obligation that 'offences [...] are punishable by [...] penalties' ('feiten worden strafbaar gesteld met [...] sancties', 'soient passibles de peines', 'Straftaten mit [...] Sanktionen bedroht sind', 'sincese castigan con peñas'). It is plain to see from these phrases that the obligation must ensure that the law provides for the sanctions required, and not that those sanctions are actually imposed. Therefore, no implicit obligation of prosecution can be inferred from the obligations regarding sanctions of Article 4 of the Framework Decision. In addition to this, the Framework Decision was adopted on the basis of Article 31(1)(e) (ex) in conjunction with Article 34(2)(b) (ex) Treaty on European Union (TEU).[62] These provisions provide the authority to adopt Framework Decisions to lay down minimum rules regarding the constituent elements of criminal offences with regard to sanctions in the area of, among other crimes, illicit drug trafficking. Thus, the provisions do not entail obligations to prosecute.

The lower limits of the maximum penalties in Article 4 the Framework Decision reflect a sliding scale with regard to the seriousness of the criminal offences in the scope of the Framework Decision. Thus, the member states are afforded some leeway in deciding the severity of the penalties to be imposed, with the proviso that the penalties must be 'effective, proportionate and

---

60 Report on Proposal Framework Decision Illegal Drug Trafficking, Brussels: European Parliament, Committee on Citizens' Freedoms and Rights, Justice and Home Affairs, Rapporteur Arie M. Oostlander, A5-0095/2004, 23 February 2004, PE 338.598, p. 7.

61 According to Arie M. Oostlander, Rapporteur European Parliament: 'Article 2 concerns attempts to offer drugs to others: this includes coffee shop policy; in particular [...]'; see Debates, European Parliament, 8 March 2004, under: Criminal acts and penalties in the field of drug trafficking, about final proposal Framework Decision illicit drug trafficking, available on: (http://www.europarl.europa.eu/sides/getDoc.do?pubRef=-//EP//TEXT+CRE+20040308+ITEM-010+DOC+XML+V0//EN).

62 These provisions were included in the Treaty on European Union as amended by the Amsterdam Treaty, *OJ* 1997 C 340 (Article 31 is pursuant to Article K.3, Article 34 is pursuant to Article K.6); see Consolidated versions of the Treaty on European Union, *OJ* 2006 C 321 E/5.

dissuasive' (Article 4(1) of the Framework Decision). To decide on the penalty, facts must be taken into consideration, such as the nature and quantity of the narcotic drugs involved, as well as the fact that the act was committed within the context of a criminal organization (Preamble under 5). Incidentally, Article 5 of the Framework Decision offers room to provide for special grounds for reducing the penalty.

Article 4(1) of the Framework Decision states that the offences referred to in Article 2 are punishable by criminal penalties of a maximum of at least between 1 and 3 years imprisonment. During the negotiations, the Netherlands proposed to include a restriction clause regarding small quantities of narcotic drugs in this article too, similar to that in Article 2(2).[63] Other delegations were opposed to this proposal; several of them were of the opinion that Article 2(2) of the Framework Decision already sufficiently satisfied the wishes of the Netherlands. A new proposal for an Article 4(6), which would mean that member states would be able to establish a lower level of penalties than that mentioned in Article 4(1) for small quantities of drugs, was accepted by the Netherlands but not by all other delegations.[64] This proposal was therefore rejected. Consequently, the obligation under Article 4(1) of the Framework Decision to provide for a maximum sentence of at least 1 to 3 years imprisonment applies for the acts referred to in Article 2(1) of the Framework Decision insofar as these were not committed exclusively for own personal consumption (because that case would be governed by the restriction clause of Article 2(2) of the Framework Decision). Cannabis cultivation for retail shops' is therefore covered by at least this obligation to punish, but a more 'serious' provision may apply to it.

Offences involving 'large quantities of drugs' (Article 4(2)(a)), 'those drugs which cause the most harm to health' or have resulted in 'significant damage' to the health of a number of persons (Article 4(2)(b), or were committed within the framework of a criminal organization (Article 4(3)), are treated as very serious. This is reflected in an increased maximum sentence of at least between five and ten years imprisonment. The Framework Decision does not specify the aggravating element of 'large quantity', which is thus left to the discretion of the individual member states.[65] The fact that offences involving large quantities

---

[63] Council of the European Union, Proposal for the Framework Decision on Illegal Drug Trafficking, Brussels, 27 May 2002, Document 8862/1/02, Rev 1, DROIPEN 31 CORDROGUE 40, file 2001/0114 (CNS), p. 3.

[64] Council of the European Union, Proposal for the Framework Decision on Illegal Drug Trafficking, Brussels, 2 October 2002, Document 10321/1/02, Rev 1, DROIPEN 42 CORDROGUE 47, file 2001/0114 (CNS), p. 12, footnote 1.

[65] The Report on the Proposal Framework Decision Illegal Drug Trafficking, Brussels: European Parliament, Committee on Citizens' Freedoms and Rights, Justice and Home Affairs, Rapporteur Arie M. Oostlander, A5-0095/2004, 23 February 2004, PE 338.598, p. 7, contains the following about these quantities: 'Of course, it is not the EU's task to set up a detailed penal code, but the jurisprudence can be expected to be quite different among the Member States.'

of drugs or those committed within the context of a criminal organization are designated as particularly serious may be relevant here, because cannabis cultivation, delivery and trafficking for the supply of retail shops' can involve organized acts and structures and larger quantities of cannabis. This does not mean, however, that the parties involved are also prosecuted for participation in a criminal organization.

Sometime after the entry into force of the Framework Decision, the European Commission noted that although the member states formally comply with the requirements regarding penalties laid down in the Framework Decision, there remain huge legislative disparities among the member states.[66] In respect of the Dutch coffee shop policy, the Commission 'has particular concerns regarding the wider problem of the supply of such coffee shops by criminal networks'.[67]

v. *Obligations Regarding Seizure*

Article 4(5) of the Framework Decision does not entail an obligation to seize cannabis or other drugs. It merely requires the member states to take the necessary measures 'to enable the confiscation of substances which are the object of offences referred to in Articles 2 and 3, instrumentalities used or intended to be used for these offences and proceeds from these offences or the confiscation of property the value of which corresponds to that of such proceeds, substances or instrumentalities'.[68] These obligations already arise from Article 5 of the Illicit Traffic Convention 1988. The term 'confiscation' in fact covers the different criminal sanctions available in the Netherlands: forfeiture, removal from use and the deprivation of illegally obtained benefits.[69]

vi. *Obligations to Prosecute: Implicit in the Framework Decision?*

Article 8 of the Framework Decision, entitled 'Jurisdiction and prosecution', only concerns itself with the requirement that member states establish jurisdiction for the prosecution of the offences referred to in Articles 2 and 3 of the Framework

66 Report from the Commission on the implementation of Framework Decision 2004/757/JHA laying down minimum provisions on the constituent elements of criminal acts and penalties in the field of illicit drug trafficking, Brussels, 10 December 2009, COM(2009)669 final, SEC(2009)1661, p. 4.

67 Report from the Commission on the implementation of Framework Decision 2004/757/JHA laying down minimum provisions on the constituent elements of criminal acts and penalties in the field of illicit drug trafficking, Brussels, 10 December 2009, COM(2009)669 final, SEC(2009)1661, p. 5.

68 Article 4(5) of the Framework Decision further stipulates that the terms 'confiscation', 'instrumentalities', 'proceeds' and 'properties' have the same meaning as in Article 1 of the Council of Europe Convention on Laundering, Search, Seizure and Confiscation of the Proceeds from Crime.

69 See section 2.3.2.i.a.V for a discussion.

Decision and does not have a bearing on the actual exercise of the powers of jurisdiction. A general obligation to prosecute is not explicitly mentioned in the Framework Decision, which is not unusual with Framework Decisions, and it is also difficult to infer from it that there is such an obligation.[70] To that extent, the government of the Netherlands seems to have a point with the previously quoted note that the Framework Decision only entails an obligation with regard to legislative measures and does not relate to the prosecution policies of the member states. The government relied on Consideration 9 of the Preamble in this respect: 'The effectiveness of the efforts made to tackle illicit drug trafficking *depends essentially on* the harmonisation *of the national measures* implementing this Framework Decision' (emphasis added). The government's reliance on this Consideration is not wholly convincing, as the term 'measures' (French: 'mesures', German: 'Maßnahmen', Spanish: 'medidas') could cover much more than merely legislation.[71] In this respect, Consideration 2 is clearer, as it does mention 'legislative action'. Also, the title of the Framework Decision ('minimum provisions on the constituent elements of criminal acts and penalties') corroborates the correctness of the Netherlands government's view more clearly. This is also true for the fact that the Framework Decision came about on the basis of Article 31(1)(e) (ex) in conjunction with Article 34(2)(b) (ex) TEU.[72] In addition, the Framework Decision – unlike the Schengen acquis, the Joint Action, the Single Convention and the Illicit Traffic Convention – does not contain general obligations to take suitable, necessary and/or effective measures to combat cannabis. So there is indeed a good reason to assume that the Framework Decision does not bear on the prosecution policies of the member states. In that situation, the Framework Decision does not necessitate prosecution for the sale of cannabis by retail shops – which was indeed the government's objective[73] – nor the cultivation of cannabis intended for those shops. However, this view is challenged and has now proved to be problematic.

For example, the Commission's explanation of the proposal – that underpins the Framework Decision – regarding Article 8 of the Framework Decision says: 'Member States that make no provision for extradition are responsible for prosecuting their own nationals who have committed offences abroad.' So here

70 This is in fact possible, for example, with provisions in the Single Convention and the Illicit Traffic Convention; see section 2.2.2.i.a.X. and 2.3.2.i.a.II.

71 The term 'measures' is not only fairly generic from a linguistic point of view, it is also used in all sorts of other Framework Decisions and Union instruments in a way that is much broader than merely 'legislative measures'; see for example the Council Framework Decision 2002/584/JHA of 13 June 2002 on the European arrest warrant and the surrender procedures between Member States.

72 See above in this section (3.4.1.iv).

73 *Kamerstukken II* 2005–2006, 30 339, nr. 3, p. 1 (MvT) (i.e., *Dutch Parliamentary Documents II* 2005–2006, 30 339, no. 3, p. 1 (Explanatory Memorandum)); see also *Kamerstukken II* 2002–2003, 23 490, nr. 246 (i.e., *Dutch Parliamentary Documents II* 2002–2003, 23 490, no. 246).

the Commission assumes an obligation to prosecute for concrete drug-related offences. In other words: the Commission does not just interpret Article 8 of the Framework Decision as an obligation on the part of the legislator to harmonize legislation with the international law principle known as 'aut dedere aut judicare', it also requires that that principle is applied in concrete cases. In addition to this, one can observe that the effectiveness of the efforts to fight illicit drug trafficking *also* depends on enforcing the harmonized penalty provisions. Consideration 9 of the Preamble also leaves room for that interpretation, as it states that that effectiveness 'essentially' depends on 'national measures'. Given the objectives of the Framework Decision, which focuses on the fight against illicit drug trafficking, is it is hard to conceive that states are not in any way obliged to prosecute in the event of offences being committed that the Framework Decision requires to be criminalized. After all, there can be no question of combating illicit drugs trafficking in that case, let alone of doing so efficiently or imposing effective, proportionate and dissuasive sanctions. Moreover, it seems hard to defend the view that this would constitute a loyal implementation of Union law (Article 4(3) TEU)[74] if a Framework Decision is only implemented by legislation and not followed up by an effective investigation and prosecution of the pertinent criminal offences referred to. Also in view of the object and purpose of the instrument that is the Framework Decision, namely the harmonization of the national systems of substantive criminal law, prosecution and penalisation are necessary to make such harmonization meaningful.[75] Furthermore, it follows from the previously quoted declaration by the Council on adopting the Framework Decision that this instrument aims to intensify the fight against all forms of drug trafficking and that this requires a strong stance against that trafficking on all levels.[76] The foregoing entails that one cannot simply suppose that the Framework Decision does not imply any obligations of prosecution. However, all that this means is that it is difficult to maintain that a state only has to implement the Framework Decision in law and can subsequently abstain from taking practical and effective action. So the above does not mean that the implicit obligation to prosecute is absolute and that states have no discretion in applying the expediency principle in their considerations. That is why the following is more important in this respect.

---

74 Pim Geelhoed, *Het opportuniteitsbeginsel en het recht van de Europese Unie* (diss. Leiden), Deventer: Kluwer, 2013, p. 370 (i.e., Pim Geelhoed, *The expediency principle and European Union law* (PhD Leiden University), Deventer: Kluwer, 2013).

75 Report from the Commission on the implementation of Framework Decision 2004/757/JHA laying down minimum provisions on the constituent elements of criminal acts and penalties in the field of illicit drug trafficking, Brussels, 10 December 2009, COM(2009)669 final, SEC(2009)1661, p. 4: 'maximum sentences are meaningful only in the context of proceedings actually initiated and penalties actually imposed by the courts.'

76 See the introduction of this section (3.4.1).

vii. Obligations to Prosecute According to Case Law of the Court of Justice of the EU

It is essential that the Court of Justice of the EU (CJEU) has explicitly confirmed the obligation to an effective and equivalent enforcement of European law.[77] In its case law, the CJEU requires consistently that member states act as energetically against infringements of Community law as in the case of enforcing similar national legislation and also that the penalties imposed by them for infringements of Community law are effective, proportionate and dissuasive. So if energetic action or such a penalty necessitates prosecution, the member state has a commitment to do so.[78] These obligations apply to European community law, or at least: for a long time, the CJEU has only been able to lay them down with regard to Union law, as a consequence of the lack of the jurisdiction of the Court in the field of police and judicial cooperation (as this field, until the entry into force of the Treaty of Lisbon, fell under the special regime of the so-called third pillar). Since the end of December 2014, however, the Court of Justice has been fully competent in this area that is relevant to criminal law. The question therefore is whether the fact that the aforementioned case law on enforcement does not apply formally to instruments regarding police and judicial cooperation in criminal cases is merely because of a procedural reason (lack of jurisdiction on the part of the CJEU) or also because of a substantive reason as a matter of principle. The latter is not immediately obvious, as we will explain below.

First, police and judicial cooperation in criminal matters is now part of the normal legal regime of the European Union. From an institutional point of view it is hard to see why the principles of equivalent and effective enforcement should not apply to EU criminal law, while in other areas of EU law they do.

---

[77] For the discussion of the obligation on the part of member states to enforce non-penal EU provisions through criminal law, see Piet Hein P.H.M.C. van Kempen, 'Communautaire doorwerking en straf(proces)recht', in: Matthias J. Borgers, Francois G.H. Kristen & Joep B.H.M. Simmelink (eds.), *Implementatie van kaderbesluiten*, Nijmegen: Wolf Legal Publishers, 2006, pp. 92–94 (i.e., Piet Hein P.H.M.C. van Kempen, 'Effect of EU Law and criminal procedural law', in: Matthias J. Borgers, Francois G.H. Kristen & Joep B.H.M. Simmelink (eds.), *Implementation of Framework Decisions*, Nijmegen: Wolf Legal Publishers, 2006, pp. 92–94); see also Pim Geelhoed, *Het opportuniteitsbeginsel en het recht van de Europese Unie* (diss. Leiden), Deventer: Kluwer, 2013, pp. 163–168 (i.e., Pim Geelhoed, *The expediency principle and European Union law* (PhD Leiden University), Deventer: Kluwer, 2013); Pim Geelhoed, 'Europeesrechtelijke eisen aan de beslissing omtrent de omvang van de vervolging', in: Jan H. Crijns, Patrick P.J. van der Meij & Jeroen M. ten Voorde (eds.), *De waarde van waarheid. Opstellen over waarheid en waarheidsvinding in het strafrecht*, Den Haag: Boom Legal Publishers, 2008, pp. 139–161 on pp. 150–153 (i.e., Pim Geelhoed in: Jan H. Crijns, Patrick P.J. van der Meij & Jeroen M. ten Voorde (eds.), *The value of truth. Essays on truth and determining the truth in criminal cases*, Den Haag: Boom Legal Publishers, 2008).

[78] See e.g. Court of Justice EU, Judgment of 21 September 1989, case C-68/88, ECLI:EU:C:1989:339, (*Commission v. Greece*), para. 24–25; Court of Justice EU, Judgment of 9 December 1997, case C-265/95, ECLI:EU:C:1997:595, (*Commission v. France*), para. 33–35.

From a substantive point of view, there is not any reason either to assume that enforcement of the criminalizations required by the Union is less needed than that of other legal measures. It is also relevant that the obligations of enforcement of criminal law ensuing from the above-mentioned case law applied to Community law other than criminal law (among other things, the free movement of goods and fisheries legislation). On a more substantive level, it is also hard to imagine that the obligation of enforcement by means of criminal law in the case of provisions that do not pertain to criminal law is more urgent and important than in the case of criminal law provisions.[79] In view of the foregoing, it is reasonable to assume that the obligation of equivalent and effective enforcement is also fulfilled in the area of police and judicial cooperation in criminal matters. More substantively, there is no reason why this should not apply to the Framework Decision on illicit drug trafficking as well. One could, however, see a formal obstacle to this, namely that the legal basis of the adoption of the Framework Decision concerns the harmonization of legislation and applicable sections (Article 31(1)(e) (ex) in conjunction with Article 34(2)(b) (ex) TEU).[80]

However, by now the CJEU has delivered judgment in the Vo[81] case in which it negates this formal obstacle by explaining that the obligation regarding equivalent and effective enforcement also applies to Framework Decisions or at any rate to the Framework Decision on unauthorised entry.[82] Just like the Framework Decision on illicit drug trafficking, the adoption of this Framework Decision is based on Article 31(1)(e) (ex) in conjunction with Article 34(2)(b) (ex) TEU). Additionally, the Framework Decision on unauthorised entry neither contains explicit obligations to prosecute or impose sanctions nor general obligations to counteract criminal acts effectively. In that respect, too, it matches the Framework Decision on illicit drug trafficking. In its judgment in the *Vo* case, the CJEU rules that the Framework Decision on unauthorised entry 'requires the Member State concerned to bring [...] a prosecution'.[83] In the view of the Court, this obligation is part of European Union law. In this case, the CJEU infers this

---

79 Piet Hein P.H.M.C. van Kempen, 'Communautaire doorwerking en straf(proces)recht', in: Matthias J. Borgers, Francois G.H. Kristen & Joep B.H.M. Simmelink (eds.), *Implementatie van kaderbesluiten*, Nijmegen: Wolf Legal Publishers, 2006, pp. 92–93 (i.e., Piet Hein P.H.M.C. van Kempen, 'Effect of EU Law and criminal procedural law', in: Matthias J. Borgers, Francois G.H. Kristen & Joep B.H.M. Simmelink (eds.), *Implementation of Framework Decisions*, Nijmegen: Wolf Legal Publishers, 2006, pp. 92–94).

80 See above in this section (3.4.1. iv).

81 Court of Justice EU, Judgment of 10 April 2012, case C-83/12 PPU, ECLI:EU:C:2012:202 (*Minh Khoa Vo*).

82 Framework Decision of 28 November 2002 on the strengthening of the penal framework to prevent the facilitation of unauthorised entry, transit and residence, 2002/946/JHA, *OJ* 2002, L 328/1.

83 Court of Justice EU, Judgment of 10 April 2012, case C-83/12 PPU, ECLI:EU:C:2012:202 (*Minh Khoa Vo*), para. 44.

obligation more specifically from the obligation in the Framework Decision 'to take the measures necessary to ensure that the infringements defined are punishable by effective, proportionate and dissuasive criminal penalties and to establish its jurisdiction with regard to the infringements committed, in whole or in part, within its territory'.[84] These obligations are also part and parcel of the Framework Decision on illicit drug trafficking. The CJEU then concludes that the member states are faced with two obligations, one of which is to 'prescribe and *enforce* effective, proportionate and dissuasive penalties against those persons' who commit the infringements defined in the Framework Decision.[85] This obligation must be fulfilled 'in such a way as to ensure that the provisions of European Union law are fully effective', where 'the national courts have a duty to seek outcomes which achieve a proper balance in relation to provisions which, if applied, might call in question the effectiveness or consistency of European Union legislation'.[86] So the obligation of criminal prosecution is connected with its contribution to an effective, proportionate and dissuasive enforcement, in particular in relation to those offences that would jeopardize the effectiveness of the underlying European policy the most.[87]

If the CJEU continues to apply the frameworks set out in the *Vo* judgment consistently, it seems there is hardly any reason to suppose that this case law would not apply to the Framework Decision on illicit drug trafficking as well. The CJEU is consistent in its unfavourable view on regarding drugs.[88] According to its settled case law, the harmfulness of narcotic drugs, including hemp products such as cannabis, is generally recognized. That is why the trade in it is prohibited in all member states, with the exception of the strictly controlled trade for use for medical and scientific purposes.[89] Narcotic drugs that are outside such a strictly controlled circuit are by their nature subject to a blanket ban on import or trade in all member states, according to the Court.[90] The fact that some states brand cannabis as a 'soft drug' and permit its sale in organizations controlled by

---

84 Court of Justice EU, Judgment of 10 April 2012, case C-83/12 PPU, ECLI:EU:C:2012:202 (*Minh Khoa Vo*), para. 43–44.

85 Court of Justice EU, Judgment of 10 April 2012, case C-83/12 PPU, ECLI:EU:C:2012:202 (*Minh Khoa Vo*), para. 45.

86 Court of Justice EU, Judgment of 10 April 2012, case C-83/12 PPU, ECLI:EU:C:2012:202 (*Minh Khoa Vo*), para. 46.

87 Pim Geelhoed, *Het opportuniteitsbeginsel en het recht van de Europese* Unie (diss. Leiden), Deventer: Kluwer, 2013, p. 369 (i.e., Pim Geelhoed, *The expediency principle and European Union law* (PhD Leiden University), Deventer: Kluwer, 2013).

88 See e.g. Court of Justice EU, Judgment of 16 December 2010, case C-137/09, ECLI:EU:C:2010:774 (*Josemans*); Court of Justice EU, Judgment of 29 June 1999, case C-158/98, ECLI:EU:C:1999:334 (*Siberië*); Court of Justice EU, Judgement of 5 July 1988, case C-289/86, ECLI:EU:C:1988:360 (*Happy Family*).

89 Court of Justice EU 16 December 2010, case C-137/09 (*Josemans*), para. 36, with reference to other case law.

90 Court of Justice EU, Judgment of 16 December 2010, case C-137/09, ECLI:EU:C:2010:774 (*Josemans*), para. 41, with reference to other case law.

the state does not alter this.[91] It is also interesting that the Court is not swayed by arguments that when once there is a policy of tolerance towards certain drug-related criminal acts, this lends a certain legitimacy to those acts: such a ban is not derogated by the simple fact that the authorities assign a lower priority to the prosecution for a certain type of trade in narcotic drugs. Illicit trafficking, even when tolerated, remains forbidden, according to the Court.[92]

The Court's judgment in the *Vo* case, however, is an isolated judgment. Therefore, one should be careful in drawing firm conclusions from it. Still, that does not alter the fact that we regard the application of the principles of equivalent and effective enforcement to obligations of criminalization as laid down in Framework Decisions or other instruments as a step that is to be expected.[93] This is mainly because European Union criminal law has become part of the normal legal regime of the European Union, whereas it is hard to think of any substantive reasons why there should be less of a need for equivalent and effective enforcement of criminal acts as required by EU law than for other legal provisions. On the basis of CJEU case law – for which not only the *Vo* judgment is pertinent – we therefore draw the conclusion that an obligation to prosecute appears to apply to the Framework Decision on illicit drug trafficking as well if its equivalent and effective enforcement requires that. Given the perspective of the *Vo* judgment and the seriousness with which the CJEU treats drug trafficking, there is in principle an even greater obligation to prosecute in the case of drug-related acts where European law requires criminalization if these are serious acts.

The follow-up question then is when that prosecution principle manifests itself more concretely. This requires a closer look at the objectives of the instrument in question. Using harmonization of legislation, the Framework Decision aims to fight illicit drug trafficking to protect the health and to improve the quality of life of the Union's citizens, and to protect the safety and stability of society. In particular, large-scale organized drug trafficking must be tackled. The Framework Decision clearly places less emphasis on acts that are exclusively aimed at personal consumption. Thus, the question whether there is a concrete obligation to prosecute appears to be answered against this background. Because joint cultivation and consumption of cannabis within Cannabis Social Clubs almost (but not quite) matches the criteria of the clause about acts strictly for personal consumption, and while there is no trade

---

91 Court of Justice EU, Judgement of 5 July 1988, case C-289/86, ECLI:EU:C:1988:360 (*Happy Family*), para. 25.

92 Court of Justice EU, Judgment of 16 December 2010, case C-137/09, ECLI:EU:C:2010:774 (*Josemans*), para. 43.

93 See also Pim Geelhoed, *Het opportuniteitsbeginsel en het recht van de Europese* Unie (diss. Leiden), Deventer: Kluwer, 2013, p. 168 and 370 (i.e., Pim Geelhoed, *The expediency principle and European Union law* (PhD Leiden University), Deventer: Kluwer, 2013).

in cannabis in case of CSC, it can be argued that the obligation to prosecute does not apply to CSC either. It is a different matter though for cannabis cultivation on a larger scale or cultivation for commercial purposes such as supplying retail shops. Such cannabis cultivation for recreational use is classed as a serious activity prohibited by virtue of the Framework Decision. In view of CJEU case law, given the scale and possibly the organised nature of cannabis cultivation, distribution and trade, the authorities will in principle have to prosecute and punish effectively whenever they are aware of the facts and know the suspected perpetrators. The question whether the current coffee shop policy in the Netherlands is still exempt from the obligations of prosecution as laid down by the CJEU requires no further discussion here.[94]

3.4.2. PERMISSIBLE EXCEPTIONS: EXEMPTIONS

The exception of 'medical and scientific purposes' from the Single Convention also applies to the Framework Decision. In this respect, it is important that the Framework Decision refers to this Convention, among other things, with regard to the meaning of drugs, whereas there are no departure points for the opposite assumption. On the contrary: the CJEU has by now repeatedly confirmed that 'narcotic drugs which are not distributed through channels which are strictly controlled by the competent authorities to be used for medical and scientific purposes are, because of their very nature, subject to a prohibition on importation and offering for sale in all the Member States.'[95] Admittedly, this case law does not refer to the Framework Decision on illicit drug trafficking, but there is no reason to assume that the Court would not consider this to be relevant if it does concern that Framework Decision. At the risk of repeating ourselves, we note here that the European Union is party to the Illicit Traffic Convention, so that it has to follow the terminology also because of this Convention, which is based on the system of the Single Convention. We already analysed the exception of 'medical and scientific purposes' in Chapter 2, so we will not elaborate on this

---

94 See, however, Pim Geelhoed, *Het opportuniteitsbeginsel en het recht van de Europese* Unie (diss. Leiden), Deventer: Kluwer, 2013, pp. 369–373 (i.e., Pim Geelhoed, *The expediency principle and European Union law* (PhD Leiden University), Deventer: Kluwer, 2013), who implies that the Dutch coffee shop policy could also be affected by these obligations of prosecution; that would have to apply *a fortiori* for regulated cannabis cultivation.

95 Court of Justice EU, Judgment of 16 December 2010, case C-137/09, ECLI:EU:C:2010:774 (*Josemans*), para. 41, 31, 36, 38, 43 and 77. See also Court of Justice EU, Judgment of 29 June 1999, case C-158/98, ECLI:EU:C:1999:334 (*Siberië*), para. 14; Court of Justice EU, Judgement of 5 July 1988, case C-289/86, ECLI:EU:C:1988:360 (*Happy Family*), para. 17 and 20; Court of Justice EU, Judgement of 28 February 1984, case C-294/82, ECLI:EU:C:1984:81 (*Einberger*), para. 15; Court of Justice EU, Judgment of 26 October 1982, case C-221/81, ECLI:EU:C:1982:363 (*Wolf*), para. 10.

here.[96] At this point, we only remind the reader that acts such as cultivation, distribution, trade, sale, purchase and possession of cannabis for recreational use falls outside the scope of this exception.

Furthermore, with respect to exceptions, it is important that Article 2 of the Framework Decision states that deliberate acts specified in the provision must be punished 'when committed without right' (French: 'lorsqu'ils ne peuvent être légitimés', German: 'ohne entsprechende Berechtigung vorgenommen wurden', Spanish: 'cuando se cometan contrariamente a Derecho', and Dutch: 'wanneer daarvoor geen rechtvaardigingsgrond aanwezig is'). It is not clear what is understood by 'when committed without right' and what the rationale is for including it. It is conceivable that this was intended in order to incorporate the exception of 'medical and scientific purposes' from the Single Convention into the Framework Decision. In any case, it is logical that the exception falls within the category of conduct for which there is a 'right' or justification. The same goes for justification under criminal law in the sense of substantive law,[97] provided – of course – that its application does not conflict with the obligation to interpret and implement European law loyally.

We have not been able to find any substantiation that the wording ('when committed without right') in Article 2(1) of the Framework Decision is to have a wider meaning. There are, however, a few indications to the contrary. In an earlier version of the proposed Framework Decision, the cultivation provision in Article 2(1)(b) seemingly referred to 'the cultivation of [...] cannabis plant *for the purpose of drug production*'. The Italian delegation proposed to delete this addition as it was redundant in the light of the clause in the preamble to the first paragraph, which says that the conduct is punishable 'when committed without right'.[98] Indeed, the addition was taken out of a later proposal. In this light, at least the production of drugs falls within the category of conduct for which there is no right/justification (at least if it does not take place for 'medical or scientific purposes' in the sense of the Single Convention). This too, does not suggest that the term 'right' or justification is intended to have a broader meaning than the exception to the Single Convention or any general grounds for justifications in accordance with relevant substantive criminal law. Another similar indication follows from the original Proposal for a Framework Decision by the Commission. In the definition of illicit drug

96 See section 2.2.3.i and section 2.6 in particular.

97 See for example the Criminal Code of the Netherlands, Book 1, Title III. See section 2.2.3.ii.

98 Council of the European Union, Proposal for a Council framework decision laying down minimum provisions on the constituent elements of criminal acts and penalties in the field of illicit drug trafficking, Brussels, 27 May 2002, 8862/1/02, Rev 1, DROIPEN 31 CORDROGUE 40, File 2001/0114 (CNS), p. 3. See also, with the same title, Brussels, 11 June 2002, 9718/1/02, REV 1, LIMITE, DROIPEN 37, CORDROGUE 45, File 2001/0114 (CNS), p. 7 (footnote 1).

trafficking that is included in it, profits and acting without authorization were central.[99] From this perspective, conduct 'committed without right' means acting without authorization, whereas there is no drug trafficking in the sense of the Framework Decision if such an authorization has been given. It is important that on account of the UN narcotic drugs conventions – to which all EU member states are party and insofar as the Illicit Traffic Convention is concerned the European Union itself as well – the authorization is only possible for cultivation, distribution, trade and sale etc. for 'medical and scientific purposes'. This indicates that in principle, without authorization, one acts 'without right' (without justification).

3.4.3. INTERMEDIATE CONCLUSION FOR THE FRAMEWORK DECISION

The Framework Decision builds on the Schengen acquis, the Joint Action and the UN narcotic drugs conventions. The rationale for the Framework Decision is the wish to harmonize the substantive criminal law provisions (crimes and penalties) in such a way that a more effective approach in fighting illicit drugs trafficking is possible. The backdrop to this is that drugs pose a threat to the health, safety and quality of life of the citizens of and the stability of the EU member states. For the definition of drugs, the Framework Decision harks back to the UN Single Convention. The Framework Decision lays down obligations to criminalize acts such as the production, extraction, offer to sell, distribution, transport, import, export, transfer as well as the cultivation of cannabis plants. Acts that are 'exclusively' for own personal consumption are excluded from this obligation of criminalization pursuant to Article 2(2) of the Framework Decision. Bearing in mind the strict wording of this clause, it would appear that in principle the obligations in the Framework Decision also apply to joint cultivation and consumption in Cannabis Social Clubs. This is also the case, albeit much more clearly, for cannabis cultivation and other drug related acts for and by retail shops. The obligations of criminalization in the Framework Decision entail that legalization or decriminalization of cannabis cultivation, supply and trafficking for recreational use by other people is not possible. Consequently, there is no room to legalize or decriminalize cultivation with a view to supplying retail shops; the same probably applies to cannabis cultivation

[99] Explanatory Statement, Proposal Framework Decision Illegal Drug Trafficking, Brussels: Commission of the European Communities, 23 May 2001, COM(2001) 259, 2001/0114 (CNS), pp. 5–6. The proposal (Article 1(1)) said: '"illicit drug trafficking" means the act *without authorisation*, of selling and marketing as well as, for profit, of cultivating, producing, manufacturing, importing, exporting, distributing, offering, transporting or sending or, for the purpose of transferring for profit, of receiving, acquiring and possessing drugs.' (emphasis added).

within a Cannabis Social Club. This does not, however, shed light on the question whether the Framework Decision only imposes an obligation with regard to legislative measures or whether it also comprises obligations of prosecution and penalization. Because of CJEU case law, it now looks as if an obligation to prosecute is applicable to acts where EU law requires criminalization – as the Framework Decision does for various acts such as cannabis cultivation. That obligation to prosecute would then in principle not apply to joint cultivation and consumption in Cannabis Social Clubs, but this would apply in the case of cannabis cultivation intended to supply retail shops, more particularly if this involves large scale commercial trade.

3.5. RESERVATIONS, DENUNCIATION AND MODIFICATIONS

The Schengen agreement does not contain provisions regarding reservations, denunciation or modifications thereof. According to Article 137 of the Schengen Implementation Agreement, reservations are not allowed with this Convention.[100] Nor has a provision regarding denunciation been incorporated in the Implementation Agreement. In view of the nature of these agreements, denunciation or withdrawal does not seem to be a possibility that was intended or envisaged by the parties. The nature of the instruments does not lend itself to this (compare Article 56 of the Vienna Convention on the Law of Treaties).[101] Article 141 of the Schengen Implementation Agreement specifies the conditions for amending this Convention. Of course, there is also a possibility to amend the Framework Decision. The Commission recently used this option by submitting a proposal for a directive amending the 2004 Framework Decision.[102] However, the amendments proposed focus on addition of new psychoactive substances and are not relevant for cannabis or, for example, its cultivation. All in all, given the nature of European law and in view of the relevant obligations ensuing from the

---

100 With the exception of the possibility as referred to in Article 60 of the Schengen Implementation Agreement, which is not relevant here.

101 See also Nota 'Het Nederlandse drugsbeleid', bijlage III, *Kamerstukken II*, 1994–1995, 240 77, nos. 2–3 (i.e., Memorandum 'The Dutch drug policy', Annex III to *Dutch Parliamentary Documents II*, 1994–1995, 240 77, nos. 2–3).

102 Proposal for a Directive of the European Parliament and of the Council amending Council Framework Decision 2004/757/JHA of 25 October 2004 laying down minimum provisions on the constituent elements of criminal acts and penalties in the field of illicit drug trafficking, as regards the definition of drug, 17 September 2013, COM(2013) 618 final, 2-13/0304 (COD). See also European Parliament legislative resolution of 17 April 2014 on the proposal for a directive of the European Parliament and of the Council amending Council Framework Decision 2004/757/JHA of 25 October 2004 laying down minimum provisions on the constituent elements of criminal acts and penalties in the field of illicit drug trafficking, as regards the definition of drug (COM(2013) 0618, C7-0271/2013 – 2013/0304(COD).

UN narcotic drugs conventions, these options do not seem suitable or effective to legalize, decriminalize, tolerate by virtue of a policy and/or otherwise regulate the cultivation of cannabis for the purpose of selling cannabis in retail shops.

3.6. CONCLUSION

The Framework Decision on illicit drug trafficking, which builds on the Schengen acquis as well as the Joint Action on illegal drug trafficking is the basic instrument within the European Union with regard to harmonization of the substantive criminal law provisions and penalties in respect of illicit drug trafficking. All these instruments confirm the obligations ensuing from the UN narcotic drugs conventions.

The obligation to penalize cultivation of cannabis for recreational use is evident from Article 2(1)(b) of the Framework Decision. This provision thus rules out legalization or decriminalization of cannabis cultivation for recreational use. The Schengen acquis and the Joint Action do not explicitly show an obligation of penalization. Article 8 of the Joint Action, however, does require states to take the most appropriate steps to combat the illicit cultivation of cannabis as well. At any rate, permitting cannabis cultivation by legalizing or regulating it in any way or by tolerating it as a matter of policy for example would be at odds with this obligation. The Schengen acquis (Agreement and Implementation Agreement) does not contain a provision referring to cultivation. Nonetheless, the obligation of Article 71(5) of the Schengen Implementation Agreement is relevant for that cultivation. The provision says that the member states shall do their utmost to prevent and combat the negative effects arising from the illicit demand for cannabis among other things. It would be a challenge to maintain that a state does its 'utmost' to prevent these negative effects of the illegal demand for cannabis, if the cultivation of cannabis were legalized or decriminalized.

The obligations arising from Article 71(5) of the Schengen Implementation Agreement and Article 8 of the Joint Action are also important for the question whether states are obliged to prosecute those who cultivate cannabis for recreational use. Taking into account the obligations in these provisions to fight the demand for and/or cultivation of cannabis, it is difficult to maintain that those obligations are fulfilled if no one is ever prosecuted for cannabis cultivation. The same logic would apply to – and is used by the Council, Commission and the CJEU – with regard to the Framework Decision. It is particularly important in this respect that an obligation to prosecute those involved in large-scale cannabis cultivation aimed at supplying retail shops seems to ensue from CJEU case law. However, it would then appear that in principle, the obligation to prosecute does not apply to joint cultivation and consumption in Cannabis Social Clubs.

CHAPTER 4

ASSESSMENT OF THE ARGUMENTS AND INITIATIVES REGARDING REGULATION OF CANNABIS CULTIVATION*

4.1. INTRODUCTION

The possibilities for and obstacles to regulated cannabis cultivation intended for recreational use are the fuel for extensive and sometimes fierce debate both in the Netherlands and in several other countries. This chapter contains an inventory and categorization of arguments and initiatives for the regulation of cannabis cultivation in and outside the Netherlands.[1] These arguments and initiatives will be analysed and assessed in the light of the UN narcotic drugs conventions and the EU laws on drugs. This is primarily done on the basis of the explanations in Chapter 2 and Chapter 3, supplemented if necessary by further discourse about international law and EU law.

The following starts with an inventory, categorization and evaluation of the legal arguments presented. It primarily concerns arguments relating to the UN narcotic drugs conventions and the EU laws on drugs. Secondly, all sorts of factual, social and political arguments set forth to legitimize the regulation of cannabis cultivation will be discussed. The last part before the conclusion constitutes an account, categorization and evaluation of modalities proposed in

* This chapter was written with the cooperation of Dr. Maartje J.M. Krabbe, who inventoried and categorized the many arguments and initiatives for regulating cannabis.

1 For the Netherlands the arguments are primarily extracted from the letters, notes and reports from 25 Dutch municipalities provided for by the Dutch Ministry of Justice and Security, see more specifically Piet Hein P.H.M.C. van Kempen & Masha I. Fedorova, *Internationaal recht en cannabis. Een beoordeling op basis van VN-drugsverdragen en EU-regelgeving van gemeentelijke en buitenlandse opvattingen pro regulering van cannabisteelt foor recreatief gebruik*, Deventer: Kluwer, 2014, Chapter 4. The municipalities in question are: *Breda*, Deventer, Doetinchem, *Eindhoven*, Enschede, *Groningen*, Haarlem, Heerlen, Kerkrade, Leeuwarden, Leiden, Maastricht, *Nijmegen*, Roermond, *Rotterdam*, Sittard-Geleen, Smallingerland/Drachten, *Tilburg*, *Utrecht*, Velsen, Venlo, Venray, Weert, Zwijndrecht and Zwolle (the seven cities of the top ten have been italicized). See also studies such as Beau Kilmer et al., *Multinational overview of cannabis production regimes*, RAND Europe/WODC, 2013; European Monitoring Centre for Drugs and Drug Addiction, *Cannabis legalization in Europe. An overview*, Luxembourg: Publications Office of the European Union, 2018.

the Netherlands and introduced in other countries for the regulation of cannabis cultivation for recreational purposes. We note that the following inevitably contains many explanations that can already be found in Chapters 2 and 3, in a slightly different context or with a somewhat different wording.

4.2. LEGAL ARGUMENTS FOR REGULATING CANNABIS

Legal arguments for the regulation of cannabis for recreational use involve claims of existing legal room under positive law to this end. In addition, there are specific arguments arguing about the existence of discretion under public international law to regulate cannabis cultivation and trade. The following is an overview of these arguments, sorted by topic, and our discussion thereof in the light of the UN narcotic drugs conventions and the EU instruments.

4.2.1. AMENDING THE RELEVANT UN NARCOTIC DRUGS CONVENTIONS

First, arguments are presented that directly put the conventions centre stage in order to answer the question how any room for legal manoeuvring can be found in order to achieve regulation of cannabis cultivation and trade for recreational use. One argument suggests that legalization of cannabis cultivation can be achieved by amending the relevant UN narcotic drugs conventions. This is possible from a legal point of view at any rate: Article 47 of the Single Convention and Article 31 of the Illicit Traffic Convention describe the procedures according to which amendments to the Convention have to take place. To assess the actual feasibility of such amendments, the following is important.

The states that are party to the Single Convention currently number 186 in total and those that are bound by the Illicit Traffic Convention 190.[2] Therefore, it will not be easy to amend these conventions – if it is possible at all – and the process would probably be drawn out for years.[3] This does not alter the fact that there are initiatives to initiate an amendment process. For example, there is *The Global Initiative for Drug Policy Reform*, which aims to bring about fundamental reform of the international drug control system. This non-governmental organization

---

2 See: http://treaties.un.org/ (Chapter VI, numbers 18 and 19) (status on 1 January 2019).

3 A similar conclusion is reached by David R. Bewley-Taylor, 'Towards revision of the UN drug control conventions. The logic and dilemmas of Like-Minded Groups', *Series on Legislative Reform of Drug Policies*, No. 19, March 2012, pp. 1–16; Scenario Team appointed by the Organization of American States, *Scenarios for the Drug Problem in the Americas 2013–2025*, Washington: Organization of American States 2013, p. 41; Robin Room & Sarah McKay, *Roadmaps for Reforming the UN Drug Conventions*, Oxford: Beckley Foundation Press, 2012, p. 10.

maintains first and foremost that the three UN narcotic drugs conventions 'lock into place a rigid, prohibitionist system of drug control' and that the 'conventions' legislation has significantly constrained various countries' efforts to experiment with alternative methods of drug control, such as the decriminalization of use and possession'.[4] The organization proposes three pragmatic options to amend the UN narcotic drugs conventions.[5] The three alternatives seek to uphold the rules and the structure of the current conventions with respect to international cooperation and controls of the international market, while at the same time offering more possibilities to national governments to introduce new drug legislation for their territories.[6] That said, *The Global Initiative* also thinks it is unlikely that there is enough international consensus between the states parties to achieve essential amendments of the conventions. States banking on amending UN narcotic drugs conventions are probably embarking on a difficult and time-consuming enterprise where there is no guarantee of success.

4.2.2. AMENDING THE STATUS OF CANNABIS THROUGH MODIFICATION OF THE SCHEDULES OF THE SINGLE CONVENTION

In order to achieve legalization or regulation of cannabis cultivation for recreational use, it has also been suggested to change the status of cannabis under the convention regime by modifying the Schedules to the Single Convention. This could involve transferring cannabis to another Schedule or to delete cannabis from the Schedules altogether.

Cannabis – in the sense of flowering and fruiting tops of the cannabis plant and cannabis resin – is included in Schedule I as well as Schedule IV of the Single Convention. This means that cannabis is subject to the strictest regime of the international drug control system, and with regard to cannabis this involves both the Single Convention and the Illicit Traffic Convention. Article 3 of the Single Convention provides for a procedure to transfer narcotic drugs from one Schedule to another or to delete it from a Schedule altogether.[7] Any attempt to modify those Schedules so as to remove obstacles on the way to legalizing, tolerating by virtue of a policy and/or otherwise regulating the cultivation of cannabis for recreational use will be fraught with various difficulties.

---

4 See The Global Initiative for Drug Policy Reform, 'Rewriting the UN Drug Conventions', available on: http://reformdrugpolicy.com/beckley-main-content/global-initiative/a-new-convention/.

5 See the website article mentioned in the previous footnote for a more elaborate discussion of the three options.

6 Ibid.

7 See for information on that section 2.2.1.

i. Is Amending the Schedules a Realistic Option?

While in general it is probably easier to transfer cannabis to a less restrictive Schedule or to delete it from the Schedules altogether than it is to change the Convention, such a modification of the schedule is not going to be easy, given the lack of consensus among the parties. As far as we could see, no state has ever initiated the transfer of cannabis to another Schedule or to have it deleted from the Schedules by means of this procedure.[8] High hopes with regard to this vested in the UN General Assembly Special Session on Drugs (UNGASS) in 2016[9] seem to not have been fulfilled.[10] At any rate, such a modification requires a majority decision in the Commission on Narcotic Drugs (CND). For the time being, this does not look easy to achieve.[11] It is therefore highly dubious whether modifying the Schedules is a realistic option.

ii. Is Transferring Cannabis to a Lighter Regime of a Different Schedule a Solution?

Even if modification of the status of cannabis through an amendment of the Schedules proves to be possible, this does not mean that the Single Convention and the Illicit Traffic Convention are no longer relevant for the discussion about cannabis cultivation. If cannabis were *transferred* from Schedule I to Schedule II and deleted from Schedule IV, nearly all obligations that currently apply to cannabis will still remain in force. By transferring cannabis from Schedule I to Schedule II, only the obligations in paragraphs 2 and 5 of Article 30 about the trade in and the dispensation of drugs (for medical or scientific purposes) would no longer apply.[12] Deleting cannabis from Schedule IV would mean that Article 2(5) of the Single Convention – to which the Netherlands does not currently attach any consequences with regard to cannabis – no longer applies.[13] In short, transferring cannabis from Schedule I to Schedule II, which would then necessitate the deletion of this drug from Schedule IV,[14] would not remove

---

8 This view is also expressed in UNODC, *A Century of International Drug Control*, Vienna: United Nations, 2008, p. 82.

9 This is noted by Marie Nougier, 'Informal Drug Policy Dialogue Report. Warsaw, Poland, 14th to 16th February 2013', May 2013, p. 27; see also Scenario Team appointed by the Organization of American States, *Scenarios for the Drug Problem in the Americas 2013–2025*, Washington: Organization of American States, 2013, p. 41.

10 See Outcome Document of the 2016 United Nations General Assembly Special Session on the World Drug Problem, 'Our Joint Commitment to effectively addressing and countering the world drug problem', A/RES/S-30-/1, New York, 19 April 2016.

11 This is hardly feasible if at all, according to Scenario Team appointed by the Organization of American States, *Scenarios for the Drug Problem in the Americas 2013–2025*, Washington: Organization of American States, 2013, p. 48; Robin Room & Sarah McKay, *Roadmaps for Reforming the UN Drug Conventions*, Oxford: Beckley Foundation Press, 2012, p. 11.

12 For more information, see the introduction to section 2.2.2.ii.a.

13 For more information, see the introduction to section 2.2.2.ii.b.

14 See Article 2(5) of the Single Convention.

any obstacles that are currently in place for cannabis cultivation with a view to recreational use.

iii. *Is Deleting Cannabis from the Schedules Completely a Solution?*

The above conclusion would be partly different in the case of a *complete removal* of cannabis from the Schedules. In that event all provisions that apply in general to narcotic drugs in the Single Convention (in particular Articles 4, 12–21, 33, 36, 37 and 38) and in the Illicit Traffic Convention (particularly, Article 3, except paragraph 1(a)ii) would no longer apply to cannabis cultivation. A total removal of cannabis from the Schedules would therefore clear a number of important obstacles for the regulation of cannabis cultivation for recreational use. However, in that event a number of relevant provisions of the Convention would still remain in force.

First of all, Article 22 of the Single Convention would still apply. Because Article 22 of the Single Convention requires a virtually outright ban on cannabis cultivation if that is necessary to protect 'public health and welfare', this provision is aimed primarily at cannabis cultivation which in itself is legal under the Convention, namely for medical and scientific purposes.[15] Such a general ban does not currently apply in the Netherlands and there does not seem to be a need for that either. Article 22 of the Single Convention has no special significance for the discussion about cannabis cultivation for the supply of points-of-sale so long as Article 36 of the Single Convention is applicable. However, if cannabis were to be deleted from the Schedules altogether – in which case Article 36 of the Single Convention would no longer apply to cannabis cultivation – Article 22 of the Single Convention could gain relevance: as we noted before, then it can be defended that a state would have to implement a prohibition (not necessarily related to criminal law) of cannabis cultivation, should that state's authorities consider that to be 'the most suitable measure' to protect 'the public health and welfare'.[16] However, if the state was genuinely of the opinion that legalization, policy-based tolerance and/or other forms of regulating cannabis cultivation for recreational use would be the most suitable measure to fight crime or reduce nuisance or on the grounds of public health,[17] then Article 22 of the Single Convention does not assume an obligation to prohibit such cultivation.

Then there is Article 28 of the Single Convention, which deals with supervision of legal cultivation of cannabis plants.[18] It can be argued that if cannabis were

---

15 See for more information section 2.2.2.ii.c.I.

16 See for more information section 2.2.2.ii.c.I.

17 See more elaborately Piet Hein P.H.M.C. van Kempen & Masha I. Fedorova, *International Law and Cannabis II. Regulation of Cannabis Cultivation and Trade for Recreational Use: Positive Human Rights Obligations versus UN Narcotic Drugs Conventions*, Cambridge: Intersentia, 2019.

18 See for more information section 2.2.2.ii.c.II.

no longer included in the Schedules, this narcotic drug would no longer qualify as illegal under the Single Convention (but this does not apply then to the Illicit Traffic Convention as well, which will be discussed below). If a state were to allow cannabis cultivation for recreational use, the consequence of that would be that Article 28 of the Single Convention requires that the obligations arising from Article 23 of the Single Convention are fulfilled. This would mean that the state would then have to establish a national government agency whose tasks would include the following. The agency decides who will be granted a licence to cultivate cannabis on a certain plot of land. Licensees are required to deliver their entire crops to this agency. The agency has the exclusive right of importing, exporting, wholesale trading and maintaining stocks of cannabis. In short: upon removal of cannabis from the Schedules, the Single Convention still requires that any permission of cannabis cultivation for recreational use takes place under the auspices of a national government agency. For a state such as the Netherlands that is also a party to the Illicit Traffic Convention, this option is not available, though. The following is important in this respect.

In Article 3(1)(a)ii, the Illicit Traffic Convention explicitly requires the states parties to criminalize intentional cannabis cultivation.[19] So even if cannabis were deleted from the Schedules, this provision about cannabis cultivation remains in force as it literally targets 'cultivation of [...] cannabis plant'. The deletion of cannabis from the Schedules will not relieve a state from its obligation to criminalize cannabis cultivation with a view to supplying points-of-sale for recreational use. This rules out the legalization and decriminalization of the cultivation of cannabis, that is to say, insofar as this would mean commercial or other than small-scale cultivation. After all, cultivation and other acts in connection with personal use fall under Article 3(2) of the Illicit Traffic Convention and are therefore outside the scope of Article 3(1)(a) under ii of the Illicit Traffic Convention.[20] Since Article 3(2) of the Illicit Traffic Convention does not explicitly refer to cannabis or the cultivation of it, the consequence of deleting cannabis from the Schedules would be that the parties to the Illicit Traffic Convention may permit cannabis cultivation for personal use. Insofar as these states are also parties to the Single Convention – like the Netherlands – they would have to ensure strict application of the regime regarding a national government agency to this 'legal' cultivation as required by Article 28 in conjunction with Article 23 of the Single Convention. From a practical point of view, permitting individual cannabis cultivation for personal use is already so much at odds with having to establish a government agency to which the crops must be handed over that a reasonable interpretation of the Convention seems to entail that such cultivation does not need to take place under the supervision

---

19 See for more information section 2.3.2.i.b.I.

20 See for more information section 2.3.2.i.b.I.

of a government agency after all.[21] Such an interpretation is warranted by Article 23 of the Single Convention as well, as this provision is clearly targeted at cultivation on a certain scale. After all, this provision refers to 'plots of land', the 'areas' of the land and 'total crops'. This argument, however, is less convincing if there is no truly small-scale cannabis cultivation. This means that if cannabis were completely deleted from the Schedules and that one could also assume that joint cultivation for personal use (for example in Cannabis Social Clubs)[22] is not covered by Article 3(1)(a) under ii of the Illicit Traffic Convention, such joint cultivation will have to be supervised by a government agency in the sense of Article 28 in conjunction with Article 23 of the Single Convention if that joint cultivation results in a significant crop. It is not easy to indicate where the line could or should be drawn in this respect. Nevertheless, arguing that cultivation in the context of a Cannabis Social Club with hundreds of members who each have one plant,[23] is not covered by Article 28 in conjunction with Article 23 of the Single Convention is never going to be easy.

Finally, there is Article 14 of the Illicit Traffic Convention, which requires the parties to take the necessary measures to fight illicit cultivation of cannabis plants among other things and to eradicate it in their own territory.[24] As we discussed before, deleting cannabis from the Schedules would not relieve the parties of their obligation in Article 3(1)(a) under ii of the Illicit Traffic Convention to criminalize intentional cannabis cultivation.[25] Cultivation within the scope of this provision is deemed illegal in the sense of the Illicit Traffic Convention, so that the obligation arising from Article 14 of the Illicit Traffic Convention applies to it as well. However, cultivation and other acts in connection with personal use fall under Article 3(2) of the Illicit Traffic Convention and are therefore outside the scope of Article 3(1)(a) under ii of the Illicit Traffic Convention.[26] The consequence of deleting cannabis from the Schedules would also be that cultivation for personal use under the Illicit Traffic Convention would no longer qualify as illicit cultivation, so that the government would not have to take measures against it in the sense of Article 14 of the Illicit Traffic Convention. However, in the case of cultivation of a commercial nature or that is not small-scale, such a deletion from the Schedules would not have any

---

21 Compare the Canadian ruling *Sfetkopoulos v. Canada* (Attorney General), 2008 FC 33 (CanLII), point 17, discussed in Beau Kilmer et al., *Multinational overview of cannabis production regimes*, RAND Europe/WODC, 2013, p. 40.

22 See for more information on that section 4.4.2.ii.

23 See for example the Belgian Social Cannabis Club 'Trekt Uw Plant' (i.e., Force Your Plant (To Flower)), which had 400 members in September 2015; see https://trektuwplant.be/trekt-uw-plant/historiek/. A Spanish Social Cannabis Club is reported to have more than 300 members in 2015, see https://www.marijuana.com/news/2018/01/the-future-of-cannabis-social-clubs-remains-uncertain-in-spain/.

24 See for more information section 2.3.2.i.b.II.

25 See for more information section 2.3.2.i.b.I.

26 See for more information section 2.3.2.i.b.I.

effect on the obligations arising from Article 14 of the Illicit Traffic Convention to combat cannabis cultivation. Although the states parties have considerable discretion for their policies in that respect, in any case it means that they cannot allow such cultivation (legalizing it or tolerating it as a matter of policy), as this would be squarely at odds with the obligation to combat it.

4.2.3. DENOUNCING THE UN NARCOTIC DRUGS CONVENTIONS AND RE-ACCESSION WITH A RESERVATION

Another proposed possibility to escape the obligations regarding cannabis cultivation pursuant to the conventions is to denounce the Single Convention and the Illicit Traffic Convention only to re-join with new reservations concerning cannabis cultivation.[27] This option will be discussed below. Let us first observe the following.

i. Final Denunciation of the UN Narcotic Drugs Conventions

Another option, albeit a far-reaching one would be for a state to leave the international drug control system or the Single Convention and the Illicit Traffic Convention completely. In our view this would involve serious disadvantages – quite apart from the fact that it is a matter for the democratic political process to consider and decide if such an approach is desirable in the first place. In the literature for example, it is pointed out that this would jeopardize the cooperation with other states and therefore the effective fight against other types of narcotic drugs or other forms of cannabis traffic, and it could at the same time damage the country's international reputation, lead to international isolation and heavy international pressure.[28] In the Netherlands, for example, such a radical step is

---

27 See for example Bjorn Arp, 'Denunciation Followed by Re-accession with Reservations to a Treaty: A Critical Appraisal of Contemporary State Practice', *Netherlands International Law Review*, vol. 1 (2), 2014, pp. 141–165; Robin Room, 'Reform by subtraction: The path of denunciation of international drug treaties and reaccession with reservations', *The International Journal of Drug Policy*, vol. 23 (5), 2012, pp. 401–406; David R. Bewley-Taylor, 'Challenging the UN drug control conventions: problems and possibilities', *The International Journal of Drug Policy*', 2003, vol. 14 (2), pp. 171–179.

28 See David R. Bewley-Taylor, 'Towards revision of the UN drug control conventions. The logic and dilemmas of Like-Minded Groups', *Series on Legislative Reform of Drug Policies*, No. 19, March 2012, pp. 1–16 on p. 3; and also The Global Initiative for Drug Policy Reform, 'Rewriting the UN Drug Conventions', available on http://reformdrugpolicy.com/beckley-main-content/global-initiative/a-new-convention/; Bjorn Arp, 'Denunciation Followed by Re-accession with Reservations to a Treaty: A Critical Appraisal of Contemporary State Practice', *Netherlands International Law Review*, vol. 1 (2), 2014, specifically pp. 144–145 and references in footnotes 12,13, 15.

considered unrealistic and therefore undesirable.[29] Apart from that, a withdrawal from the UN narcotic drugs conventions does not remove the obligations such as the criminalization of cannabis cultivation imposed on the member states under European Union law.

ii. Denouncing and Re-Accession with a Reservation

The Single Convention provides for the possibility (in Article 46) to denounce the Convention[30] and does not explicitly raise obstacles to re-joining after denunciation (see Article 40(3)). Nor does the Convention explicitly rule out the possibility to formulate a reservation upon re-accession. The Convention, however, does explicitly impose limitations to the possible content of such reservations.[31] Insofar as this is relevant for cannabis cultivation, Article 49 of the Single Convention offers states parties at the time of signature, ratification or accession the possibility to reserve the right to allow the use of cannabis, cannabis resin, extracts and tinctures of cannabis for non-medical purposes. This permissive stance should be of a temporary nature, though. Moreover, Article 49(2)(f) in conjunction with Article 49(1) of the Single Convention stipulates that the use of cannabis for purposes other than medical and scientific ones must be discontinued within twenty-five years from the coming into force of the Convention in accordance with Article 41(1) of the Single Convention, which means that the Convention has ruled out any reservations regarding cannabis for recreational use after 1989. Flouting this provision would also be a breach of Article 19(b) of the Vienna Convention on the Law of Treaties. Apart from that, states like the Netherlands would never have been able to use the reservation, because Article 41(2)(a) of the Single Convention stipulates that the activities referred to by the reservation are traditional and were permitted on 1 January 1961 in the country that formulates the reservation. Not only could the aforementioned cannabis cultivation as well as other cannabis activities hardly be labelled as traditional in the Netherlands, but it is also important that these acts cannot be qualified as 'permitted' either, as they have always been punishable in the Netherlands. That is why the situation regarding cannabis in the Netherlands is different from the one in Bolivia with respect to the coca leaf.[32] Should the Bolivian reservation with regard to 'traditional' consumption

---

29 Commissie Van de Donk, *Geen deuren maar daden. Nieuwe accenten in het Nederlands drugsbeleid*, Advies Commissie Drugsbeleid, 2009, p. 44 (i.e., Van De Donk Commission, *Deeds instead of doors. New accents in Dutch drug policy*, Advice Commission Drug Policy, 2009).

30 Nevertheless, see also Article 46 of the Single Convention, from which it follows that denunciation is not possible until two years after the date the Convention came into force.

31 See also section 2.2.4.

32 See for more information section 2.4.v.

of the coca leaf be legitimate, which is rather dubious given the twenty-five year period[33] and which has been challenged by the Netherlands itself, that would not imply that a reservation with respect to cannabis cultivation is or could be acceptable. The conclusion is that a state, such as the Netherlands, cannot in good faith use a reservation to escape in a legally sound manner from the obligations pertaining to cannabis cultivation ensuing from the Single Convention (this concerns in particular Articles 4, 33, 36, 37 and 38 of the Single Convention).[34] For the sake of completeness and apart from the foregoing, we also note that such a reservation would hardly be compatible with the object and purpose of the Single Convention, which is required by virtue of Article 19(c) of the Vienna Convention on the Law of Treaties. The fact is, what we are going to present below with regard to the object and purpose of the Illicit Traffic Convention, applies to a large extent (mutatis mutandis) to the Single Convention as well.

The Illicit Traffic Convention does not contain explicit limitations to any reservations to be formulated and does not even contain a provision about reservations.[35] That does not change the fact that any reservation will have to be in accordance with international public law, for which the Vienna Convention on the Law of Treaties is decisive and which is reflected in the Guide to Reservations and Commentaries by the International Law Commission (ILC).[36] This means that a reservation must in any case be compatible with the object and purpose of the convention, according to Article 19(c) of the Vienna Convention on the Law of Treaties.[37] As illustrated above, not only must the reservation as such be acceptable, but also its application in practice.[38] In section 2.3.4.iv, it has already been explained why it would be difficult in this light to maintain that the reservation already made by the Netherlands vis-à-vis the Illicit Traffic

33 See also David R. Bewley-Taylor & Martin Jelsma, 'The Limits of Latitude. The UN drug control conventions', *Series on Legislative Reform of Drug Policies*, No. 18, March 2012, p. 16; David R. Bewley-Taylor, 'The Contemporary International Drug Control System: A History of the UNGASS Decade', in: John Collins (ed.), *Governing the Global Drug Wars*, London: London School of Economics, 2012, pp. 49–55 on p. 54. For a more positive view, see the IDPC Advocacy Note, 'Bolivia's legal reconciliation with the UN Single Convention on Narcotic Drugs', International Drug Policy Consortium, July 2011, available on: https://www.tni.org/files/publication-downloads/idpc-advocacy-bolivia-july2011.pdf.

34 Incidentally, it is perhaps possible to formulate a legally valid reservation upon re-accession in the case of for example Article 28 in conjunction with Article 23 of the Single Convention, which stipulate that the granting of permits for supervision of and collection of the crops of legal cannabis cultivation should be in the hands of a government agency. Such a reservation, however, is fairly pointless as long as there is no escape from the prohibitions regarding cannabis cultivation, and for that reason we will not look any further into the question whether such a reservation is permissible.

35 However, see Article 32(4) of the Illicit Traffic Convention, which is not relevant here, but which deals with parties rejecting procedures for settling disputes and the advisory role of the International Court of Justice.

36 For more information about the International Law Commission see section 2.1.ii.

37 See also Guideline 3.1 ILC Guide to Reservations.

38 See for more information section 2.3.4.iv.

Convention can be used to tolerate the cultivation, delivery and trade in cannabis for the supply of coffee shops or to regulate it in other ways on the basis of a policy; we will come back to this in section 4.2.3.ii. Is it possible then, taking into account the object and purpose of the Illicit Traffic Convention, to formulate a new reservation that ensures that relevant obligations arising from the provisions of this Convention are no longer applicable to tolerating cannabis cultivation or at least no longer form an obstacle to this objective? This is particularly so – but not exclusively – with regard to Article 3(a) under i (an obligation to criminalize all sorts of activities with cannabis), under ii (an obligation to criminalize intentional cannabis cultivation) and under iv (an obligation to criminalize intentional production and distribution of equipment, materials and certain substances for cannabis cultivation), Article 3(2) (an obligation to criminalize cannabis cultivation for personal consumption), Article 3(6) (an obligation to achieve maximum effectiveness in prosecuting persons also with regard to cannabis cultivation) and Article 14 (an obligation to take the appropriate measures against cannabis cultivation).

Seen from the perspective of the object and purpose of the Illicit Traffic Convention it is relevant that the Convention is explicitly aimed against illicit traffic, given the title, the preamble and various provisions. According to Article 1(m) of the Illicit Traffic Convention, all activities described in Article 3(1) and 3(2) of the Illicit Traffic Convention constitute illicit traffic. This includes in any event – though not exclusively – commercial cannabis cultivation, deliveries and trade and therefore also cannabis cultivation for supplying retail shops with a view to selling cannabis to consumers for recreational use. In addition to this, it is important that next to coca products and poppy products, cannabis products are the main object of this Convention, since these are mentioned explicitly not only in the Schedules of the Convention, but in the Convention itself as well. Moreover, as illustrated by the text, system and rationale of the Convention, the Illicit Traffic Convention seeks to provide further reinforcement of the complete prohibition of the circulation of illegal cannabis among other things, by means of the required criminalizations, enforcement through criminal law and cooperation in criminal matters,[39] and in the context of the Convention this means: all flowering and fruiting tops of cannabis plants, cannabis resin and cannabis plants for non-medical and non-scientific purposes. Combating cannabis use for recreational purposes and 'eradication of illicit traffic' in cannabis is a primary objective ('purpose') of the Convention. Even if we only look at this fact, a reservation the object of which is to make it possible to tolerate cannabis cultivation can hardly be argued to be compatible with the 'object and purpose' of the Illicit Traffic Convention. However, there is more to it than that. Considering that the Netherlands with its current coffee shop policy

39 See for more information section 2.6.

already tolerates the sale of cannabis to consumers for recreational use, allowing the cultivation of cannabis as well (legalizing or regulating it in any way or by tolerating it as a matter of policy) would result in a situation where an entire domestic cannabis economy from cultivation to selling aimed at recreational use is tolerated. This tolerance would also include cultivation, trading and selling on a serious scale. A reservation that attempts to achieve this would therefore neutralize the Illicit Traffic Convention for huge quantities of narcotic drugs in a key area of the Convention: combating cannabis for recreational use and the illicit traffic in it. It is hard to see how this could be compatible with the object and purpose of the Illicit Traffic Convention.[40] Therefore, we do not think it is possible to formulate such a reservation in good faith.

4.2.4. THE GENERAL PUBLIC HEALTH INTEREST AND THE EXCEPTION OF 'MEDICAL AND SCIENTIFIC PURPOSES'

Many arguments for the regulation of cannabis, especially in the Netherlands, are based on considerations of public health. The more factual, practical and policy-related arguments about this will be dealt with in section 4.3.1. Here, we limit ourselves to arguments directly concerning the UN narcotic drugs conventions and/or EU law or those that have a legal slant anyway. For example, there are arguments that are based on the public health interest and/or the exception of medical or scientific purposes that apply to the UN narcotic drugs conventions. What follows is an inventory of these arguments and their assessment in the light of the relevant drug conventions.

i. The Public Health Interest in Article 22 of the Single Convention

Article 22 of the Single Convention stipulates that if one state party is of the opinion that a prohibition of the cultivation of cannabis is the appropriate way to serve the public health and welfare, this avenue must be followed. One could therefore also argue – a contrario – that, since public health is actually served by a regulated and supervised method of cannabis cultivation, cultivation should not be prohibited, actually, on the basis of Article 22 of the Single Convention.

---

40 It is worth mentioning that Vietnam formulated reservations with respect to extradition obligations in the Single Convention (Article 36(2) and the Illicit Traffic Convention (Article 6), and that Sweden, Finland, Austria, France and Germany and – not explicitly – the United Kingdom and the United States also objected to those reservations with regard to one or both conventions on account of the object and purpose. This is interesting, because the extradition obligation seems to be less central to these conventions than the actual prohibition and prosecution activities and combating cannabis; after all, extradition is only one of the additional instruments to that end.

In itself, it is true that if the general public health interest is not served by a prohibition in the sense of Article 22 of the Single Convention according to a party, that party does not have to implement such a prohibition. This does not mean, however, that that party is no longer required to prohibit cannabis cultivation for recreational use. The fact is that the reasoning underlying this argument is based on an incorrect interpretation of Article 22 of the Single Convention and the argument collapses.[41] The provision requires a near-total prohibition of cannabis cultivation if that is necessary for protecting 'the public health and welfare'. If such a necessity exists, the provision requires parties to prohibit even the cannabis cultivation that is legal under the terms of the Convention for 'medical or scientific purposes' almost[42] entirely. As a consequence, – a contrario – the state does not have to implement such a near-total ban that also includes medical cannabis if the protection of 'public health and welfare' does not require this. In short: the party may continue to permit cannabis cultivation for 'medical and scientific purposes'. The fact that there is no obligation to implement a near-total ban of course does not imply that there will no longer be a ban of cannabis cultivation that is illegal under the Convention – that is to say: cultivation for recreational use. In other words: the mere fact that a party does not need to implement the prohibition of Article 22 of the Single Convention, does not relieve the party from its obligations arising from all other provisions of the Convention. Therefore, Article 22 of the Single Convention does not provide any possibilities to justify legalization, policy-based tolerance and/or other forms of regulating cannabis cultivation for recreational use. Consequently, it is irrelevant who would be involved in such cultivation (government, private persons, or Cannabis Social Clubs) and for whom that cultivation would take place (retail shops, state run shops, shared consumption or private persons).

ii. Cannabis Cultivation for Recreational Use under the Exception of 'Medical Purposes'

As we observed before, many arguments for the regulation of recreational cannabis are based on considerations of public health. It is pointed out that legalization, policy-based tolerance and/or other forms of regulating cannabis cultivation would have all sorts of benefits for public health (see section 4.3.1), without any explanation as to how this relates to the UN narcotic drugs conventions and European law based on these conventions. Could a state by using the evolutive or the 'living instrument' interpretation method, in a

41 See for more information section 2.2.2.ii.c.I.

42 The exception involves: 'small quantities required [...] for scientific or research purposes', where 'scientific or research purposes' in itself is already more restricted than 'medical or scientific purposes', and at the same time it can only involve small quantities; see for more information section 2.2.2.ii.c.I.

legally valid way and in good faith, arrive at an extension of the exception that general public health policy could be included under the umbrella of 'medical purposes'? If that were the case, and provided that it could be made plausible that legalization, policy-based tolerance or other forms of regulating cannabis cultivation for recreational use would indeed benefit public health, then allowing cultivation under that exception would be possible.[43]

This thought experiment is undoubtedly exciting, but various arguments lead us to the conclusion that the approach suggested is not possible under the UN narcotic drugs conventions after all. The same also applies to the EU laws on drugs, which after all are based on the regime of those conventions.[44] Section 2.2.3.i. contains an elaborate explanation about the scope of the exception of 'medical or scientific purposes'. The conclusion of that explanation – based on the text of the convention, the drafting history, the rationale for the convention, the convention system, and the UN Commentary – is that in the final analysis, the exception of medical or scientific purposes is limited to the use of narcotic drugs as meaningful and/or effective medicine in concrete cases, the use of narcotic drugs to produce medicines for such cases, and scientific research for the aforesaid medicinal use, the aforesaid production of medicines or medical science.

Admittedly, the 'living instrument' interpretation is applied in practice in international public law norms, but they primarily concern open, general and/or vaguely formulated provisions mostly in human rights treaties. In this case, though, we are not looking at an interpretation building on something offered by the Convention in general terms, but an interpretation that is hard to reconcile with the fairly hermetic text of the Convention and that also explicitly goes against the explicit and express intention of the states parties to keep the exception limited and truly medical. We also note that a considerably more liberal interpretation also runs counter to the Single Convention where this provides for a further tightening of the cannabis combating regime twenty-five years after it came into force in 1964.[45] With respect to the 'living instrument' interpretation, it is also important that it is not a specifically designated

43 See Piet Hein P.H.M.C. van Kempen & Masha I. Fedorova, *International Law and Cannabis II. Regulation of Cannabis Cultivation and Trade for Recreational Use: Positive Human Rights Obligations versus UN Narcotic Drugs Conventions*, Cambridge: Intersentia, 2019, where we base our argument for legal room for states to regulate cannabis for recreational on positive human rights obligations and not on an extensive interpretation of the medical and scientific purposes-clause.

44 See the introduction of section 3.2.2, the introduction of section 3.3, the introduction of section 3.4.1 and section 3.4.2. The last section refers to Court of Justice EU, Judgment of 16 December 2010, case C-137/09, ECLI:EU:C:2010:774 (*Josemans*), para. 31, 36 and 77, and also 38, 41 and 43, in which the Court considers that the harmfulness of narcotic drugs, including hemp products such as cannabis, is generally recognized, so that the trade in it is prohibited in all member states, with the exception of the strictly controlled trade in cannabis that is used for medical and scientific purposes.

45 See section 2.2.4.

international organization that comes to such an interpretation, but merely one of the states parties out of a total of 186.[46] The Convention explicitly provides for other options for these parties, such as the procedure to transfer narcotic drugs from one Schedule to another or to delete it from a Schedule altogether.[47] If individual states parties had the room to bring about a substantial modification of the Convention single-handedly via interpretations (which would then in principle be possible for other areas in the Convention and for other types of narcotic drugs), then the Convention with its strict wording and strict object and purpose would lose much of its impact. This would have adverse effects on the international legal obligations for a state, which partly arise from Articles 26 and 31 of the Vienna Convention on the Law of Treaties. For all these reasons, we conclude that it is legally impossible to stretch the exception of 'medical purposes' to include 'public health purposes' so as to permit cannabis cultivation and all other activities aimed at the sale of cannabis for recreational use.[48]

Moreover, there is something else at play. We just noted that the proposed public health interpretation is actually that of one state or a few states, not that of a specifically appointed international organization. This is very much a problem in the case of the Single Convention, because this Convention specifies such official supervisory bodies, of which the International Narcotics Control Board (INCB) is particularly relevant with respect to the supervision of the implementation of the Single Convention and the other UN narcotic drugs conventions.[49] The Board uses an interpretation and application of the exception which matches its wording in the Convention and it is therefore limited to genuine medical use of cannabis.[50] An interpretation of the exception of 'medical purposes' in the sense of 'public health purposes' is flatly rejected by this supervisory body. Were a state to proceed with applying such an interpretation, in doing so it would ignore the text, the system, the object and purpose and the thrust of the Convention and also square up to the INCB.

---

46 See: http://treaties.un.org/ (Chapter VI, numbers 18 and 19) (current situation December 2018).

47 See for information on this section 2.2.1.

48 See also David R. Bewley-Taylor & Martin Jelsma, 'The Limits of Latitude. The UN drug control conventions', *Series on Legislative Reform of Drug Policies*, No. 18, March 2012, p. 15, who, despite trying to interpret the conventions in as liberal a way as possible, still conclude that such a broad interpretation of the medical exception cannot currently be maintained. It is also interesting that Robin Room & Peter Reuter, 'How well do international drug conventions protect public health?', 379 *The Lancet* 2012 (January 7), pp. 84–91, argue that the UN narcotic drugs conventions should address public health interests much better than they actually do now, but that this is not possible under the current conventions, because of, among other things, the limited nature of the exception for medical use of drugs and that therefore amendment of the Convention is called for. They too, see no way out via the exception of 'medical or scientific purposes'.

49 For information on the task, status and limitations of the INCB see the introduction to section 2.4.

50 See for more information section 2.4.iii.

iii. Cannabis Cultivation for Recreational Use under the Exception of 'Scientific Purposes'

It has also been suggested that it is possible under the international conventions to devise a scientific experiment which is aimed at a closed circuit of cultivation for personal recreational use by adults. This is really an experiment with a Cannabis Social Club. The assessment of the extent to which the UN narcotic drugs conventions and the EU laws on drugs allow the legalization, policy-based tolerance and/or other forms of regulating cannabis cultivation in the context of joint cultivation and consumption for personal use ('shared consumption') and/or a Cannabis Social Club will be carried out in section 4.4.2.ii Here, we focus our attention on the question whether experiments with cannabis cultivation for recreational use are possible under the exception of 'scientific purposes' in the sense of the UN narcotic drugs conventions.

As observed above, section 2.2.3.i. contains an elaborate explanation about the scope of the exception of 'medical or scientific purposes'. We also repeated the ensuing conclusion with regard to the content and scope of this exception as a whole. What is particularly important here is that the explanation in that section concerning the element of 'scientific purposes' results in the conclusion that this partial exception is also meant to be fairly limited and that it refers in principle to medicines or medical science. For example, research can mean specifically authorized controlled clinical trials, where those experiments involve the narcotic drugs themselves and the patients.[51] The experiment may be aimed at discovering the therapeutic or medical value of the drug. Taking this into consideration, the exception of 'scientific purposes' does not lend itself to including experiments with cannabis cultivation for recreational use. After all, in that case it is not the cannabis that is the subject or instrument of the scientific research, but rather, among other things, the control and organization of the cultivation and the distribution of the yield. Furthermore, the aim of the research is not the advancement of medical science or the development of cannabis in order to produce a useful and/or effective medicine.

iv. Regulation of Cultivation Ties in with the Distinction between Soft Drugs and Hard Drugs as Made in the Dutch Opium Act

Municipalities in the Netherlands have pointed out that the regulated tolerance of cannabis cultivation would do justice to the distinction between soft drugs and hard drugs that is made in the Dutch Opium Act. It is noted that there

[51] See United Nations, 'Conference for the adoption of a Single Convention on Narcotic Drugs, New York, 24 January–25 March 1961, Official Records, Volume II', *UN Doc.* E/CONF. 34/24/Add. 1, pp. 3, 33 and 81–82.

is a tension between the risk assessment regarding soft drugs in international conventions and that of the Netherlands.

The existence of this distinction in the Dutch Opium Act and the Dutch drug policy in itself is irrelevant for the question which obligations ensue from the UN narcotic drugs conventions and EU law concerning drugs. Even if we assume that this distinction is made on good and solid grounds (and it is outside the scope of this book to assess whether this is indeed the case), it cannot affect in any way obligations pursuant to international and European law. After all, national law needs to be consistent with international and European law rather than the other way round. Incidentally, we need to point out that the distinction between cannabis and hard drugs is not reflected in the UN narcotic drugs conventions anyway. On the contrary: with its inclusion in Schedule I as well as Schedule IV of the Single Convention, cannabis – in the sense of flowering and fruiting tops of the cannabis plant and cannabis resin – together with, for example, heroin is subjected to the strictest regime known to the UN narcotic drugs conventions.[52] The Court of Justice of the EU (CJEU) also seems to take a rather dim view of it.[53] While this may be incomprehensible from the Netherlands point of view – but not necessarily from that of other countries inside and outside Europe[54] – it does not make a difference.

4.2.5. THE EXPEDIENCY PRINCIPLE, THE RESERVATION REGARDING THE ILLICIT TRAFFIC CONVENTION AND THE CURRENT POLICY OF TOLERANCE TOWARDS COFFEE SHOPS IN THE NETHERLANDS

There are various arguments put forward by the municipalities in the Netherlands that build on the expediency principle, in connection with the current policy of tolerance regarding the sale of cannabis to consumers for recreational use and/or the Dutch reservation regarding the Illicit Traffic Convention. These three categories of arguments will now each be discussed in turn, but it must be stressed that both the arguments and the individual discussions are interconnected.

i. Do the UN Narcotic Drugs Conventions and European Law Offer Sufficient 'Room for Expediency' to Proceed to Permit Cannabis Cultivation?

One argument is that the UN narcotic drugs conventions and European law admittedly prohibit the selling, trade, production and possession of cannabis,

---

52 See also e.g. INCB Report 2016, p. 42 (no. 323).

53 See section 3.4.1.vi.

54 According to Beau Kilmer et al., *Multinational overview of cannabis production regimes*, RAND Europe/WODC, 2013, pp. 42 and 45, cannabis and heroin are now treated in the same way in countries such as France and Chile.

but that it is up to the states parties to decide to what extent the law is enforced and these criminal offences are prosecuted. The notion is that this would allow for a system of permissiveness for cannabis cultivation based on the expediency principle.

The Single Convention and the Illicit Traffic Convention contain obligations for criminalization of all forms of cannabis cultivation aimed at recreational use. These obligations of criminalization cover both small-scale cultivation for personal use (see Article 36(1) of the Single Convention (which is not entirely clear), and the indisputable Article 3(2) of the Illicit Traffic Convention) and cultivation that is not small-scale and/or is not intended for personal use (see Article 36(1) of the Single Convention and Article 3(1) of the Single Convention).[55] The question then is to what extent the UN narcotic drugs conventions require enforcement of these criminalizations of cultivation through prosecution.

There is no provision in the Single Convention that explicitly contains a general obligation of prosecution. However, as we will explain in section 2.2.2.i.a.IX, the Convention does assume in various ways that there are obligations of prosecution. For example, it follows from the Convention that effect must be given to criminalization, which seems impossible without prosecuting persons for offences (see Article 4(a) and (c) in conjunction with Article 36 of the Single Convention); that serious offences, which include in principle cannabis cultivation that is not small-scale for recreational use, must be penalized under criminal law, which implies prosecution (Article 36(1)(a) and (b) of the Single Convention); and that such serious offences committed by nationals of foreigners 'shall be prosecuted' in principle by the party in whose territory the offences were committed (Article 36(2)(a) under iv of the Single Convention). The Single Convention does not imply here that there is in general room for applying the expediency principle or something similar (incidentally, neither in Article 36(4) of the Single Convention, which after all has no bearing on it[56]). The above-mentioned paragraph results in the conclusion that one can hardly argue that tolerating cannabis cultivation in order to supply coffee shops in general or as a matter of policy is permissible on the grounds of the expediency principle under the Single Convention. Since the reservation that the Netherlands created to protect the expediency principle applies to the Illicit Traffic Convention, that reservation is not relevant for this conclusion as it refers to Single Convention.

Apart from that reservation, in section 2.3.2.i.a.II for the Illicit Traffic Convention in respect of implicit obligations of prosecution, we reach a conclusion similar to that for the Single Convention. In that sense, both conventions largely corroborate each other. It is more important, though,

---

55 For a discussion of these provisions, see sections 2.2.2.ii.a.IV (about Article 36 of the Single Convention) and 2.3.2(a) under i (about Article 3 of the Illicit Traffic Convention).

56 See section 2.2.2.ii.a.VII and section 4.2.6 below.

that in contrast with the Single Convention, the Illicit Traffic Convention in Article 3(6) does contain a provision about discretionary legal powers for deciding whether or not to prosecute persons for offences criminalized by the Convention. The provision requires that such powers are used in such a way that maximum effectiveness in the investigation and in law enforcement is realized with regard to these punishable offences (incidentally, Article 3(11) of the Illicit Traffic Convention, the equivalent of Article 36(4) of the Single Convention, does not detract from that as this provision too does not seek to provide freedom of policy[57]). The elaboration on Article 3(6) of the Single Convention in section 2.3.2.i.a.II leads to the conclusion there is no room based on general policy to refrain from prosecution for offences if the authorities are aware of the facts and know who the perpetrators are. This applies at any rate to more serious drug-related activities, that is to say: activities involving drugs that are not small-scale and/or are not intended for personal use. Therefore, cannabis cultivation for supplying coffee shops cannot be tolerated under criminal law according to Article 3(6) of the Illicit Traffic Convention (this does not yet answer the question whether this is different for the Netherlands in view of the reservation). In the case of possession, purchase and cultivation for personal use, the authorities appear to have a little more room for manoeuvre.[58]

This is confirmed by what the INCB, as the official supervisory body, states about obligations of prosecution and the application of the expediency principle. The Board appears to be even less stringent than the text, the system and the rationale of the Convention seem to presuppose.[59] The INCB appears to leave some room for considerations of expediency *in concreto* for serious criminal drug related offences, but not for a general policy intended to refrain from prosecution for a certain category of such offences. In the case of cannabis-related offences involving personal consumption – including cultivation for personal consumption – there is a little more room to refrain from prosecution. For such offences, the INCB considers non-prosecution also permissible on the basis of a general policy. One can hardly argue, though, that this could also include cannabis cultivation for supplying coffee shops. The question whether this is different in connection with Cannabis Social Clubs and/or shared consumption, will be discussed in more detail in section 4.4.2.ii.

From a European law point of view, it is relevant that the EU laws on drugs do not contain any explicit obligations of prosecution, but they come to the fore in case law of the Court of Justice of the European Union. It would appear from that case law that there is also an obligation of prosecution for the criminalizations

57 See section 2.3.2.i.a.VI and section 4.2.6 below.

58 The same view is expressed by David R. Bewley-Taylor & Martin Jelsma, 'The Limits of Latitude. The UN drug control conventions', *Series on Legislative Reform of Drug Policies*, No. 18, March 2012, p. 6.

59 For information on those INCB views see section 2.4.iv.

required by the Framework Decision Illicit Drug Trafficking – including cannabis cultivation for non-personal use[60] – if this is necessary on the grounds of effective law enforcement.[61] If such an obligation of prosecution applies, it even appears to be absolute in the case of serious cannabis-related offences, so that there is little room for expediency in that case. The Public Prosecutions Service will then have to prosecute effectively for cannabis cultivation intended to supply points-of-sale, depending on the scale in particular and/or the possibly organized nature of that cannabis cultivation, and the distribution and trade that goes with it, if they are aware of the facts and know the suspected perpetrators.

Finally, it is important to observe that some appear to be labouring under the misunderstanding that it will be possible to permit cannabis cultivation as soon as a state manages to wriggle out of its obligation of prosecution. That is not the case. If an obligation of prosecution under criminal law no longer applies, this does not mean that other obligations to enforce law – that in principle do not pertain to criminal law – also cease to apply all of a sudden. In this subsection (under Re: 4) we will elaborate on this point.

ii. Does the Reservation of the Netherlands Regarding the Illicit Traffic Convention Leave Sufficient Room to Proceed to Permit Cannabis Cultivation?

Another argument for regulating cannabis in the Netherlands is that regulating cannabis cultivation is possible under the reservation that the Netherlands formulated with regard to the Illicit Traffic Convention.

We conclude that the reservation regarding the Illicit Traffic Convention leaves insufficient room to proceed to permit cannabis cultivation. Any other conclusion is precluded by each of the following legal obstacles: 1. The obligations of criminalization and prosecution under the Single Convention; 2. The international public law fixation of the content and functioning of reservations, which resists later expansion of its implementation; 3. The object and purpose of the Illicit Traffic Convention; 4. The obligations that in principle do not pertain to criminal law, regarding the fight against cannabis cultivation and use (Articles 4, 33, 37 and 38 of the Single Convention, and Article 14 of the Illicit Traffic Convention). We will now address these four points.

- *Re: 1. Obligations of criminalization and prosecution under the Single Convention.* The content, context, meaning and scope of the reservation formulated by the Netherlands in respect of the Illicit Traffic Convention has been dealt with extensively in section 2.3.4. In connection with that scope, it is important to realize that the reservation does not refer to the

60 See Article(1)(b) of the Framework Decision.

61 See section 3.4.1.vii.

Single Convention. Therefore, it does not affect in any way the obligations of criminalization and prosecution for cannabis cultivation among other things, which arise from that Convention, nor can it. This means at any rate that any cannabis cultivation that is not small-scale and/or not aimed at private personal use must be criminalized (Article 36 of the Single Convention). In addition to this, the Single Convention implies an obligation of prosecution for serious offences.[62] When push comes to shove, one can hardly argue that tolerating cannabis cultivation in order to supply points-of-sale in general or as a matter of policy is permissible on the grounds of the expediency principle under the Single Convention.[63] However, it is possible to defend the view that these obligations pursuant to the Single Convention do not apply for possession, selling and cultivation for one's own private use, but this is without any relevance for the cultivation for, supply to and selling by retail shops. The Single Convention alone makes it difficult to maintain that tolerating cannabis cultivation for the supply of retails shops in whichever form can be permitted.

- *Re: 2. Limitations of reservations.* With regard to the content and function of the reservation, the first important observation is that it applies to the room for discretion in prosecution decisions (the expediency principle) and does not affect in any way obligations of criminalization. Therefore, it does not eliminate the obligation to criminalize cultivation of cannabis for one's own personal consumption and recreational purposes (Article 3(2) of the Illicit Traffic Convention) and of all other cannabis cultivation for recreational use (Article 3(1) of the Illicit Traffic Convention). Cannabis cultivation for the supply of retail shops – which comes under the first paragraph – will also have to be criminalized. There can be no doubt that the reservation does provide room for a policy of refraining from prosecution for cannabis cultivation intended for personal consumption, with an appeal to the expediency principle.[64] However, this is not relevant for cannabis cultivation for the supply of retail shops, because such cultivation is evidently subject to the first paragraph (whether this cultivation in the context of Cannabis Social Clubs and/or shared consumption is a different scenario, will be explored in section 4.4.2.ii).

The question that presents itself is whether the reservation can now be used to justify non-prosecution for cannabis cultivation for the supply of retail shops. To answer that question, we must first and foremost understand what

---

62 See for the detailed discussion section 2.2.2.ii.a.IX.

63 Ibid.

64 See for more information section 2.3.4. Incidentally, this is already possible to some extent on the grounds of the Illicit Traffic Convention itself, in view of the system of Article 3 of the Illicit Traffic Convention and the position of the INCB on discretion. With respect to Article 3 of the Single Convention section 2.3.2.i.a.III and with respect to the INCB, see section 2.4.iv.

that reservation is about. In section 2.3.4 we concluded that the reservation is about ensuring room for considerations of expediency – also as a general policy – in the case of criminal behaviour aimed at personal consumption in the sense of Article 3(2) of the Illicit Traffic Convention. The notion that the reservation was also aimed at securing the sale of cannabis by retail shops to consumers is not borne out by the reservation itself, nor by the Dutch Parliamentary Documents about this, nor by the 'Understanding' from the Netherlands with respect to the Illicit Traffic Convention. For the other states parties – to whom the reservation is actually addressed – it is not clear if such a consequence of the reservation was intended. It is certain, however, that the reservation did not a priori intend to create extra room for any future application of the expediency principle to the supply side of the drug economy nor by implication to cannabis cultivation, delivery and trade for the supply of Dutch coffee shops.

What matters is that according to general public international law, a reservation which is formulated so as to protect national law relates to a law that is in force at the time when the reservation is formulated. It is not possible to formulate or use a reservation to allow for any future initiatives. The Netherlands did not formulate the reservation for that purpose anyway.[65] The reservation is therefore fixed in relation to the law that applies at the time of its wording.[66] If the Netherlands were to proceed with adopting a policy to refrain from prosecution for cannabis cultivation, delivery and trade for the supply of coffee shops, this would constitute a significant change in policy with regard to the enforcement of criminal law pertaining to cannabis-related offences. After all, it would imply that the Netherlands would suddenly permit an entire domestic cannabis economy from cultivation to selling, aimed at recreational use. Therefore, it is difficult to defend that the Dutch reservation to Article 3(6) of the Illicit Traffic Convention offers room to proceed to such a general policy of tolerance after all.

- *Re: 3. The object and purpose of the Illicit Traffic Convention.* As we have repeatedly observed, the content and application of a reservation must be compatible with the object and purpose of the convention; see Article 19(c) of the Vienna Convention on the Law of Treaties.[67] It is also interesting that Bewley-Taylor & Jelsma in spite of the Dutch reservation question

---

65 For more information on this, see section 2.3.3.iii.

66 The question whether a state that changes its constitution would be covered by the constitutional clause of Article 36 of the Single Convention ('Subject to its constitutional limitations, each Party shall [...]' is of a different category altogether, because in that case one does not appeal to the reservation but to the Convention itself. Even if this is possible (which question does not need answering here), that does not imply that the same is allowed with a reservation; the aforementioned already illustrates that this is not the case either.

67 See also Guideline 3.1 ILC Guide to Reservations.

whether the current coffee shop policy can be qualified as implementing the conventions in good faith.[68] We have also already come to that conclusion[69] (see also the next paragraph). It would be even more problematic to tolerate cultivation to supply coffee shops as well, as we have explained earlier in this chapter.[70] The conclusion we drew there (and its substantiation) of course also applies in this case: it is hard to see how such penal tolerance could be compatible with the object and purpose of the Illicit Traffic Convention. This is why in our view it is not possible to apply the current reservation in this way in good faith.

- *Re: 4. Other obligations that in principle do not pertain to criminal law.* If the state managed to wriggle out of its obligation of prosecution, this does not mean that the authorities are allowed to permit the cultivation of cannabis, as we have stated before. Even if one could defend that the expediency principle can be applied fully to (certain modalities of) cannabis cultivation for recreational use, then this implies nothing more or less than that the Public Prosecutions Service is authorized to refrain from prosecuting persons for that cultivation. The expediency principle – also by virtue of Article 167(2) of the Dutch Code of Criminal Procedure and Article 3(6) of the Illicit Traffic Convention – is only relevant with regard to prosecution for criminal offences: it does not derogate from obligations of criminalization under the Convention, nor does it touch on obligations that do not pertain to criminal law which are imposed on the state by the Convention.

  So even if the Netherlands were able to defend in good faith that it is not required to prosecute persons for cannabis cultivation, this does not detract from, for example, the general obligation to limit actively the production, distribution, trade, use and possession of cannabis among other things, to medical and scientific purposes (Article 4 of the Single Convention); obligations to prohibit and seize cannabis (Article 33 of the Single Convention and possibly Article 37 of the Single Convention); the obligation to take measures against cannabis use (Article 38 of the Single Convention); and the obligation to fight the cultivation of cannabis (Article 14 of the Illicit Traffic Convention).[71]

68 David R. Bewley-Taylor & Martin Jelsma, 'The Limits of Latitude. The UN drug control conventions', *Series on Legislative Reform of Drug Policies*, No. 18, March 2012, p. 15. This view is also propounded more emphatically by Hub Hennekens, 'Grenzen aan het opportuniteitsbeginsel. Een verkenning in relatie tot het drugsbeleid', in: Jan W. Fokkens, Piet Hein P.H.M.C. van Kempen, Henny J.B. Sackers & Paul C. Vegter (eds.), *Ad hunc modem. Opstellen over materieel strafrecht* (Machielse-bundel), Deventer: Kluwer, 2013, p. 104 (i.e., Hub Hennekens, 'The limits of the expediency principle. An exploration in connection with the drug policy', in: Jan W. Fokkens, Piet Hein P.H.M.C. van Kempen, Henny J.B. Sackers & Paul C. Vegter (eds.), *Ad hunc modem. Essays on substantive criminal law* (Machielse bundle of essays), Deventer: Kluwer, 2013, p. 104).

69 See section 2.3.4.iv.

70 See section 4.2.3.ii.

71 See Chapter 2 for a detailed discussion about all these obligations.

However, a policy of tolerating and actually permitting cannabis cultivation would imply that these obligations are not fulfilled, whereas the Netherlands is also legally bound to do so. After all, the reservation has no bearing on that, since it explicitly concerns only the sixth (and the seventh and the eighth) paragraph of the criminal law related Article 3 of the Illicit Traffic Convention. The obligations mentioned are therefore an obstacle to permitting the cultivation of cannabis to supply coffee shops as a matter of policy, or to go even further, to grant permission for it explicitly by issuing licences.

It is interesting that the difference between enforcement that is related to criminal law and enforcement that is not is also expressed in various ways in Dutch law. For example, the Aanwijzing Opiumwet (Instruction regarding the Dutch Opium Act) stipulates, on the one hand, that in certain cases, prosecution will not take place in principle, and, on the other hand, that when it is established that a criminal offence has been committed, the Opium Act requires that all substances found that are mentioned on Schedule I and/or II must be confiscated, if nothing else.[72] In short: here too, there most certainly is an obligation to enforce the law, although that enforcement is not by definition through criminal law. Additionally, it is settled case law of the Dutch Supreme Court that the mere fact that a licence for the exploitation of a coffee shop has been issued by the relevant authorities does not mean that the Public Prosecutions Service loses its independent decision-making powers (that have been bestowed by virtue of Article 167(1) of the Dutch Code of Criminal Procedure) to prosecute persons complying with the conditions of the licence issued to them.[73] This too confirms that the circumstance that a certain form of law enforcement does not take place does not mean that another form of law enforcement may or must also be refrained from.

iii. Is there Extra 'Room for Expediency' because of Public Health Interests?

It has also been argued that the Public Prosecutions Service may refrain from investigation and prosecution on the basis of the so-called expediency principle, if this serves the public interest, namely public health. This argument does not diminish what we have discussed above, for example the obligations that are not related to criminal law in principle, as the expediency principle does not

72 College van procureurs-generaal openbaar ministerie, 'Aanwijzing Opiumwet (2015A003)', *Stcrt.* 2015/5391 (i.e., Board of Procurators General of the Dutch Public Prosecutions Service, 'Instruction regarding the Opium Act (2015A003)', Dutch Government Gazette, 2015/5391), with effect from 1 March 2015.

73 See Piet Hein P.H.M.C. van Kempen, annotation to Supreme Court of the Netherlands 2 July 2013, ECLI:NL:HR:2013:137, *Netherlands Jurisprudence* 2013/563 (*Checkpoint*), referring to Supreme Court of the Netherlands 9 April 2002, ECLI:NL:HR:2002:AD8737, *Netherlands Jurisprudence* 2002/535, annotated by Buruma.

apply to these. Apart from that, the Netherlands could not justify permitting the cultivation of cannabis for the supply of coffee shops for recreational use with this argument. At the heart of this argument lies the assumption – which is correct in itself[74] – that the cultivation of cannabis for recreational use does not fall under the exception of 'medical or scientific purposes'. After all, if that were the case, one would not need to invoke the expediency principle in order to try and create room for permitting cannabis cultivation for recreational use. Therefore, it is important – as discussed before – for which type of acts and within which limits a state can refrain from prosecution for such cannabis cultivation under the conventions on the basis of the expediency principle. The international legal obligation to implement conventions in good faith implies that this principle can only be applied insofar as the authorities have a good reason to use the so-called room for expediency. Interests of public health can possibly be such a reason, as well as all sorts of other public interests for that matter. Considerations of public health can therefore play a part within the room allowed by conventions to apply the expediency principle. However, it does not work the other way round: such considerations cannot create room for expediency not allowed by the conventions. Previously, taking into consideration the reservation made by the Netherlands with respect to Article 3(6) of the Illicit Traffic Convention, we saw that it is difficult to argue that conventions leave room for applying the expediency principle to cannabis cultivation other than for one's own personal consumption. Therefore, there is no room either for such an application on the basis of public health considerations or other public interests.

It is more complicated for the obligation of prosecution which appears to arise from the case law of the Court of Justice of the European Union (CJEU).[75] It is significant in this respect that the CJEU might consider it permissible to refrain from prosecution on account of considerations of public health. European law does provide opportunities for that, as the protection and improvement of public health is one of the spheres of competence of the European Union.[76] But the question is whether the CJEU could be convinced that penal tolerance of the cultivation of cannabis for the market of recreational users would benefit public health. This is far from certain. For example, the preambles of the EU drug instruments and the jurisprudence of the CJEU demonstrate that illicit drug trafficking in cannabis is a threat to the health, safety and the quality of life of the citizens of the Union, and that the very protection of that health requires combating narcotic drugs.[77]

---

74 See sections 4.2.4 and 2.2.3.i.

75 For more information on the obligation, see this section (4.2.5.ii) and particularly section 3.4.1.vii.

76 See Article 6 (a) of the TFEU.

77 See (with additional references) Court of Justice EU, Judgment of 16 December 2010, case C-137/09, ECLI:EU:C:2010:774 (*Josemans*), par. 67 and 68, and also the introduction to section 3.4 and section 3.4.1.vii.

Without so much as a convincing argument based on facts that a policy of non-prosecution for cannabis cultivation for coffee shops is genuinely beneficial to public health, it is hardly conceivable that the CJEU would not uphold the obligations of prosecution that it established itself.

iv. Can Cannabis Cultivation also be Considered Permissible on Account of the Current Coffee Shop Policy in the Netherlands?

Other arguments relate to the current policy of tolerance with regard to cannabis sales by coffee shops to consumers in the Netherlands. It is argued that the inclusion of cannabis in the Schedules of the Single Convention does not form any obstacle to the current policy of tolerance; it is not clear then why extending the policy of tolerance to production and distribution should do just that. Of a similar nature is the argument that if tolerating possession and the selling of cannabis as a matter of policy is possible within the international framework of obligations (and the Dutch government has for years been claiming this), then this would also be true for tolerating cultivation of cannabis. According to the proponents of this view, there are no legal or principal arguments to justify the difference between selling and possession on the one hand and cultivation on the other. It is also observed that the Articles of the Single Convention do not form an insurmountable obstacle to extending the policy of tolerance.

These arguments are based on the following three propositions presented as arguments. 1. The current policy of tolerance with regards to cannabis sales to consumers by coffee shops is not a violation of the UN narcotic drugs conventions and European law; 2. Extending the policy of tolerance with regard to coffee shops to include cannabis cultivation for coffee shops is such a small step that, if the current policy of tolerance is permissible, then such an extension should also be permissible; 3. Policy-based tolerance of cannabis cultivation for coffee shops – whether or not this is influenced by the government policy – in itself is already permissible under the UN narcotic drugs conventions and European law. On the basis of the discussion below of each of these three arguments, we draw the conclusion that these statements will hardly make an impact, if at all. Based on these arguments, it is not possible to achieve the goal of permitting cannabis cultivation for the supply of coffee shops – in the sense of penal and administrative tolerance – in good faith within the framework of the UN narcotic drugs conventions and European law.

- *Re: 1. Current coffee shop policy compliant with UN narcotic drugs conventions and European law?* Regarding the current coffee shop policy of tolerance (that is to say, the selling of cannabis by coffee shops to consumers for recreational use), we came to the conclusion that it is questionable whether the current coffee shop policy can be qualified as implementing the conventions in good faith.[78] The reasons for this are the following:

The selling of cannabis by coffee shops to consumers for recreational use cannot be subsumed under the exception of 'medical and scientific purposes'.[79] This is important, because the conventions aim to eliminate the narcotic drugs subject to those conventions – or at any rate activities involving those drugs such as cannabis cultivation – that are not covered by the exception. This is particularly true for cannabis in the sense that the fight against it together with coca products and poppy products are central to the conventions. The aim of eradication is reflected in the preambles (the use of drugs outside the aforementioned exception is seen as 'abuse' or even an 'evil' that must be fought, 'eradication of illicit traffic' is a joint responsibility of all parties), in the title of the Illicit Traffic Convention ('Against Illicit Traffic in Narcotic Drugs'), in the general obligation to active limitation of the production, distribution, trade, use and possession of cannabis among other things, to exclusively medical and scientific purposes (Article 4 of the Single Convention), in the estimate system, the objective of which is to limit forcefully the availability of narcotic drugs to only those drugs that are necessary for medical and scientific purposes (see Articles 12–21 of the Single Convention), in the obligation to criminalize cultivation that is not small-scale and/or does not relate to personal use (see Articles 36(1) of the Single Convention and Article 3(1) of the Single Convention),[80] in all sorts of obligations of prosecution ensuing from the conventions applicable to cannabis cultivation that is not small-scale and not meant for personal use, and in various obligations that in principle do not pertain to criminal law, such as obligations to prohibit and seize cannabis (Article 33 of the Single Convention and possibly Article 37 of the Single Convention), in the obligation to take measures against cannabis use (Article 38 of the Single Convention) and in the obligation to fight the cultivation of cannabis (Article 14 of the Illicit Traffic Convention).[81]

---

78 See section 2.3.4 under iv. See also David R. Bewley-Taylor & Martin Jelsma, 'The Limits of Latitude. The UN drug control conventions', *Series on Legislative Reform of Drug Policies*, No. 18, March 2012, p. 15. This view is also propounded more emphatically by Hub Hennekens, 'Grenzen aan het opportuniteitsbeginsel. Een verkenning in relatie tot het drugsbeleid', in: Jan W. Fokkens, Piet Hein P.H.M.C. van Kempen, Henny J.B. Sackers & Paul C. Vegter (eds.), *Ad hunc modem. Opstellen over materieel strafrecht* (Machielse-bundel), Deventer: Kluwer, 2013, p. 104 (i.e., Hub Hennekens, 'The limits of the expediency principle. An exploration in connection with the drug policy', in: Jan W. Fokkens, Piet Hein P.H.M.C. van Kempen, Henny J.B. Sackers & Paul C. Vegter (eds.), *Ad hunc modem. Essays on substantive criminal law* (Machielse bundle of essays), Deventer: Kluwer, 2013, p. 104).

79 See sections 4.2.4.ii and 2.2.3.i.

80 It is not relevant for cultivation for 'coffee shops' that there is also an obligation to criminalize small-scale cultivation for personal use (see Article 36(1) of the Single Convention (which is not entirely clear), and the indisputable Article 3(2) of the Illicit Traffic Convention).

81 The content and scope of all these obligations are discussed extensively in Chapter 2.

The conventions aim to achieve this eradication of narcotic drugs for recreational use in the interests of public health and to fight crime. As we will see later, the conventions set out to achieve those objectives through this prohibitive, repressive and consequently also one-sided approach.[82] This means that approaches serving public health or fighting crime in other ways do not fit in with the convention. Indeed, if those other approaches detract from the fulfilment of the prohibitive and repressive obligations in the, they are actually in conflict with it. This also applies to tolerating the cultivation, distribution and selling of cannabis. In addition to this, most of the concrete obligations mentioned also refer to the selling of cannabis, some more emphatically than others, and therefore also play a part in being a legal obstacle to permitting it. There is another argument, namely that the International Narcotics Control Board consistently finds that the current Dutch coffee shop policy violates the UN narcotic drugs conventions. That is hardly surprising in view of the foregoing. With regard to the UN narcotic drugs conventions the conclusion is that it is difficult to defend that the current state of affairs in the Netherlands, where the selling of cannabis to consumers by coffee shops on a serious scale and as general policy is tolerated, is permissible under these conventions. This applies *a fortiori* to permitting cannabis cultivation.

From the point of view of European law, it is particularly relevant that given the text, purpose and scope of the Framework Decision Illicit Drug Trafficking, the EU member states are obliged to criminalize activities – including cannabis cultivation – that are not exclusively aimed at personal consumption and must counteract these activities with effective, proportionate and dissuasive sanctions.[83] That obligation includes without any doubt the sale of cannabis by coffee shops, witness the case law of the CJEU.[84] According to the Explanatory Memorandum to the Dutch Implementation Act for the Framework Decision as well as the EU report on the deliberations about the proposal for the Framework Decision, the Framework Decision has no impact on the Dutch coffee shop policy. It is unclear what this finding is based on. It cannot be the exception for acts that are exclusively intended for one's own personal consumption (Article 2(2) of the Framework Decision). After all, sales by coffee shops can hardly be regarded as such.[85] However, in the

82 See also section 2.6.

83 See also Article 8 of the Joint Action, which requires states to take the most appropriate steps to combat the cultivation of cannabis (see section 3.3.1.i for more about this), while more implicitly that obligation also follows from Article 71(5) of the Schengen Implementation Agreement (see section 3.2.2. ii).

84 See for example Court of Justice EU, Judgment of 16 December 2010, case C-137/09, ECLI:EU:C:2010:774 (*Josemans*), par. 31, 41–42.

85 This also follows from Court of Justice EU, Judgment of 16 December 2010, case C-137/09, ECLI:EU:C:2010:774 (*Josemans*), par. 39 and 42.

above-mentioned Explanatory Memorandum, the government also observes that the Framework Decision only invokes obligations of legislation, not enforcement, so that there is no obligation of prosecution for selling cannabis in coffee shops. This position is not unassailable.[86] Even if the Framework Decision does not imply obligations of prosecution with regard to the criminalizations it prescribes, such obligations appear to apply according to the case law of the CJEU. This raises the question whether the Netherlands is also bound under current European law to prosecute the selling of cannabis in coffee shops if it involves substantial amounts. Much will depend on the stance taken by the CJEU (for example in infringement proceedings[87] initiated by the Commission or another country). The deciding factor can be the extent to which the Court lends weight to the negotiations preceding the Framework Decision, which show that the Netherlands managed to safeguard its coffee shop policy in relation to the other EU member states. Another consideration will be whether the CJEU wishes to give priority to the text of the Framework Decision and its own case law or to this political negotiation reservation.

We must also point out that the notion that the Framework Decision Illicit Drug Trafficking has no bearing on the regulation of cannabis cultivation, because this Framework Decision only applies to drug trafficking for profit and without a licence, is seriously flawed. This notion is based on an incorrect reading of the Framework Decision. As we observed before, the Framework Decision requires the EU member states to criminalize, among other things, the intentional cultivation of cannabis which is not intended for personal use but for recreational purposes (in other words not intended for medical or scientific purposes), using effective, proportionate and dissuasive sanctions. Trading in cannabis *for profit* is not a condition for the criminalizations required by the Framework Decision, and is not mentioned anywhere in it at all.[88] Where small-scale cultivation of cannabis exclusively for one's own personal use falls outside the scope of this obligation (see Article 2(2) of the Framework Decision) and the small-scale (be it commercial or not) sale of cannabis to third parties can be subsumed under the expediency principle (as in the case of

86 See for more information section 3.4.1. vi.

87 See articles 258–260 of the TFEU.

88 It is interesting that the Proposal for a Framework Decision by the Commission contained a definition of 'illicit drug trafficking', which read as follows: the act *without authorisation*, of selling and marketing *as well as*, *for profit*, of cultivating, producing, manufacturing, importing, exporting, distributing, offering, transporting or sending or, for the purpose of transferring *for profit*, of receiving, acquiring and possessing drugs.' (emphasis added); see Proposal Framework Decision Illicit Drug Trafficking, Brussels: Commission of the European Communities, 23 May 2001, COM(2001) 259, 2001/0114 (CNS), p. 15, or Proposal Framework Decision Illicit Drug Trafficking, *OJ* 2001 C 304 E/172 (Article 1(1)). As the final Framework Decision shows, this definition, which would have limited the scope of the Framework Decision, did not make it into the final version.

'small-time' dealers), none of this applies to the cannabis cultivation which is not small-scale and intended to supply coffee shops. Even if that cultivation is non-commercial in nature, it is covered by the obligation of criminalization, and the room for expediency will be more limited, the more serious that production of cannabis through that cultivation is. Relevant considerations in this respect can be whether cultivation is of a commercial nature and whether it takes place in an organized structure. However, there are no indications that these criteria are decisive, not in the Framework Decision itself, nor in the case law of the CJEU regarding obligations of prosecution. On the contrary, as the Framework Decision only excludes acts aimed at personal use from the obligation of criminalization (Article 2(2) of the Framework Decision). In addition to this, the Joint Action on Illegal Drug Trafficking (explicitly, see Article 8 of the Joint Action) and the Schengen Implementation Agreement (more implicitly, see Article 71(5) of the Schengen Implementation Agreement) requires parties to take appropriate measures to fight cannabis cultivation. Only if the cultivation is carried out for medical and scientific purposes, and this is done with a 'licence' from the government, is it legally possible to permit cultivation under the obligations arising from international law, including European law. Since the cultivation of cannabis for recreational use cannot be subsumed under the scope of this exception in good faith, there can be no 'licence' from the government for such cultivation.

- *Re: 2. Is an extension of the policy of tolerance to cover cannabis cultivation merely a difference of degree?* There is the argument that extending the current policy of tolerance with regard to coffee shops to include cannabis cultivation for coffee shops is such a small step that, if the current policy of tolerance is permissible, then such an extension should also be allowable. This argument fails since – as we have explained earlier – it cannot be argued that the policy of tolerating coffee shops is permissible. However, even if that were the case, it seems to be difficult to maintain that extending the policy to organized cannabis cultivation is only a small step, because there are no legal or principal arguments that justify the difference between selling and possessing cannabis on the one hand and cultivation on the other.

  The idea that such a difference does not exist, is incorrect in the sense that there are various provisions that intend to limit the production of drugs, while such provisions less explicitly exist (if at all) regarding selling. The clearest of these provisions is Article 14(2) of the Illicit Traffic Convention, which constitutes an obligation to take measures against cannabis cultivation. Additionally, one can point out the provisions about the national government agency (Article 28 in conjunction with Article 23 of the Single Convention), which emphatically aim to control cultivation for medical or scientific purposes and limit this to what is necessary. Then there is Article 28 of the Single Convention about the introduction of a near total prohibition (which even covers cultivation for medical purposes) if this is deemed to be necessary. Article 3(1) of the Illicit Traffic Convention – preamble and (a) under ii – must also be mentioned: it specifically requires the criminalization of cultivation of the 'cannabis plant', whereas such an explicit provision does not exist for the sale of cannabis (the obligation to criminalize this follows from Article 36(1) of the Single Convention and Article 3(1) of the Illicit Traffic Convention – preamble and (a) under ii – in combination with the inclusion of cannabis in the Schedules).

What is more important, though, is that it is hard to argue that an extension of the policy of tolerance to include cannabis cultivation would not constitute an essential change but only a gradual one. To begin tolerating cannabis cultivation for the sake of coffee shops fundamentally implies not only tolerating that cultivation itself, but also the (whole) sale and distribution of it. We have repeatedly observed that this would mean that an entire domestic cannabis economy would be tolerated in the Netherlands, from cultivation to selling, aimed at recreational use. This tolerance would also include cultivation, trade, distribution and selling on a serious scale. It also means that the Netherlands would all of a sudden directly tolerate the creation of new quantities of cannabis, whereas the current policy only implies that the selling of existing drugs is tolerated. Of course, tolerating such sales would actually also generate the production of drugs, but even so, there is not just a principal difference. After all, at present, there is an all-out fight against cannabis cultivation. If the policy of tolerance were extended to include cannabis cultivation, that fight would at any rate be discontinued for a part of the cannabis production.

Once again, the publication of Bewley-Taylor & Jelsma merits our attention. We have already noted that in spite of the Dutch reservation they question whether the current coffee shop policy can be qualified as implementing the conventions in good faith.[89] They also note, however, that if the current policy of tolerance with regard to coffee shops can be based on the expediency principle, it would be difficult to find a reason why the same discretion could not be applied to cannabis cultivation for the supply of coffee shops under certain conditions as well. 'It would mean stretching the art of interpretation a little further but within the same limits.' It is not clear how this argument can legitimize tolerating cannabis cultivation on legal grounds. The key point, after all, which they themselves make, remains that the current policy of tolerating coffee shops is problematic given the conventions. Apart from that, as we have explained just now, it is difficult to maintain that an extension of the policy of tolerance to include cannabis cultivation is not an essential change but merely makes a gradual difference.

89 David R. Bewley-Taylor & Martin Jelsma, 'The Limits of Latitude. The UN drug control conventions', *Series on Legislative Reform of Drug Policies*, No. 18, March 2012, p. 15.

Finally, as discussed in the previous section 4.2.5.ii. (Re: 4), the fact remains that any room to apply the expediency principle to cannabis cultivation for recreational use, only implies that the Public Prosecutions Service has the authority to refrain from criminal prosecution for that cultivation. It does not diminish the various relevant obligations that in principle do not pertain to criminal law ensuing from the conventions (see in particular Article 4 of the Single Convention, Article 33 of the Single Convention, Article 37 of the Single Convention, Article 38 of the Single Convention and Article 14 of the Illicit Traffic Convention). Moreover, all those obligations apply to cultivation for personal use and to any other cultivation for recreational use.

Finally, a few comments about European law. We have seen before[90] that it is questionable that the Netherlands would not be bound by current European law to prosecute for the sale of cannabis in coffee shops under criminal law if the quantities involved were significant, given the case law of the CJEU. If that is the case, then as we have observed before, it will depend on the extent to which the Court might be prepared to lend weight to the fact that the Netherlands managed to safeguard its coffee shop policy in relation to the other EU member states in the negotiations on the Framework Decision. The possibility of tolerating cannabis cultivation for recreational use by third parties never played a part in those negotiations. In view of the fact that the current coffee shop policy is problematic already given the jurisprudence of the CJEU, there is little reason to assume that the Court would want to exclude commercial, large-scale and/or export oriented cannabis cultivation from the obligation of prosecution, if the Court applies those obligations to the Framework Decision.

- *Re: 3. Regulation of cannabis cultivation already possible now under the UN narcotic drugs conventions and European law?* It follows from the foregoing that the argument that tolerating cannabis cultivation for coffee shops is permissible in itself under the UN narcotic drugs conventions and European law unravels under close scrutiny. The fact that the government in the Netherlands leaves the municipalities room to customize local coffee shop and safety policies does not change that.

  First, this does not imply that the government also intends to tolerate cannabis cultivation. Even if that were the case, though, national government policy cannot derogate from the obligations arising from the conventions and European law, which the Netherlands has assumed. Incidentally, it must be mentioned here that the Commission on Narcotic Drugs (CND) – in which the Netherlands has a seat – has in several Resolutions urged member states to take measures against illicit cultivation of cannabis plants.[91] In that respect,

---

90 See under Re: 1.

91 See for more information on this section 2.4.i.

the 'Political Declaration and Plan of Action on International Cooperation towards an Integrated and Balanced Strategy to counter the World Drug Problem', which was adopted by the CND in 2009[92] and later that year also by the General Assembly of the United Nations, is of importance.[93] The General Assembly calls for the parties to take measures that are necessary for a full implementation of the actions agreed.[94] The 'Political Declaration' entails among other things: 'We, the States Members of the United Nations, [...] 36. Decide to establish 2019 as a target date for States to eliminate or reduce significantly and measurably: (a) The illicit cultivation of opium poppy, coca bush and cannabis plant [...].'[95] That commitment was reaffirmed in the Outcome document of the Special Session of the General Assembly 2016 (UNGASS 2016) called 'Our joint commitment to effectively addressing and countering the world drug problem'.[96]

4.2.6. PROVISIONS IN THE CONVENTIONS TO PROTECT NATIONAL LAW AND POLICY

There is also the question whether provisions in the Single Convention and the Illicit Traffic Convention that protect national law – so-called 'safeguard clauses' – also create room for a state's own legislation or policy on cannabis cultivation for recreational use.

We fail to see how the conventions offer any room or basis for that assertion. One must realize first and foremost – contrary to what seems to be assumed sometimes – that Article 36(4) of the Single Convention and Article 3(11) of the Illicit Traffic Convention are not relevant in this respect. These provisions imply the need to transpose and implement the law of the Convention to national law and seek to ensure that none of the provisions in the Convention is

---

92 CND, Report on the fifty-second session (14 March 2008 and 11–20 March 2009), *UN Doc.* E/2009/28, E/CN.7/2009/12, p. 5 (para. 3). The 'Political Declaration and Plan of Action' were adopted on 12 March 2009 by the ministers and government representatives in the CND; see p. 119, para. 154. For a more recent confirmation, see CND Resolution 56/10, *UN Doc.* E/2013/28, E/CN.7/2013/14, p. 38 on p. 39.

93 UN General Assembly Resolution 64/182, 'International cooperation against the world drug problem', adopted 65th plenary meeting on 18 December 2009, *UN Doc.* A/RES /64/182, 30 March 2010.

94 Ibid, p. 2, para. 1.

95 *UN Doc.* E/2009/28, E/CN.7/2009/12, pp. 37 and 44.

96 CND Resolution 59/1, adopted by the General Assembly on 19 April 2016 at the thirtieth special session, 'Our joint commitment to effectively addressing and countering the world drug problem', A/RES/A-30/1, 4 May 2016, p. 9 (d) ('Increase cooperation at all levels and enhance measures to prevent and significantly and measurably reduce or eliminate the illicit cultivation of opium poppy, coca bush and cannabis plant used for the production of narcotic drugs and psychotropic substances, including through eradication, within the framework of sustainable crop control strategies and measures; ...').

self-executing in countries where the constitution provides for the direct operation of international law. These Articles do not create an additional clause to offer parties room for their own laws or policies. They only constitute an obligation of transposition.[97] Article 2(1) of the Illicit Traffic Convention is not relevant either: it follows from the drafting history, the system of the convention and the wording of the clause in this provision that its aim is not to give the parties additional freedom of policy in implementing and fulfilling their obligations arising from the conventions.[98]

What is relevant is that the obligation of criminalization in Article 36(1) of the Single Convention is subject to the 'constitutional limitations' of each state party. This really refers to constitutions. This follows not only from the linguistic meaning of these concepts, but also from the analyses in the UN Commentary.[99] It is also evident from the system of the Convention, as it distinguishes between Constitutional law ('constitutional limitations') and ordinary law ('legal system and domestic law'), as we will discuss in a short while. It is hard to see why the current Dutch constitution should presently be an obstacle to the criminalization of cannabis cultivation among other things. We have not been able to find any literature containing the arguments that, and why this is (possibly) the case either. It is also important that the obligations in Article 36(2) of the Single Convention (such as the obligation to criminalize participation and attempt, and obligations regarding the proper administration of justice in international law) are subject to the 'legal system and domestic law' of the state as well as 'constitutional limitations'. The second paragraph of Article 36 of the Single Convention, however, is not directly relevant with regard to fighting cannabis cultivation. Apart from that, this clause does not derogate from the obligations as such, but it implies among other things that states are not beholden to adapt their domestic law concepts to the terminology of the Convention.[100]

A similar situation applies to the Illicit Traffic Convention. Admittedly, the obligation of criminalization of cannabis cultivation among other things in Article 3(1)(a) and (b) of the Illicit Traffic Convention is not explicitly subject to a 'constitutional' clause, but it can be argued that it also applies to the provision because and to the extent that part of this provision refers explicitly to the Single Convention. However, even in that case it is hard to assert that the current Dutch constitution presently forms an obstacle to the criminalization of cannabis cultivation among other things. Additionally, the

---

97 See section 2.2.2.ii.a.VII for more information (Article 36(4) of the Single Convention) and section 2.3.2.i.a.V (Article 3(11) of the Illicit Traffic Convention).

98 See section 2.3.2.i.a.VI for more information.

99 United Nations, *Commentary on the Single Convention on Narcotic Drugs, 1961*, New York: 1973, p. 429 (nos. 11–13).

100 See section 2.2.2.ii.a.VI for more information.

obligations in Article 3(1)(c) of the Illicit Traffic Convention (obligations to criminalize, among other things, participation, attempts and possession of property, equipment or materials or substances for cultivation among other things) are subject to its 'constitutional principles and the basic concepts of its legal system'. As demonstrated in Chapter 2, the point is that the parties can implement this obligation within the structure of their own system and it does not offer any justification for refraining from criminalization altogether.[101] The same 'safeguard clause' occurs in Article 3(2) of the Illicit Traffic Convention (obligation to criminalize intentional possession, purchase or cultivation of cannabis for personal consumption). Seeing that it is difficult to defend that criminalization of intentional cannabis cultivation for personal use runs counter to the 'constitutional principles and the basic concepts' of the legal system in the Netherlands, this clause too offers no room to decriminalize or legalize personal possession, purchase by consumers, (for example in a coffee shop) and personal cultivation of cannabis. The question whether the clause allows the application of the expediency principle to such offences of 'personal use' is more complicated. While it is true that this principle can be considered a 'basic concept' of the Dutch system of criminal procedure, prosecution for these offences in itself does not conflict with this principle, since the expediency principle is essentially a discretionary power and not an obligation to refrain from prosecution. Therefore, the obligation of prosecution must be fulfilled under the regime of the expediency principle as well. This discussion is not very important for the Netherlands, as the application of the expediency principle to offences in the category of 'personal use' is already a possibility under the reservation for the Single Convention.[102] As noted before, this is however not relevant for cannabis cultivation for the supply of coffee shops, because such cultivation is evidently subject to the first paragraph of Article 3 of the Illicit Traffic Convention and not to the second paragraph (whether this cultivation in the context of Cannabis Social Clubs and/or shared consumption is a different scenario, will be explored in section 4.4.2).

To conclude, a few comments about the obligations ensuing from Article 4 of the Single Convention and Article 14(2) of the Illicit Traffic Convention to take the necessary or appropriate measures respectively to combat cannabis cultivation for recreational use. It is true that these provisions do not contain 'safeguard clauses', but because these provisions are not very specific in how these obligations should be fulfilled, the states parties have considerable discretion for their own individual approach. However, it would be squarely at odds with these obligations to fight cannabis cultivation if cannabis cultivation for recreational use was legalized or permitted in any other way.

---

101 See section 2.3.2.i.a.I.

102 See section 4.2.5.ii.

4.2.7. INTERMEDIATE CONCLUSION

The foregoing and also Chapter 2 show that the UN narcotic drugs conventions and the EU laws on drugs contain many obstacles to permitting through legalization, decriminalization, policy-based tolerance and other regulation of cannabis cultivation intended for recreational use. Even if one managed to remove one of those obstacles, for which there are some possibilities with regard to cannabis cultivation for personal use, then there still remain several other legal obstacles with respect to permitting cannabis cultivation. Insofar as it does not concern cannabis cultivation for one's own personal use, all the legal obstacles discussed apply. At the same time, none of the 'safeguard clauses' in the UN narcotic drugs conventions detract from those obligations. This means that permitting cannabis cultivation so as to supply retail shops cannot be realized on the basis of any of the arguments put forward, for example by the Dutch municipalities, without violating the UN narcotic drugs conventions and European law. Whether that cannabis cultivation takes place for the sake of relatively private (closed) and/or small-scale retail shops is not a significant difference. After all, all obligations remain applicable to these retail shops too, because it does not involve cultivation for personal use (the question whether there is room for another conclusion in the event of such personal use will be explored in section 4.4.2.ii in relation to Cannabis Social Clubs and/or shared consumption).

4.3. FACTUAL, SOCIAL AND/OR POLITICAL ARGUMENTS

In addition to the above-mentioned legal arguments, a wide range of factual, social and/or political arguments is presented in the Netherlands and other countries. Most of these arguments reflect the numerous problems that local authorities face in connection with the cultivation, distribution, trade, selling, purchase and use of cannabis. It is particularly because of those problems that many municipalities in the Netherlands emphasize that there is an urgent need for regulated permission of cannabis cultivation. It is argued that the highly repressive approach towards cannabis growers over the past few years has led to a dramatic deterioration of the entire coffee shop scene, while cannabis use is alleged to be on the rise.

The following is an overview by topic of factual, social and/or political arguments and presents a detailed picture of the problems experienced in, for example, the municipalities in the Netherlands. Fundamentally, the purpose is to discuss these arguments in the light of the relevant the UN narcotic drugs conventions and the EU laws on drugs. As we explained in Chapter 1, the discussion in this book is as strictly legal as possible. This means that we are not going to assess the arguments of a factual, social and/or political nature which are presented by municipalities and put forward in literature on the accuracy of their content or their validity. We assume that these arguments are sound and on that premise we evaluate whether they could justify the regulation of cannabis cultivation under the UN narcotic drugs conventions and European laws on drugs.

4.3.1. IMPROVING PUBLIC HEALTH BY REGULATING CANNABIS CULTIVATION

An important type of argument put forward to justify regulating cannabis cultivation for personal use concerns the promotion of public health. This argument asserts first of all that through regulation the government creates an opportunity to control the production of cannabis and to improve its quality. It is argued that this benefits the health of the consumer, the producer and stakeholders. For example, in the Netherlands, cannabis growers feel a constant pressure because of the possibility of a police raid, so they feel they have to harvest rather sooner than later. This may result in drugs of poorer quality. Another point is that illegal hemp nurseries are currently often located in residential areas and consequently cause dangerous situations. The unsafe wiring of the electrical installations and the theft of power increase the risk of fire. In addition to this, there is a direct risk of seriously harmful infections, like Legionella infection, for local residents as a result of the high humidity in combination with high temperatures.

Municipalities in the Netherlands thus not only maintain that regulation would put an end to unhealthy and unsafe situations, they also argue that with regulation, clear requirements can be laid down for the entire process of cannabis cultivation. Requirements could relate to fire risks, the technical installations, the packaging of cannabis, the security of the nursery, the quantity and quality of the pesticides, the THC content, the THC/CBD ratio, the HSE requirements for employees, the integrity of the entrepreneur and education for users. A system of regulated cultivation would also mean that the above-mentioned requirements can be checked. Also, the prohibition on use by youths could be better maintained in such a system. It is noted that there are hardly any risks for public health if cannabis cultivation is regulated; an increase of consumption by regulating supply does not seem likely.

Another argument mentioned with regard to public health is that regulating cannabis cultivation contributes to a clear differentiation between soft drugs and hard drugs. After all, if the entire cannabis chains regulated, hard drugs will not be available any more from sellers or growers of soft drugs. The idea is that a soft drug user as a consequence of regulation is less likely to slide down the slippery slope towards hard drugs. This argument is also at the heart of the current soft drugs policy in the Netherlands. That is why Dutch municipalities find it remarkable that the government does not extend this logic to the cultivation of soft drugs.

And finally, regulating cannabis would contribute to the individual freedom of choice regarding intoxication. According to some, cannabis is significantly less risky than legal substances such as alcohol and tobacco.

Aspects of public health are more prominent in the Single Convention than in the Illicit Traffic Convention. From a distant perspective, the above arguments seem to be compatible with the conventions. However, from a legal point of view we must check if these arguments hold up under scrutiny. It is important to recognize that the drugs conventions seek to protect public health only in a limited way and partly with a one-sided and rigid approach.

As became clear earlier,[103] the UN narcotic drugs conventions aim to serve public health interests in the following three areas: 1. To guarantee the availability of narcotic substances as useful and/or effective medicine or research into this;[104] 2. To concentrate on treatment and care for drug users to help them wean themselves off drugs; 3. To protect society against narcotic drugs by fighting and eliminating the production, trade, possession and use of these drugs for recreational purposes using criminal law and many other kinds of prohibitions and measures. With regard to the latter point, it is important that nowhere under the conventions is the interest of general public health recognized as a ground to circumvent or alleviate the repression of narcotic drugs required by the conventions, whereas conversely that same interest can very well necessitate an even more forceful repression of narcotic drugs than is already required by default. This latter point is emphatically made in Article 22 of the Single Convention:[105] this provision contains the requirement to prohibit cultivation of plants yielding drugs that in itself is permitted (i.e., for medical or scientific purposes) if that is necessary 'for protecting the public health and welfare and preventing the diversion of drugs into the illicit traffic'.[106]

This unilateral and rigid prohibitive approach of the protection of public health means that even if states have well-founded views regarding

103 See section 2.6. See also sections 4.2.4 and 2.2.3.i above.

104 Incidentally, it must be noted that the 1971 Convention on Psychotropic Substances explicitly states the requirement of 'usefulness of the substance in medical therapy' if the question is whether narcotic drugs must be included in the international control system (which aims to guarantee the availability for medical and scientific purposes and to fight all other uses); see Article 2(4).

105 See for more information about this section 2.2.2.ii.c.I.

106 A similar obligation also applies to narcotic drugs on Schedule IV – such as cannabis – by virtue of Article 2(5)(b) of the Single Convention. See section 2.6 for more information.

public health policy, this will still prove futile under the conventions. Even if the arguments are factually correct, they will not be valid legally to permit cultivation of cannabis for recreational use – whether or not it is limited and/or subject to conditions – for supplying points-of-sale. The numerous obligations to eradicate cannabis for recreational use are obstacles in the way. In short, and for good measure, once again, it is particularly the general obligation to pursue actively the limitation of the production, distribution, trade, use and possession of cannabis as well to medical and scientific purposes (Article 4 of the Single Convention), from the obligation to criminalize cultivation that is not small-scale and/or does not relate to personal use (see Articles 36(1) of the Single Convention and Article 3(1) of the Illicit Traffic Convention),[107] all sorts of obligations of prosecution ensuing from the conventions applied to cannabis cultivation that is not small-scale and not meant for personal use, and various obligations that in principle do not pertain to criminal law, such as obligations to prohibit and seize cannabis (Article 33 of the Single Convention and possibly Article 37 of the Single Convention), the obligation to take measures against cannabis use (Article 38 of the Single Convention) and the obligation to fight the cultivation of cannabis (Article 14 of the Illicit Traffic Convention).[108]

The INCB firmly affirms the conventions' position.[109] Repeatedly the INCB emphasized that regulating the use of cannabis for recreational (as non-medical/scientific) use contravenes the UN drugs system:

> We note with concern [...] proposals [...] that would allow the cultivation and consumption of cannabis for non-medical purposes. [...] Proponents of such initiatives ignore the commitment that all Governments have made to promote the health and well-being of their communities, and such initiatives run counter to the growing body of scientific evidence documenting the harm associated with drug abuse, including occasional use, particularly among young people during their formative years. Furthermore, such initiatives would create a false sense of security and would send a false message to the public, in particular children, regarding the health impact of abuse of drugs.[110]

---

107 It is not relevant for cultivation for retail shops that there is also an obligation to criminalize small-scale cultivation for personal use (see Article 36(1) of the Single Convention (which is not entirely clear), and the indisputable Article 3(2) of the Illicit Traffic Convention).

108 The content and scope of all these obligations are discussed extensively in Chapter 2.

109 See for more information section 2.4.i, which also features a long quotation from the INCB, of which the following is a part.

110 INCB Report 2012, pp. v–vi. See also e.g. INCB Report 2016, pp. iii, 42–43 (nos. 319–326, 323: 'The Board wishes to remind all States that, in recognition of the public health risks associated with its abuse, cannabis has been subjected to the highest levels of control under the international drug control treaties through its inclusion in Schedules I and IV of the 1961 Convention.').

The INCB is of the opinion that public health is best served by fighting drug abuse. To tolerate cannabis cultivation for recreational use as a means to achieve this end is something that this body sees no possibilities for.[111]

The conclusion therefore is that under the UN narcotic drugs conventions, the above presented considerations of public health cannot lead to a justification of tolerating cannabis cultivation for recreational use to supply retail shops or other points of sale, whether or not that cultivation is limited and/or subject to conditions. Can the European laws on drugs make any difference in this respect? There is a little more nuance in European law. It cannot be ruled out that the Court of Justice of the European Union will leave the Dutch authorities more room for expediency if they are able to make a convincing case supported by facts that a policy of non-prosecution of cannabis cultivation for coffee shops is genuinely beneficial to public health. That is a heavy burden of proof. However, it is not plausible that the Court would settle for anything less, because, as we have seen above, European law is based on the premise that the illicit trafficking of cannabis constitutes a threat to health and that the protection of that health actually requires combating narcotic drugs.[112]

Finally, we observe that it is argued in the literature that the one-sided and rigid approach manifested in the conventions actually results in a less than optimal protection of public health around drugs use than is desirable. For example, Room & Reuter posit: 'The adoption of national policies that are more aligned with the risks of different drugs and the effectiveness of controls will require the amendment of existing treaties, the formulation of new treaties, or withdrawal of states from existing treaties and re-accession with reservations.'[113] This underlines the above conclusions once more, from a different angle. By the way, with regard to the latter observation (denunciation of the conventions and re-accession with a newly worded reservation), it has been explained above that states parties and any rate the Netherlands, will still find it hard to escape from the obligations arising from the conventions if they go down this road.[114]

4.3.2. FIGHTING ORGANIZED CRIME BY REGULATING CANNABIS CULTIVATION

It is claimed that more and more money circulating in the criminal circuit is earned from cannabis cultivation and that regulating cannabis cultivation will

111 See for more information section 2.4.

112 See section 4.2.5 under iii.

113 Robin Room & Peter Reuter, 'How well do international drug conventions protect public health?', 379 *The Lancet* 2012 (January 7), pp. 84–91 on pp. 84 and 89.

114 See section 4.2.3 and also section 4.2.5.

reduce crime. By regulating cultivation it will be taken out of the illegal sector. For the Netherlands it would mean that this market will become less attractive to organized crime as coffee shop owners will no longer have any reason to be dealing with criminals. Because the tax authorities can check regulated buying and selling of cannabis, the cannabis market will also be less interesting for criminal networks. The export of soft drugs will consequently decrease, it is argued. The export of soft drugs will also decrease by matching demand (by retail shops) with supply (by growers), so no produce will be left over (closed system). Since retail shops can better manage the quality, continuity and diversity of the supply-side if cannabis cultivation is regulated, they can prevent their customers from going underground. It is also argued that regulation will also lead to a reduction of indirect crime such as the theft of electrical power, corruption, money laundering, criminal involvement of sectors such as real estate, the violent settling of scores between drug gangs and the use of drug money for illicit arms trafficking. The problem of bribery and intimidation is relevant too: socially disadvantaged citizens in deprived neighbourhoods are roped in by criminals for the production of soft drugs, as a result of which entire areas are in the grip of organized crime.

The Illicit Traffic Convention in particular aims to combat drug-related crime, particularly organized crime. The Preamble to this Convention mentions various threats from such crime that also come to the fore in the above arguments. For example, the Preamble states that the 'magnitude of and rising trend' of the illicit traffic 'pose a serious threat to the health and welfare of human beings and adversely affect the economic, cultural and political foundations of society'. It is also considered, among other things, that this illicit traffic succeeds in making 'steadily increasing inroads into various social groups', that the 'links between illicit traffic and other related organized criminal activities [...] undermine the legitimate economies and threaten the stability, security and sovereignty of States,' and that illicit traffic is 'an international criminal activity'.

So far, the rationale of the Illicit Traffic Convention seems to closely match the considerations pro regulation of cannabis cultivation. However, in respect of the way in which the proponents of regulation on the one hand and the UN narcotic drugs conventions on the other hand intend to prevent and fight this (organized) crime, they choose diametrically opposed approaches. The proponents advocate – mostly subject to conditions and with limitations – that cannabis cultivation for the supply of retail shops be permitted. The conventions on the other hand impose a prohibitive and repressive system with obligations for the states parties which, among other things, aim to eradicate the cultivation of cannabis for recreational use completely. Within this one-sided and rigid approach, there is no room for permitting cannabis cultivation with the exception of medical and scientific purposes, simply because any tolerance of such cultivation runs counter to the wide range of obligations under the UN narcotic drugs conventions, which have been discussed above and in Chapter 2 and which have been summarized in the preceding subsection.

As the official supervisory body for the UN narcotic drugs conventions, the International Narcotics Control Board makes it clear it believes that the approach manifested in the conventions is the right one. The INCB also touches upon the arguments that are in fact used by the proponents:[115]

> Some have argued that these proposals would eliminate the illicit markets and organized crime associated with drugs of abuse. Yet, even if such initiatives were implemented, organized criminal groups would get even more deeply involved, for instance by creating a black market for the illicit supply of newly legalized drugs to young people. To target the organized crime and violence associated with the illicit trade in drugs, the most effective tool is primary prevention of drug abuse, coupled with treatment and rehabilitation, and complemented by supply reduction measures, as provided for in the conventions.[116]

What it boils down to is that the INCB is of the opinion that permitting cannabis cultivation will mean that organized crime that is currently responsible for the cultivation will create new criminal markets. It could involve a shift to more serious crime. In addition, the Board warns states for cross-border criminal activity and the spill-over effect that legalization may have in neighbouring states. As far as the Board is concerned, the remedy is therefore: the prevention of drug abuse combined with combating drug production.

It is clear, also if one did not take the views of the INCB into consideration, that from a legal point of view that the above arguments to combat crime cannot, with due regard for international law, create room for tolerating cannabis cultivation for recreational use to supply retail shops, whether or not such cultivation is limited and/or subject to conditions. Nonetheless, it is worth mentioning that the EU laws on drugs confirm and endorse the premises with regard to combating drug traffic as they are expressed in the United Nations framework. As observed, the starting point is that illicit drug traffic is a repugnant offence that constitutes a threat to the safety of EU citizens, among

---

[115] See for more information section 2.4.i, which also features a long quotation from the INCB, of which the following is a part.

[116] INCB Report 2012, pp. v–vi. See more recently INCB Report 2016, p. 42 (no. 325) ('One of the central arguments advanced by proponents of the legalization of the use of cannabis for non-medical purposes is that the creation of a regulated licit market for cannabis intended for non-medical use would contribute to reducing drug trafficking by criminal networks. That argument fails to take into account the spill-over effect that legalization may have in neighboring jurisdictions where the use of cannabis for non-medical purposes remains illegal. Countries where legislative measures to permit and regulate the non-medical use of cannabis have been adopted or are being considered should also be aware of the risk that they will be targeted by criminal networks seeking to use them as transit countries for trafficking to other jurisdictions where the non-medical use of cannabis is not permitted.').

other things.[117] The EU drug instruments are strongly based on this position and from this perspective they encourage states to harmonize penalty provisions and aim to reinforce cooperation in the area of criminal law so as to combat the illicit traffic in narcotic drugs. European law therefore chooses the same approach as that of the Illicit Traffic Convention in particular.

4.3.3. OTHER INTERESTS IN REGULATING CANNABIS CULTIVATION

The arguments relating to the protection of public health and the fight against (organized) crime discussed above appeared to tie in the most with the rationale of this international and European law when looking at the UN narcotic drugs conventions and the EU laws on drugs from a distant perspective. This is less the case for many other factual, social and political arguments, which will now be presented one by one per category and then discussed jointly.

i. Reduction in Nuisance and Damage

Apart from the nuisance caused by crime and endangering public health, illegal hemp cultivation also causes other forms of nuisance. Because illegal cultivation sites are poorly set up, they lead to stench, noise, and flooding. Then there is also the illegal dumping of cultivation-related waste. All these problems would be reduced by regulating cannabis cultivation. Municipalities in the Netherlands point out that the current policy of tolerance is partly based on the attempt to reduce nuisance. This policy has proved successful. The various problems could be tackled even more efficiently, though, if the cultivation of cannabis were also regulated. It is also argued that regulation will also reduce a number of recurring costs, such as irrecoverable damage to rented property and losses to energy companies, which are now recovered by higher charges for all energy users.

ii. Taxation and Other Economic Advantages

Regulating cannabis cultivation also has economic advantages, it is argued. The entire cannabis retail sector (EU wide) can be taxed. Regulation also boosts employment (for low-skilled workers) and generates tax revenue and social security contributions. Furthermore, regulation will lead to a significant

[117] See Declaration for entry in the Council minutes, in: Annex to Council of the European Union, Adoption of the Council Framework Decision illicit drug trafficking, Brussels: 28 September 2004, 2001/0114 (CNS), 12451/04, DROIPEN 47, CORDROGUE 63, quoted in the introduction to section 3.4.

reduction in the workload for the police and the judiciary. After all, the nuisance caused by illegal cultivation sites will decrease and the investigative capacity will no longer be taken up by easy targets (the small scale grower). Finally, regulation would promote a stable market: retail shop owners could offer various types of weed at competitive prices without having to worry about business continuity, because they can get their products delivered in time and in sufficient quantities.

iii. Administrative Control

It is argued that other advantages would result from a regulated and therefore controllable cultivation of cannabis. A tighter control at points-of-sale of cannabis for example, where violations of cultivation agreements could be sanctioned by an administrative measure. Regulation could also increase the authority of the administration: the contradictory soft drugs policy in the Netherlands – the regulated sale of cannabis on the one hand and the illegal supply and cultivation on the other hand – affects the credibility of the local government. Finally, from the point of view of administration, it is also undesirable that the lack of regulation causes uncertainty for both coffee shop owners and the government.

iv. The User and the Coffee Shop Owner

Other advantages of the regulation of cannabis cultivation mentioned by municipalities in the Netherlands are a reduction of the stigma attached to the user, the interest of the cannabis user in not supporting criminal networks and realising ideological objectives, such as increasing the freedom of choice of the citizen. As far as coffee shop owners are concerned, it is pointed out that illegal cultivation of cannabis forces them to do business with criminals. Additionally, the lack of regulation of cannabis cultivation also causes uncertainty among coffee shop owners.

v. Assessment

The foregoing clearly shows the problems that local authorities face in connection with the cultivation, distribution, trade, selling, purchase and use of cannabis. Nevertheless, these arguments have one thing in common (probably even more so than the arguments regarding protecting public health and fighting (organized) crime): they do not affect or diminish in any legal way the many obligations mentioned and discussed repeatedly in this chapter and in Chapters 2 and 3 (obligations such as general eradication of narcotic drugs for recreational use, criminalization, prosecution, seizure and combating cannabis cultivation). That is not to say that these arguments presented above are not valid, or nonsensical. It is just that from a legal point of view, under the

UN narcotic drugs conventions, they cannot lead to a justification of tolerating cannabis cultivation for recreational use to supply retail shops or other points of sale, whether or not that cultivation is limited and/or subject to conditions. In principle, the same applies to European law.

With regard to the suggested taxation of cannabis cultivation, there is the additional problem under European law that drug trafficking cannot simply be taxed, as this traffic is prohibited. The case law of the Court of Justice of the European Union states 'that no liability to turnover tax arises upon the unlawful supply of narcotic drugs within the territory of a Member State in so far as the products in question are not confined within economic channels strictly controlled by the competent authorities for use for medical and scientific purposes.' And also: 'That also applies to the unlawful supply of narcotic drugs derived from hemp even where, pursuant to a selective prosecution policy, the authorities of a Member State do not systematically bring criminal proceedings against small-scale retail dealing in such drugs.'[118]

Apart from this, for some of the above-mentioned problems, there is a risk that the INCB or the Court of Justice of the European Union will take the view that the government brings these problems down on its own head by tolerating cannabis cultivation. This is conceivable, for example, for arguments that the illegal cultivation of cannabis forces coffee shop owners to do business with criminals, that the lack of regulation causes uncertainty for coffee shop owners and the government, and that the authority and credibility of the administration suffers from the current contradiction between the regulated sale of cannabis on the one hand and the illegal supply and cultivation on the other. Arguments that regulation can reduce the stigma of the cannabis user and that it would increase the freedom of choice of the citizen for his use of substances will most certainly be an abomination to the INCB. After all, the Board warns that tolerating drug use gives a 'false sense of security' and 'would send a false message to the public, in particular children, regarding the health impact of abuse of drugs'.

4.4. REGULATING MODALITIES IN AND OUTSIDE THE NETHERLANDS

Some municipalities in the Netherlands outline how regulating cannabis cultivation should be achieved or they present plans for experiments for regulating cannabis cultivation. More concrete forms of legalized, permitted or at any rate regulated cannabis cultivation can be found in some other countries than the Netherlands. Generally, developments in Belgium, Portugal, Spain, the

118 Court of Justice EU, Judgement of 5 July 1988, case C-289/86, ECLI:EU:C:1988:360 (*Happy Family*).

Czech Republic, Uruguay, federal states of the United States (such as California, Colorado and Washington) and South America are pointed at.

4.4.1. THE RAND OVERVIEW 2013

A detailed analysis of initiatives concerning regulating cannabis cultivation for recreational use in the above-mentioned countries and in a few other states is presented in: Beau Kilmer, Kristy Kruithof, Mafalda Pardal, Jonathan P. Caulkins & Jennifer Rubin, *Multinational overview of cannabis production regimes*, RAND Europe/WODC, 2013 (hereinafter to be referred to as: RAND overview). This report was compiled partly for the purpose of this study. It provides a multinational overview of initiatives for cannabis cultivation with a specific focus on identifying and describing official points of view and/or legal rulings about these initiatives aimed at cannabis cultivation. The RAND overview describes how these initiatives have developed in *Belgium*, *Spain*, *Uruguay* and the federal states of *Washington* and *Colorado* of the United States, and examines whether official statements have been made in these countries or federal states about if and how the new policy fits in with the international legal framework. The report also discusses in less detail schemes and proposals for schemes thereto or policy practice in *Canada*, *Chile*, *Denmark*, *Germany*, *France*, *Israel*, *Portugal*, *the Czech Republic*, the *United Kingdom*, *Switzerland* and the two capitals *Copenhagen* and *Mexico City*. It must be emphasized once more that the explanations and legal analyses below regarding the initiatives in all the above-mentioned jurisdictions, as far as the content and argumentation of these initiatives are concerned, are almost exclusively based on information provided by the RAND overview on these subjects. We assume that this information is correct and we have not carried out essential research to supplement this information.

In principle, the RAND overview does not assess whether these countries fulfil their obligations arising from the international conventions. As we have said already, an assessment of initiatives in countries other than the Netherlands will be conducted below. However, this will not involve a detailed description of legislation and/or policy in those countries. We refer the reader to the RAND overview for this. Nor does the following provide an assessment in detail of that legislation and/or that policy. We will assess whether the cannabis systems that have been implemented or proposed are or could be fundamentally permissible, taking into account any arguments that have been propounded to support the systems as presented in the RAND overview. Moreover, in light of the scope of this study the systematic assessment of these initiatives will not be carried out for each initiative individually, but similar regulating modalities will be grouped together, so that a discussion per category is possible. The discussion will also include proposals for schemes and pilots as presented in the Netherlands.

4.4.2. DEVELOPMENTS IN OTHER COUNTRIES AS ARGUMENTS FOR REGULATING CANNABIS CULTIVATION?

The countries discussed in the RAND overview have been chosen by the authors of the overview because of the developments there towards legalization, liberalization, decriminalization, or other forms of regulating the cannabis market or parts of it. The value of that is that one can see how certain regulating modalities or the arguments on which they are founded relate to the UN narcotic drugs conventions and/or European law. This can provide further insight in the content and scope of international and European law and the room it leaves for permitting cannabis cultivation. The developments in those countries and federal states do not, however, provide any legal argument that something is permitted under international or European law. This is worth noting, because municipalities in the Netherlands and also some authors seem to base their views on these developments in other countries in this way. In the same way that one could not draw the conclusion that the UN narcotic drugs conventions should be applied much more stringently than the rationale, the text and the system of these conventions stipulate because of the repressive approach by some states parties, the liberalising developments in various other state parties are insufficient grounds to arrive at the opposite conclusion. After all, in general the rationale, the text and the system of the convention are the yardstick, unless another meaning is to be given through generally accepted interpretations of the conventions or state practice.[119] To establish such generally accepted interpretations or state practice, all states parties – from the most liberal to the most repressive – are equally important in principle from a public international law point of view. The resolutions of the Commission on Narcotic Drugs and of the General Assembly of the United Nations which we have mentioned before, and which contain the decision 'to establish 2019 as a target date for States to eliminate or reduce significantly and measurably […] [t]he illicit cultivation of […] cannabis plant […]'[120] confirm that the initiatives discussed below cannot currently qualify as generally accepted interpretations of conventions or as relevant state practice. In this respect, it is also important that there have been various proposals within the CND for even stronger resolutions pertaining to cannabis.[121] Admittedly, they were not adopted, but they do illustrate that there

119 See for information on that section 2.5.

120 See CND, Report on the fifty-second session (14 March 2008 and 11–20 March 2009), *UN Doc.* E/2009/28, E/CN.7/2009/12, p. 119, para. 154. See for the General Assembly of the United Nations *UN Doc.* E/2009/28, E/CN.7/2009/12, pp. 37 and 44. For more information see section 2.5 and section 4.2.6 above.

121 See David R. Bewley-Taylor, 'The Contemporary International Drug Control System: A History of the UNGASS Decade', in: John Collins (ed.), *Governing the Global Drug Wars*, London: London School of Economics 2012, pp. 49–55, in particular on p. 53.

are also states which want an even stricter regime than the one established by the current United Nations conventions and that the initiatives below will not be approved by many states. The countries discussed below in principle commit wrongful acts from a public international law point of view to the extent that they act in contravention of their obligations under the United Nations conventions and/or European laws on drugs. We will now look at the question whether they also act in breach of these conventions.

i. Cannabis Cultivation for Recreational Use via Regulated Legalization

Uruguay is the first state in the world and also the first and so far only nation that is a party to the UN narcotic drugs conventions that has formally legalized cannabis production, distribution and possession aimed at recreational use.[122] This happened with the enactment of Bill No. 19.172 on 20 December 2013.[123] The first jurisdictions in the world that implemented such legalization – in 2012 – however, were the federal states of Washington and Colorado in the United States. As far as these federal states are concerned, there is no full legalization: all cannabis-related activities in these two jurisdictions as well as in the rest of the United States are still prohibited by virtue of the federal Controlled Substances Act.[124]

Uruguay and the federal states of Colorado and Washington allow commercial companies (enterprises seeking profits) to cultivate, distribute and sell cannabis on a large-scale subject to a licensing system and these companies have to pay taxes.[125] Uruguay and Colorado also legalized cultivation at home: in both cases up to six plants.[126] In Uruguay that is only for one's own personal consumption, whereas in Colorado one is allowed to transfer 28.35g (one ounce) to another adult. In Colorado and Washington, adults (21 years of age or older) may possess 28.35g (one ounce) of cannabis and larger quantities of drinks and food

122 For the relevant law in Uruguay, see Beau Kilmer et al., *Multinational overview of cannabis production regimes*, RAND Europe/WODC, 2013, pp. 31–37.

123 The implementation of that law took until July 2017, when pharmacies started selling non-medical cannabis to registered users. See e.g. INCB Report 2017, p. 36 (no. 183).

124 According to Beau Kilmer et al., *Multinational overview of cannabis production regimes*, RAND Europe/WODC, 2013, p. xiv.

125 Beau Kilmer et al., *Multinational overview of cannabis production regimes*, RAND Europe/WODC, 2013, p. xvii and the paragraphs in the report about these jurisdictions. In the meantime, other US states have legalised recreational cannabis use: Colorado (2012) and Washington (2012), Oregon (2014), Alaska (2014), Maine (2016), Massachusetts (2016), Nevada (2016), California (2018), Vermont (2018) and Michigan (2018). See https://en.wikipedia.org/wiki/Legality_of_cannabis_by_U.S._jurisdiction. The amount of allowed cannabis possession or the number of plants allowed for cultivation per household vary slightly around 1 ounce and 4–6 plants.

126 Many proposals for legalization or decriminalization of cultivation and possession of cannabis for personal use that by now have failed were made in Chile, Portugal and Switzerland;

containing cannabis extract. In Uruguay, adults can buy up to 40g of cannabis for recreational use from a dispensing chemist. Uruguay has also legalized joint cultivation in collective 'Cannabis Clubs'. These clubs have between 15 to 45 members and are allowed to grow up to 99 plants in total, in proportion to the number of members.

We will now address in a general way the question whether these initiatives towards legalization are legally viable under the UN narcotic drugs conventions and EU laws on drugs. Subsequently, we will pay attention to some arguments used to underpin these initiatives.

a. About Legalization in General

It is not clear whether Uruguay and several federal states of America are of the opinion that they are acting in accordance with the UN narcotic drugs conventions with this regulated legalization of cannabis cultivation. As far as Uruguay is concerned, that is not evident from the RAND overview, while also a statement from the Uruguayan Ministry of Foreign Affairs is not conclusive about that.[127] It is somewhat different in the case of Colorado and Washington. There is a complex discussion going on about this in the United States, the main issue being whether federal states within the federal structure of the United States are bound by the international conventions that the federal state has signed.[128] That American discussion on the federal structure is not relevant for other states, but it is another matter with regard to relevant international law. It must be noted that pursuant to Article 27 of the Vienna Convention on the Law of Treaties, a state party is not allowed to appeal to the provisions of its domestic law so as to justify non-implementation of the Convention and that Article 29 of this Convention says that a treaty between one or more states binds each state party for its entire territory. In addition to this, 'a State cannot adduce as against another State its own Constitution with a view to evading obligations incumbent upon it under international law or treaties in force'.[129] Furthermore, 'the international responsibility of a State is engaged by the action of the competent organs and authorities acting in that

see Beau Kilmer et al., *Multinational overview of cannabis production regimes*, RAND Europe/ WODC, 2013, pp. 46, 48, 49 and 50.

127 'Statement' dated 4 February 2014, of the Minister of Foreign Affairs of Uruguay, to the Members of the International Narcotics Control Board, about the relationship between the INCB and Uruguay in recent months and the newly enacted law number 19.172, available in Spanish on: http://www.mrree.gub.uy/ (hereinafter to be referred to as: Statement Uruguay to INCB, 4 February 2014).

128 Beau Kilmer et al., *Multinational overview of cannabis production regimes*, RAND Europe/ WODC, 2013, pp. 29–31.

129 Permanent Court of International Justice, Advisory opinion of 4 February 1932, *P.C.I.J.* 1932 Series A/B, no. 44, p. 24 (para. 62) (*Treatment of Polish Nationals and Other Persons of Polish Origin or Speech in the Danzig Territory*).

State, whatever they may be'.[130] The latter stipulation was considered by the International Court of Justice in a case where the 'competent organs and authorities acting in that State' had a bearing on (the governor of) a federal state in the United States; the Court ruled that the federal state 'is under the obligation to act in conformity with the international undertakings of the United States'. For the Netherlands, for example, this means that municipalities are also bound by international public law to comply with the conventions entered into by the Netherlands.

Do the approaches taken by Uruguay and the federal states of the United States provide an opportunity for other states, such as the Netherlands to legalize cannabis cultivation while respecting the UN narcotic drugs conventions and EU laws on drugs? In our opinion, that is not the case because of the following. Incidentally, the International Narcotics Control Board also sees the legalization by Uruguay, the federal states of the United States and more recently Canada as a violation of the UN narcotic drugs conventions.[131]

Article 36(1) of the Single Convention and Article 3(1) of the Illicit Traffic Convention require the criminalization of cannabis cultivation among other things.[132] At any rate, these obligations apply to cultivation that is not intended for one's own personal use. This means that legalization and also decriminalization of cannabis cultivation for recreational cannabis use by third parties clashes with this provision. It also means that regulated cannabis cultivation, distribution and selling by commercial enterprises via licences is not legally permissible under the conventions. In the case of personal use or joint cultivation for personal use – through Cannabis Social Clubs for example – legalization and decriminalization are not legally permissible either. After all, Article 3(2) of the Illicit Traffic Convention requires this to be criminalized (the question whether joint cultivation eventually comes under Article 36 of the Single Convention and/or Article 3(1) of the Illicit Traffic Convention will be addressed in section 4.4.2.ii). Moreover, legalizing all cannabis cultivation for recreational use in principle runs counter to the obligation (that in principle does not pertain to criminal law) in Article 33 of the Single Convention and the obligation to fight cannabis cultivation pursuant to Article 14 of the Illicit Traffic Convention, and such legalization is also hard to defend given the general obligation to limit in an active way the production, distribution, trade

---

130 International Court of Justice, Order of 3 March 1999, Provisional Measures, *I.C.J. Reports* 1999, p. 9 on p. 16 (para. 28) (*LaGrand – Germany v. United States of America*).

131 For more information see section 2.4 under v; Beau Kilmer et al., *Multinational overview of cannabis production regimes*, RAND Europe/WODC, 2013, pp. 36 and 29; Recently, Statement by the INCB on the entry into force of Bill C-45 legalising cannabis for non-medical purposes in Canada, Vienna, 17 October 2018, https://www.incb.org/incb/en/news/press-releases/2018/statement-by-the-international-narcotics-control-board-on-the-entry-into-force-of-bill-c-45-legalising-cannabis-for-non-medical-purposes-in-canada.html. See more generally INCB Report 2017, p. 29 (no. 198) and p. 35 (no. 180).

132 See section 2.2.2(a) under vi for more information (Article 36(1) of the Single Convention) and section 2.3.2(a) under i (Article 3(1) of the Illicit Traffic Convention).

in, use and possession of cannabis as well to only medical and scientific purposes (Article 4 of the Single Convention); the obligations to seize cannabis (Article 33 and 37 of the Single Convention) and the obligation to take measures against cannabis use (Article 38 of the Single Convention).[133] For EU states, in addition, the EU laws on drugs also play an important part. We can be brief about this. Such legalization clashes with the obligation in the Framework Decision to criminalize cannabis cultivation, if it is not exclusively intended for personal use, and to punish this with effective, proportionate and dissuasive sanctions with a maximum of at least between one and three years of imprisonment (Article 2(1) and Article 4(1) of the Framework Decision).

Or can the arguments put forward by Uruguay and the federal states in the United States for the legalization of commercial cannabis cultivation detract from the conclusion that legalization of cannabis cultivation is not possible under the current regime of the UN narcotic drugs conventions and EU laws on drugs? The following demonstrates it will be hard to maintain that this is the case. Consequently, in our opinion, the state and government bodies cannot assume control of the cultivation of cannabis for recreational use themselves. In the light of the UN narcotic drugs conventions and EU laws on drugs, that would mean that the government itself is directly responsible for the prohibited acts and thereby would act against the international law in the most direct and overt manner, and under the conventions, this conduct would qualify as a punishable offence.

b. Regulation through Supervision and a Licensing System

It is because municipalities in the Netherlands sometimes legitimize their plans for experiments or pilots by pointing out that those plans include a regulation or licensing system, that it is interesting that such systems are also part of initiatives in other countries.[134]

In Uruguay, a new agency, the Instituto de Regulacion y Controle del Cannabis (IRCCA), has been assigned the task of effecting the regulation. The IRCCA is responsible for granting licences to commercial companies for cannabis cultivation, distribution and selling to found a Cannabis Club, and for the registration of users, home growers and participants in the Cannabis Clubs. In other states, for example the federal states of Colorado and Washington, commercial cannabis cultivation is also subject to licensing. According to Uruguayan law, commercially cultivated cannabis – for both medical and recreational purposes – can only be sold by pharmacies. In the case of cannabis for recreational use, the pharmacies may only sell to adults and there is a limit of 40g per month per individual user. In Colorado and Washington, cannabis is sold by retail stores which have the appropriate licence.

---

133 See Chapter 2 for a detailed discussion about all these obligations.

134 See the paragraphs below for those municipal plans and proposals.

We will not assess the extent to which the regulation systems of Uruguay and the federal states in the United States procedurally match the licensing system required by the Single Convention. However, we do note that the licensing system under the Convention applies to cultivation, manufacture, trade in and distribution of narcotic drugs for 'medical and scientific purposes'. That most certainly is not the case with cannabis for recreational use, so a regulation system that involves cannabis for recreational use does not lie within the scope of the Convention. The same applies to European law.[135] From a substantive point of view, a licensing system for the cultivation, manufacture, and trade in and distribution of cannabis for recreational use does in a sense tie in with the Convention, because such a system leads to control and thereby to management and limitation of the drugs market. At the same time, such a system implies that this market is also permitted up to a point. And that results in a violation of the above-mentioned provisions detailing obligations under the Convention. The fact that regulation limits the extent of the violation does not alter that fact. So under the Single Convention, a licensing system cannot legally legitimize cannabis cultivation for recreational use. Indeed, such licences emphasize that the state actually permits the very thing that they are required to prohibit and fight by virtue of the conventions.

One could argue that if the conventions are violated as Uruguay chooses to do – which from a legal perspective is not an option and which, from the point of view of international law, in principle constitutes a wrongful act towards the other parties – then a regulated violation at least still manages to meet most of the objectives of the Convention. However, there is another side to this. In the previous subsection, we argued that the state and government bodies cannot undertake the cultivation of cannabis for recreational use themselves, as this would mean – from the perspective of the UN narcotic drugs conventions and the EU laws on drugs – that the government itself would be directly responsible for the prohibited acts. These acts also qualify as punishable offences under the conventions.[136] One might argue that even government regulation is a punishable offence, as it allows others to commit drug-related offences. In our opinion there is not anything that can immediately be put forward to counter that claim.

---

[135] See for section 4.2.5 under iv.

[136] See the annotation of A.H. Klip to Court of Justice EU, Judgment of 16 December 2010, case C-137/09, ECLI:EU:C:2010:774 (*Josemans*), *Netherlands Jurisprudence* 2011/290, at 22, who raises the legitimate question whether the government in the Netherlands, in creating and administering a pass system ('weed pass', see https://en.wikipedia.org/wiki/Coffeeshop_(Netherlands)) that was used a short while in the Netherlands, does not actually commit an offence, namely by allowing others to commit drug-related offences.

c. Democratic Decisions as Justification for the Legalization of Cannabis Cultivation

In states that have taken steps towards relating cannabis for recreational use, the regulated legalization of cannabis cultivation among other things came about in a democratic manner.[137] In the Netherlands too, there is support for regulating the cultivation of cannabis.[138] Can a state appeal to an internal democratic process and/or majority support in order to wriggle out of its obligations under the conventions to prohibit and combat cannabis cultivation? Yes and no. No, because the opinions of the majority of the population or the electorate as such do not derogate from the obligations which a state has assumed by signing an international treaty – and therefore also towards other states. Non-fulfilment of such obligations under international law constitutes a wrongful act. It is of no consequence that the 'act' itself meets with the approval of the population or is even based on a democratic decision. However, this is not to say that obligations under a convention trump democracy. After all, a state joins a convention within a democratic process, in particular if the obligations under the conventions were assumed by ratification of the convention. A democratic process can also result in the state rejecting the obligations under the convention by denouncing the convention. So in this respect, the answer to the question above is yes. However, as long as there is no denunciation by the state, it remains bound by public international law to act in agreement with the UN narcotic drugs conventions. Likewise, as long as the state is part of the European Union, the same applies to European law.

d. Other Arguments to Justify the Legalization of Cannabis Cultivation

The Uruguayan Act No. 19.172 aims to reinforce public safety and public health.[139] According to Uruguay, the object of the Illicit Traffic Convention is to fight illicit traffic and in particular to combat the harmful effects of the drugs trade. This objective, it is argued, would be achieved better through this Act.[140] Uruguay invokes general obligations regarding human rights – without specifying which rights – that it is bound by. Uruguay also argues that drug use and possession of cannabis for personal consumption is not prohibited under the Single Convention.

137 For information on the democratic processes and the support in these jurisdictions, see the Beau Kilmer et al., *Multinational overview of cannabis production regimes*, RAND Europe/ WODC, 2013, pp. 25–27 and pp. 31–34.

138 See the introductory part of section 4.3.

139 Beau Kilmer et al., *Multinational overview of cannabis production regimes*, RAND Europe/ WODC, 2013, p. 32.

140 Statement Uruguay to INCB, 4 February 2014. See also: https://en.wikipedia.org/wiki/Cannabis_in_Uruguay#Commercial_distribution.

The arguments presented by Uruguay for legalizing commercial cannabis cultivation for recreational use fail to justify that legalization from a legal perspective. Uruguay's claim that there is no obligation to criminalize drug use is correct in itself, but that is irrelevant with regard to cannabis cultivation. Nor is it correct that such an obligation does not apply to possession of drugs for personal use: the criminalization of that is required at any rate by Article 3(2) of the Illicit Traffic Convention. This means that in relation to recreational cannabis use the legalization or even decriminalization of home cultivation or cultivation in the context of Cannabis Social Clubs and/or shared consumption is not legally possible under the conventions.[141] However, it is more important here that none of this is relevant for permitting commercial cannabis cultivation for recreational use, since it does not fall under the regime of cultivation for one's own personal use at any rate.

The way in which Uruguay intends to adhere to the object and purpose of the Illicit Traffic Convention, cannot relieve the country from its obligations under the Convention either, since the Convention actually states that these obligations need to be met in order to achieve the aims of the Convention.[142] For that reason, the factual, social and political arguments discussed above could not stand up to a legal scrutiny either, no matter how valid they may have been otherwise. Such arguments may be relevant from the point of view of human rights, though. Whether or not the obligations under the UN narcotic drugs conventions should give way to obligations undertaken by the state in the context of human rights treaties, cannot be established on the basis of the scant remarks by Uruguay on that point. But even if this were different, such an assessment is beyond the scope of this study.[143] Irrespective of the result of such an assessment, Uruguayan legislation – and for that matter, that of the federal states in the United States – is in conflict with the UN narcotic drugs conventions and the same goes for acting on the basis of that legislation.

ii. Cannabis Cultivation and Joint Consumption in Cannabis Social Clubs

In various countries, so-called Cannabis Social Clubs (CSCs) are already active, in which the members of the club jointly cultivate and use cannabis. Also in the Netherlands there have been a few proposals from municipalities to permit this kind of club in order to arrive at regulated cannabis cultivation in that way. Before we assess whether permitting such clubs is a viable legal option under the

---

141 For more information on Cannabis Social Clubs, see section 4.4.2.

142 For more information, see the sections 4.2.4 and 4.3 above.

143 See section 1.4. We addressed this question in another study, see Piet Hein P.H.M.C. van Kempen & Masha I. Fedorova, *International Law and Cannabis II. Regulation of Cannabis Cultivation and Trade for Recreational Use: Positive Human Rights Obligations versus UN Narcotic Drugs Conventions*, Cambridge: Intersentia, 2019.

UN narcotic drugs conventions and the EU laws on drugs, it is a good idea to get a clearer picture of this phenomenon first.

a. Cannabis Social Clubs in Uruguay, Belgium and Spain

We saw earlier that joint cultivation in collectives or clubs has been legalized in Uruguay. These clubs have between 15 and 45 members and are allowed to grow up to 99 plants in total, in proportion to the number of members. The club must have a licence from the Instituto de Regulacion y Controle del Cannabis, which body also registers the members of the club.[144]

Belgium and Spain also know so-called Cannabis Social Clubs (CSCs), but these have not been legalized. Various CSCs are active in Belgium. The first one was a not-for-profit organization established in 2006 operating under the name of 'Trekt Uw Plant'. It had 400 members in September 2015.[145] In the club, members collectively grow cannabis in areas that are not open to the public, where the total number of plants does not exceed the number of members.[146] Every member has his or her own plant and he or she receives its yield. Members pay a membership fee for the costs of cultivation. Membership is open to adults resident in Belgium, and they can be medical as well as recreational cannabis users. The organization also carries out research into cannabis cultivation, so as to minimize risks to public health, and informs its members about the results of the research. Unlike the coffee shops in the Netherlands for example, the Belgian CSCs are not regulated by specific licensing terms or policy guidelines tailored to them. Government officials do not play a role in the production and distribution. The CSCs actually operate in a grey area. Cannabis cultivation as such is prohibited in Belgium and punishable under criminal law with a fine or prison sentence.[147] Both cultivation of cannabis for personal consumption and recreational purposes and cultivation for use by others are covered by criminal law. According to a 2005 guideline from the Justice Minister and the Board of Procurators General, the possession of cannabis of up to 3g or one plant for adults should however be given the lowest investigation priority and not lead to seizure of the cannabis products. This only applies if it does not involve disturbance of public order or other aggravating circumstances. A decision by the Antwerp Court of Appeal indicates that the acts within the CSC qualify as acts for personal use.[148] This would mean that CSCs operating under the lowest

144 Beau Kilmer et al., *Multinational overview of cannabis production regimes*, RAND Europe/ WODC, 2013, pp. xvii and 34–35; see also pp. 48–49, where the reader learns that there has also been a proposal to legalize CSCs in Portugal, but this was rejected.

145 See https://trektuwplant.be/trekt-uw-plant/historiek/.

146 Beau Kilmer et al., *Multinational overview of cannabis production regimes*, RAND Europe/ WODC, 2013, p. 18.

147 Ibid, pp. xv, 16–17 and 19.

148 Ibid, p. 19.

investigation priority are not threatened with seizure of the plants. The State Secretary for Justice in Belgium makes it clear however, that the CSC 'Trekt Uw Plant' violates Belgian criminal law and international conventions, and that the activities of the club do not conform with the guideline because the club facilitates the possession of cannabis for others and also drug use by others.[149] With respect to the CSC, the State Secretary notes that this involves facilitating the drug use of another person and this constitutes an infringement. He goes on to say that the aim of the organization clearly does not meet the description of the guideline and the facts give rise to prosecution.[150] Since then, several actions have been taken against the Belgian CSCs.[151]

Spain has more than four hundred Cannabis Social Clubs. The Spanish Federation of Cannabis Social Clubs defines a CSC as an association of adults producing and sharing cannabis together without distributing it to third parties.[152] A CSC can function as such if the venue is only accessible to members, there is no trade among members, the cannabis can only be used in the CSC and only a small amount needs to be paid.[153] With regard to domestic law, the Spanish CSCs have a little more room than the ones in Belgium. The possession and use of cannabis is prohibited in Spain, but a breach of the prohibition is not a punishable offence, at any rate not if small quantities are involved and consumption takes place in the private sphere.[154] Judicial authorities usually interpret the relevant legislation in a way that permits shared consumption and joint cultivation for personal use, because it is in effect personal consumption.[155] This has led to acquittals for members of CSCs among other things.

149 Ibid, p. 20.

150 Belgische Kamer van Volksvertegenwoordigers 2011, Beknopt Verslag Commissie voor de Justitie, *CRABV* 53 COM 190 (Antwoord Staatssecretaris Carl Devlies op Vraag van de heer Bert Schoofs aan de minister van Justitie over 'de Cannabis Social Club' (nr. 3651)), p. 12 (i.e., Belgian Chamber of Parliamentarians 2011, Brief Report Commission for Justice, *CRABV* 53 COM 190 (Answer State Secretary Carl Devlies to Question from Mr. Bert Schoofs for the Minister of Justice about 'the Cannabis Social Club' (no. 3651)), p. 12).

151 See e.g. 'Opnieuw politie-inval bij Mambo Social Club, *De Wereld Morgen*, 25 January 2014 (i.e., 'Another raid on Mambo Social Club), 25 January 2014), available on: http://www.dewereldmorgen.be/blogs/marccuyvers/2014/01/25/opnieuw-politie-inval-bij-mambo-social-club, and earlier 'Politie neemt "legale cannabis" Mambo Social Club in beslag', *Het Belang van Limburg*, 20 December 2013 (i.e., 'Police seizes "legal cannabis" Mambo Social Club'), 20 December 2013), available on: http://www.hbvl.be/limburg/hasselt/politie-neemt-legale-cannabis-mambo-social-club-in-beslag.aspx. See more recently: https://www.voc-nederland.org/2017/05/grote-politie-actie-tegen-oudste-belgische-cannabis-social-club-trekt-uw-plant-3-bestuursleden-nog-vast/.

152 Beau Kilmer et al., *Multinational overview of cannabis production regimes*, RAND Europe/WODC, 2013, p. 9. See also https://en.wikipedia.org/wiki/Cannabis_in_Spain.

153 See for more information Beau Kilmer et al., *Multinational overview of cannabis production regimes*, RAND Europe/WODC, 2013, p. 10.

154 Ibid, pp. 6, 8.

155 Ibid, pp. 8–9 and 12–13. But see the recent Supreme Court decisions: https://sensiseeds.com/en/blog/new-decisions-constitutional-court-end-cannabis-tolerance-spain/.

The arguments that seem to play a part are that the CSC does not pursue a commercial interest, that the cultivation qualifies as a demonstration of collective will in the context of personal autonomy, that consumption takes place in enclosed places, that small quantities are involved,[156] that the CSC has a small number of members, that little is shared among members, that consumption takes place immediately after receiving the crop, that the members are cannabis users. If, however, cultivation takes place to stimulate, promote or facilitate illegal drug use by making the crop available to third parties, then this is a criminal offence, even if it is committed by CSCs.[157] Spain has no additional legislation or guidelines defining the regime in which cannabis cultivation is permissible.[158]

b. Cannabis Social Clubs Permissible under the UN Narcotic Drugs Conventions and the EU Laws on Drugs?

The criminalization of cultivation, possession and purchase of narcotic drugs – including cannabis – for personal use is required in any case by Article 3(2) of the Illicit Traffic Convention.[159] A less stringent regime than usual applies to acts covered by this stipulation, partly because states have a little more room to refrain from prosecution on the basis of expediency considerations. For all other acts involving cannabis, the more stringent standard regime of Article 36(1) of the Single Convention and Article 3(1) of the Illicit Traffic Convention applies. These provisions require the criminalization of cultivation, production, manufacture and possession of cannabis which is not intended for personal use. This includes all commercial activities with cannabis for recreational use, because by definition these do not concern cultivation, possession and purchase for one's own personal use.[160] It also shows from the fact that Article 36(1) of the Single Convention and Article 3(1) of the Illicit Traffic Convention require the criminalization of trade, distribution, offering and selling

156 The case in question revolved around 239g per member per year, that equals approximately 20g per month.

157 Beau Kilmer et al., *Multinational overview of cannabis production regimes*, RAND Europe/WODC, 2013, p. 9.

158 Ibid, pp. 9 and 10. Several attempts to regulate cannabis consumer associations, has been deemed unconstitutional and legally void by the Constitutional Court in Spain, see for example: https://www.ara.cat/en/Constitutional-Court-overturns-Catalan-cannabis_0_2096190465.html (website article of 287 September 2018). See also Martin Barriuso, 'The end of cannabis tolerance in Spain, 2 January 2018, on: http://www.undrugcontrol.info/en/weblog/item/8135-the-end-of-cannabis-tolerance-in-spain.

159 Possibly the same applies to Article 36(1) of the Single Convention, where it can be argued that this is not the case (see for more information section 2.2.2(a) under vi and section 2.5 under ii); we therefore assume for the following that acts for personal use do not fall under Article 36(1) of the Single Convention.

160 The fact that Article 3(2) of the Illicit Traffic Convention only refers to 'personal consumption' has been explained in section 2.3.2.i.a.I (see: Behaviours for personal cannabis use).

of cannabis. Moreover, the cultivation, possession and purchasing of larger quantities then could reasonably be needed for one's own private consumption can hardly be treated as intended for personal consumption, so that for such quantities the standard regime for Article 36(1) of the Single Convention and Article 3(1) of the Illicit Traffic Convention applies. To that extent, cannabis cultivation that is not small-scale is therefore subject to the standard regime.

Because there is a more lenient regime for Article 3(2) of the Illicit Traffic Convention (among other things for cultivation for personal consumption) than for Article 3(1) of the Illicit Traffic Convention and Article 36(1) of the Single Convention (cannabis cultivation not for personal use), it is important to establish which regime applies to joint cultivation within a CSC. There are at least two possible ways of reasoning.

A strict and formal way of reasoning would be that cannabis cultivation for one's personal use implies that someone cultivates cannabis purely for himself, and that consequently cultivation will be entirely at his own expense and that he uses the cannabis crop himself and does not share it with others. This seems to be the approach taken by the State Secretary for Justice in Belgium in explaining that the Belgian CSC 'Trekt Uw Plant' is not covered by the Belgian guideline for prosecution, because the club facilitates drug use by another person.[161] Cultivating cannabis together and/or using it from the joint crop within the club does not qualify in the strict interpretation as cultivation for personal use, so that the standard strict regime of Article 3(1) of the Illicit Traffic Convention and Article 36(1) of the Single Convention applies.

A more flexible and more substantive way of reasoning would be that in fact it is cultivation for personal use, seeing that the result of a CSC on balance is the same as when each member grows one plant at home for himself and consumes the yield. After all, within the club each member has one plant, the yield of the plants is the same in principle as the total yield if all members grew their plants at home and the route from cultivation to consumption constitutes a closed system, because only the club members consume the yield. To put it differently: in principle, the scale of cultivation within a CSC is the same as that of the cumulative scale of all individual members cultivating a plant at home, while consumption of the yield takes place by those individuals in a private setting, so in that respect there is also cultivation for personal use by the members, where no yields are provided to third parties, so there are no commercial activities. This is even more obviously the case if everyone only consumes the yield of his or her plant.

In our opinion, this second way of thinking is approximately as valid as the first one from a legal perspective. One consideration in this respect is that the text of the conventions and the preparatory history do not offer decisive points

---

[161] See for more information this section under i.

of departure that clearly advocate one angle or rather the other. Against this background, states parties can choose either way of thinking in good faith and therefore choose the interpretation of the Convention that they consider to be the most convincing. This would be different if one were to qualify CSCs as criminal organizations, because of the cooperation between multiple persons in the criminal cultivation of cannabis for recreational use. That might be possible from a formal legal point of view. The INCB seems to approach the issue from this perspective. When evaluating Spain's approach to cannabis, the INCB reiterates its position in general terms that the establishment of 'cannabis consumption clubs' is not consistent with the UN drugs conventions.[162] The Board notes that possession, consumption and cultivation of cannabis are liable to criminal sanctions in Spain and that 'associations that pursue aims or use methods classified as criminal are illegal.'[163] However, if the offences committed by the members in a CSC are not directed at or against the outside world, but merely serve to facilitate each other's cannabis use (which does not need to be criminalised according to the drugs conventions), while the CSC does not seek to influence third parties either nor pursues financial profit, this has in essence very little to do with a criminal organization. Therefore, the above-mentioned formal possibility to treat CSCs as criminal organizations does not materially diminish the validity of the more flexible and substantive way of thinking in our opinion.

This means that a party can conclude that the activities of CSCs should only be punishable by virtue of Article 3(2) of the Illicit Traffic Convention, so that there is some room to refrain from prosecuting – the members of – such clubs as part of a policy.[164] Unlike other countries, the Netherlands in principle is completely free to apply the expediency principle. There are two important points in this respect. The first is that the Dutch reservation regarding Article 3(6) of the Illicit Traffic Convention is meant to ensure the freedom for considerations of expediency – also as general policy – in the case of offences involving personal use. In view of the fact that the more substantive way of thinking presented above is defensible, it can also be argued convincingly that non-prosecution of CSCs is fairly consistent with the room for expediency that the Netherlands managed to ensure by means of this reservation. Then there is the second point. Because the reservation does not diminish the obligations under the Single Convention, it is relevant that the obligations of prosecution arising from this Convention in principle only relate to 'serious offences'.[165] It is exactly because of the fact that CSCs are not about trade and only exist for personal use of cannabis by adults that it would be rather difficult to assert that such serious offences are taking

162 INCB Report 2016, p. 28, no. 188.
163 INCB Report 2016, p. 28, no. 187.
164 See section 2.3.2.i.a.III and section 2.4.v.
165 See section 2.2.2.ii.a. X and section 2.4.v.

place there. In short: under the UN narcotic drugs conventions, in principle, the Netherlands has the discretion to decide on the basis of considerations of expediency whether or not to prosecute CSCs and to make that a general policy. If such a policy means that CSCs are not prosecuted in principle (penal tolerance), then it is only logical that the investigation policy is shaped accordingly.

Also with respect to European law, Cannabis Social Clubs are covered by the obligations of criminalization, while eventually there is also room for expediency to refrain from prosecuting (the members of) these clubs. First and foremost, all acts mentioned in Article 2 of the Framework Decision, must be criminalized. This includes cannabis cultivation, among other things. According to Article 2(2) of the Framework Decision, acts involving cannabis that take place 'exclusively' for personal consumption are exempt from this obligation of criminalization. A linguistic interpretation of the Framework Decision implies that the obligations included also apply to joint cultivation and consumption in Cannabis Social Clubs, because there is no cultivation for exclusive personal use in the case of joint cultivation. In addition to this, the number of plants in such a club can be regarded as not small, so that cultivation in the club for that reason does not meet the criteria of the provision of Article 2(2) of the Framework Decision.[166] However, as such cultivation does not need to qualify as 'serious' for the above-mentioned reasons, there is also room to refrain from prosecution as a matter of policy on the grounds of considerations of expediency, also as far as the obligations of prosecution adopted by the Court of Justice of the European Union are concerned, assuming that they are applicable to the Framework Decision.[167]

The fact that a state has room to refrain from prosecuting CSCs, does not mean that it can permit them (for example administratively). After all, here too all sorts of obligations in the conventions would preclude that: the general obligation to limit actively among other things the production, use and possession of cannabis to medical and scientific purposes (Article 4 of the Single Convention), the obligations to prohibit and seize cannabis (Article 33 of the Single Convention and possibly Article 37 of the Single Convention), the obligation to take measures against cannabis use (Article 38 of the Single Convention) and the obligation to fight the cultivation of cannabis (Article 14 of the Illicit Traffic Convention).[168] From the perspective of European law, it is relevant that the parties are bound explicitly by Article 8 of the Joint Action on Illegal Drug Trafficking and bound implicitly by Article 75(5) of the Schengen Implementation Agreement to take appropriate measures to fight cannabis cultivation. In respect of explicitly permitting CSCs, it would be hard to defend that this would not constitute a violation of obligations under international law.

166 See section 3.4.1.ii.

167 See section 3.4.1.vii.

168 See Chapter 2 for a detailed discussion about all these obligations.

This also means that under UN conventions, there is no room to impose conditions on CSCs or to regulate them in other ways. For that too would imply an explicit recognition of the CSCs and permission. Paradoxically, a party that leaves CSCs alone, without any attempt to regulate them (something which is a less attractive option given the rationale for drug control), would be less blatantly in breach of the provisions regarding the obligations under the conventions. In that case, there can be policies and regulations that discourage – participation in – CSCs and thereby fulfil the obligations under the Convention, without it necessitating intensive efforts to dismantle such clubs. Where there is no place for CSCs from a legal point of view, they could function de facto in a grey area. However, the moment the authorities know where such a cannabis club is located, a decision to forgo acting against it in a factual or at least in an administrative way would conflict with said obligations. It is also relevant in this respect that there seems to be a fundamental difference between cultivation at home and cultivation in a CSC: taking into account the right of privacy, among other things, where it would be disproportionate to enter, for example, the homes of a 100 persons so as to seize just one cannabis plant in each home, qualifying the application of the power of seizure as disproportionate is much less obvious or perhaps even a misnomer if the plants of these persons exist side-by-side in a hall or on a plot of land. We conclude that it is possible to refrain from prosecution of CSCs as a policy (penal tolerance), but that tolerating them under an administrative policy (administrative tolerance) would be hard to defend from a legal point of view, also because of the obligations that do not pertain to criminal law (mostly based on UN conventions).[169]

iii. Cannabis Cultivation for Recreational Use by Commercial or Non-Profit Producers

Another argument of proponents of cannabis regulations that we encountered concerns the difference between commercial and non-commercial or non-profit cultivation of cannabis. The question whether cannabis cultivation takes place on commercial or non-commercial basis can be relevant in deciding which regime of the conventions applies. In the case of commercial cultivation for recreational use, Article 36(1) of the Single Convention and Article 3(1) of the Illicit Traffic Convention always apply. However, this can also be the case for non-commercial cultivation.[170] This is because neither the Single Convention

169 Interestingly, a 2013 bill in Spain provides administrative fines of up to €30,000 for the possession of small quantities of cannabis for personal use; see Inés Giménez, 'A step back in Spanish drug policies. A de facto criminalisation of cannabis use?', 19 December 2013, on: http://www.undrugcontrol.info/en/weblog/item/5227-a-step-back-in-spanish-drug-Policies.

170 The assumption that the UN narcotic drugs conventions only counter the commercialization of cannabis, an argument used in the Portuguese parliament, is therefore incorrect: see Beau Kilmer et al., *Multinational overview of cannabis production regimes*, RAND Europe/WODC, 2013, p. 49.

nor the Illicit Traffic Convention make this kind of distinction. The distinctions made by the conventions are those between 'serious offences' and offences that are not, and between acts aimed at personal consumption (this can only be cultivation, possession and purchase) and all other acts. Cultivation that does not take place for personal consumption is subject to the criminalization of Article 36(1) of the Single Convention and Article 3(1) of the Illicit Traffic Convention and consequently to the strict standard regime. This also applies to the non-commercial cultivation. The crucial element is that the cultivation takes place for the purpose of recreational use by third parties. The fact that such non-commercial cultivation is possibly afflicted with fewer disadvantages than commercial cultivation does not affect its unlawfulness. As it involves significant quantities, it will probably also qualify as 'serious'. It follows more directly from the provisions of the conventions themselves that non-commercial cultivation also falls under these provisions. After all, they constitute obligations to criminalize not only cannabis cultivation, but also offering, offering for sale, distribution, selling, delivery on any terms whatsoever and transport of cannabis for recreational use.

Consequently, the entire range of obligations arising from the conventions also apply where cannabis cultivation for recreational use by third parties is not commercial in nature. As we have observed repeatedly, it is particularly the general obligation to pursue actively the limitation of the production, distribution, trade, use and possession of cannabis as well for medical and scientific purposes (Article 4 of the Single Convention), the obligation to criminalize cultivation that is not small-scale and/or does not relate to personal use (Article 36(1) of the Single Convention and Article 3(1) of the Illicit Traffic Convention),[171] the various obligations of prosecution ensuing from the conventions applicable to cannabis cultivation that is not small-scale and not meant for personal use, and various obligations that in principle do not pertain to criminal law, such as obligations to prohibit and seize cannabis (Article 33 of the Single Convention and Article 37 of the Single Convention), the obligation to take measures against cannabis use (Article 38 of the Single Convention) and the obligation to fight the cultivation of cannabis (Article 14 of the Illicit Traffic Convention).[172] There would be a conflict with all these obligations if a non-profit organization were permitted to cultivate cannabis for recreational use by third parties, even if this happened because of a policy of tolerance. As a matter of fact, the positions taken by the International Narcotics Control Board and the resolutions of the

171 It is not relevant for cultivation for retail shops that there is also an obligation to criminalize small-scale cultivation for personal use (see Article 36(1) of the Single Convention (which is not entirely clear), and the indisputable Article 3(2) of the Illicit Traffic Convention).

172 The content and scope of all these obligations are discussed extensively in Chapter 2.

Commission on Narcotic Drugs leave no room for cannabis cultivation for recreational use by third parties.[173]

With regard to European law, it can be added that it does not make a distinction either between commercial and non-commercial cannabis cultivation, even though it is clear that the Framework Decision is primarily aimed at the first category. All acts that are mentioned in Article 2 of the Framework Decision must be criminalized and penalized with effective, proportionate and dissuasive sanctions. However, the Framework Decision does not have the obligation to criminalize acts involving cannabis that are 'exclusively' intended for personal recreational use; see the exception of Article 2(2) of the Framework Decision. Cultivation for retail shops, however, takes place for recreational cannabis use by third parties, so that even if non-commercial producers are responsible for the cultivation, these would absolutely be outside the aforementioned exception. If that cultivation is not small-scale, which the scale of cultivation for the supply of retail shops readily suggests, it could also qualify as serious, despite the non-commercial nature of the producer. Also under European law, an obligation of prosecution could apply.

iv. Cannabis Cultivation for Recreational Use under Medical Programmes

The conventions leave room to permit the use of cannabis as a medicine. In various countries – including the Netherlands, Canada, Chile, the Czech Republic, France and Israel – the opportunity to cultivate and/or use medicinal cannabis is also provided by fairly to severely restrictive systems.[174] In federal states of the United States systems exist that provide for easy access to cannabis (be it intentionally or unintentionally) for recreational users in addition to patients.[175] In the USA cannabis is included in Schedule I of the federal Controlled Substances Act (CSA). This means that there is no federal recognition that cannabis may have a medicinal use and that each use according to that federal legislation – and therefore across the United States – is prohibited.[176] At least in this respect, the United States complies with the requirements under the convention, with regard to the exception of 'medical and scientific purposes'. Nevertheless, most states create exceptions to the federal prohibition by permitting the use and in some case the production and selling of cannabis if the user has a recommendation that cannabis consumption could be medically beneficial.

173 See for more information section 2.4 in particular.

174 See Beau Kilmer et al., *Multinational overview of cannabis production regimes*, RAND Europe/WODC, 2013, pp. 39–43.

175 See for an elaborate discussion http://en.wikipedia.org/wiki/Medical_cannabis_in_the_United_States.

176 Beau Kilmer et al., *Multinational overview of cannabis production regimes*, RAND Europe/WODC, 2013, p. 22.

The schemes vary from severely limited access for patients to fairly broad access, including recreational users to all intents and purposes.[177] The US Department of Justice – which state, unlike its federal states, is a direct party to the UN narcotic drugs conventions – has indicated that law enforcement and possibly prosecution of commercial companies that in violation of federal legislation market and sell cannabis for-profit will remain a priority.[178] On the other hand, prosecution of individuals suffering from cancer or another serious disease who violate federal laws is qualified as unlikely.

We have explained before[179] that the exception of medical or scientific purposes is rather limited in scope and basically only leaves room for the use of narcotic drugs as meaningful and/or effective medicine in concrete cases, the use of narcotic drugs to produce medicines for such cases, and scientific research for the aforesaid medicinal use, the aforesaid production of medicines or medical science. We also concluded that it is legally impossible under the Convention to stretch the exception of 'medical purposes' to include 'public health purposes' so as to permit cannabis cultivation and all other activities aimed at the sale of cannabis for recreational use. Insofar as medical programmes grant recreational users access to cannabis intentionally or unintentionally, these programmes are not covered by the exception. This means that such programmes do not comply with the wide range of obligations under the conventions that have been listed before.[180] Therefore, legally there is no room to permit the cultivation of cannabis for recreational use under the guise of medical programmes. The International Narcotics Control Board urges states parties to prevent this and to combat abuse of medical programmes.[181] This also applies to European law, since the EU drug instruments and the Court of Justice of the European Union follow the UN narcotic drugs conventions with regard to the exception of 'medical or scientific purposes'.[182]

v. Cannabis Cultivation for Recreational Use under Scientific Programmes

It is also advocated to regulate the cultivation of cannabis for recreational use by means of a pilot or experiment. A controlled experiment would help

---

177 See also http://en.wikipedia.org/wiki/Medical_cannabis_in_the_United_States.

178 Beau Kilmer et al., *Multinational overview of cannabis production regimes*, RAND Europe/WODC, 2013, pp. 24–25. See also http://en.wikipedia.org/wiki/Medical_cannabis_in_the_United_States, with reference to the so-called *Ogden Memo* of 2009 and the *Cole Memo* of 2011 from the U.S. Department of Justice and the enactment of the Rohrabacher-Farr amendment in 2014, which offers important protections for state-legal medical cannabis activities. The Cole Memorandum was rescinded by Attorney General Sessions in January 2018 (https://en.wikipedia.org/wiki/Cole_Memorandum).

179 See section 4.2.4 above and sections 2.2.3.i and 2.4.iii.

180 See section 4.4.3.

181 See section 2.4.iii.

182 See section 3.4.2.

to establish the consequences of regulating both cultivation and trade of cannabis for recreational use. There seem to be opportunities in Germany, the United Kingdom and Switzerland to conduct scientific research into cannabis.[183] The possibilities are limited, though, and there appears to be no room for research that is not focused on the narcotic drug itself nor for any projects concerning cannabis cultivation for recreational use.

We have repeatedly pointed out[184] that the exception of 'scientific purposes' has a fairly limited scope and does not lend itself to including experiments with cannabis cultivation for recreational use. With all the pilots and experiments proposed by the municipalities, it is not the cannabis that is the subject or instrument of the scientific research, but rather, among other things, the control and organization of the cultivation and the distribution of the yield. Furthermore, the aim of the research is not the advancement of medical science or developing cannabis in order to produce a useful and/or effective medicine. These pilots therefore fall outside the exception of 'scientific purposes' and come up against the wide range of obligations of criminalization, prosecution, obligations to prohibit and seize cannabis and obligations to fight cannabis cultivation, which have been mentioned repeatedly.[185] Even if the exception had a wider scope, it would still be quite challenging to justify the trials and experiments with regulated cannabis cultivation for recreational use. If the proposed projects resulted in knowledge about the best possible form of regulating cannabis cultivation for recreational use in view of the relevant interests, that form could not be implemented after all. Once again, that implementation would run counter to the various convention obligations that preclude cannabis cultivation for recreational use. From the perspective of the UN narcotic drugs conventions and European law, these pilots actually seek to achieve what is in essence an unacceptable objective.

4.5. CONCLUSION

This chapter contains an inventory and categorization of arguments and initiatives (legislation or proposals) for the regulation of cannabis cultivation in and outside the Netherlands. These arguments and initiatives have been analysed and assessed in the light of the UN narcotic drugs conventions and European law. The analysis of these arguments and initiatives is important, because it illustrates the considerable extent of problems the authorities face regarding cultivation, trade, distribution, sale, purchase, possession and consumption

---

183 Beau Kilmer et al., *Multinational overview of cannabis production regimes*, RAND Europe/WODC, 2013, pp. 43–45.

184 See section 4.2.4 above under iii and earlier sections 2.2.3.i and 2.4.iii.

185 See section 4.4.2.iii.

of cannabis. The importance of this analysis also lies in the fact that it forms the basis of a systematic and analytical assessment of the arguments and initiatives in the light of international law. The assessment consisted of three parts: an evaluation of the legal arguments; an evaluation of the factual, social and/or political arguments; and the assessment of the various regulating modalities as proposed in the Netherlands by the municipalities or as they are implemented in other countries.

The legal arguments mainly relate to amendments of the Single Convention, denunciation of the Convention with a view to formulating a new reservation before re-accession, the application of the exception of 'medical and scientific' use on the grounds of public health interests and the application of the expediency principle. The assessment on the basis of international law shows that the UN narcotic drugs conventions and European law (EU laws on drugs and case law of the Court of Justice of the European Union) present many obstacles for permitting (legalization, decriminalization, policy-based tolerance and other regulation) of cannabis cultivation intended for recreational use. The conclusion is that permitting cannabis cultivation so as to supply retail shops cannot be realized on the basis of any of the arguments put forward without violating the UN narcotic drugs conventions and the EU laws on drugs. By the way, Chapter 2 and Chapter 3 show that these conventions and this legislation do not offer any room for this, regardless of the arguments.

The same conclusion must be drawn in respect of the factual, social and/or political arguments. The most important interests featuring in those arguments are those of public health and crime control, and regulated cannabis cultivation would serve those interests. Strictly speaking, the UN narcotic drugs conventions and European law are also intended to protect those interests. The prohibitive and repressive obligations to eradicate cannabis for recreational use imposed by international law so as to serve those interests, however, are diametrically opposed to the regulation solutions advocated by the municipalities. The municipal arguments as regards public health, fighting crime and looking after other social interests cannot be a justification under international law for permitting cultivation of cannabis for recreational use – whether or not it is limited and/or subject to conditions – for supplying any points of sale.

The last part of the assessment relates to the various regulating modalities as they have been applied in several countries. This involves regulated legalization (Uruguay and several federal states of the United States, in particular Colorado and Washington), joint cultivation in Cannabis Social Clubs (Belgium, Spain and Uruguay), cannabis cultivation by non-profit growers or by commercial parties with a licence, and cannabis cultivation for recreational use dressed up as medical or scientific programmes. The conclusion with regard to these modalities is that the international legal framework for fighting drugs does not leave any room for legalization, decriminalization, policy-based tolerance and other regulation of such cultivation. Nevertheless, only with respect to Cannabis Social Clubs will states which let such clubs operate de facto and therefore without any regulation be less likely to contravene the obligations pursuant to the UN narcotic drugs conventions and European law.

The overall conclusion therefore is that legalization, decriminalization, policy-based tolerance and other regulation of cannabis cultivation for the recreational user market is not permissible under the UN narcotic drugs conventions and European law. This also means that regulating cannabis cultivation for supplying retail shops is not possible with due regard for international law, regardless of the manner in which such cultivation were to take place.

CHAPTER 5
CONCLUSION

5.1. INTRODUCTION

The need of citizens to have access to cannabis for recreational use poses all sorts of challenges to the authorities. In the Netherlands, for example, not only does the so-called soft drugs policy almost continually give rise to discussions, but it also brings up the legal, social and political conundrum of how the authorities should deal with the cultivation of cannabis for the supply of retail shops. Meanwhile, new phenomena are developing that generate similar questions. For example, the joint cultivation and consumption in so-called Cannabis Social Clubs. In several countries around the globe there are issues around cultivation, trade, distribution, sale and purchase of cannabis for recreational use. This makes the subject of this book topical, much-talked about and at any rate, socially relevant.

The key question in this book, which strictly focuses on matters from a legal point of view, is whether legalization, decriminalization, policy-based tolerance and/or other forms of regulating cannabis cultivation for recreational use is permissible under international law on drug control. The assessment expressly also focuses on the question to what extent the arguments and initiatives for the regulation of cannabis cultivation in and outside the Netherlands can be squared with relevant international law such as European law and the UN narcotic drugs conventions. More specifically, this concerns the UN 1961 Single Convention on Narcotic Drugs as amended by the 1972 Protocol, the UN Illicit Traffic Convention, the so-called EU Schengen acquis, the EU 1996 Joint Action on Illegal Drug Trafficking and the EU 2004 Framework Decision on Illicit Drug Trafficking. The book does not look at the question of how cannabis use and the fight against this relate to individual freedoms and the duties of the state with respect to international human rights law.

To arrive at substantiated answers to the questions addressed in this book, the preceding chapters contain an elaborate and detailed explanation and analysis of relevant international law. Apart from the above-mentioned international legal instruments, we have also reviewed the findings and opinions of the international bodies that are designated to supervise the said instruments, particularly those of the International Narcotics Control Board (INCB), the Commission on Narcotic Drugs (CND) and the Court of Justice of the European Union (CJEU). Within the ensuing framework under international law, the arguments and initiatives for the regulation of cannabis for recreational use in and outside the Netherlands have been evaluated from a legal perspective. This last chapter aims to provide an overview of the most important findings and conclusions.

5.2. INTERNATIONAL LEGAL FRAMEWORK OF CANNABIS CULTIVATION FOR RECREATIONAL USE

5.2.1. UN NARCOTIC DRUGS CONVENTIONS

The aim of the United Nations drug control system is to restrict the use of narcotics such as cannabis to purely medical and scientific purposes. Any use of cannabis on account of its narcotic effects that is not covered by this exception is deemed to be for recreational purposes. The eradication of cannabis for recreational use is the 'object and purpose' of these conventions, in view of the Preamble, the body of the text, the system and the history of deliberations of the Single Convention and the Illicit Traffic Convention. At the heart of this aim of eradication lies the assumption that the interests of public health and crime control are most adequately served by achieving this aim. For this book, it is of importance that next to coca and poppy products, cannabis products are the main object of these conventions, since these are mentioned explicitly not only in the Schedules of the Conventions, but in the Conventions themselves as well. This objective of eradication, which also explicitly targets cannabis, cannot be reconciled with permitting cannabis cultivation for recreational use by legalization, decriminalization, policy-based tolerance and/or other forms of regulation of such cultivation.

In order to achieve this aim of eradication, the conventions provide for a prohibitive, repressive and multi-layered enforcement system, which imposes a wide range of diverse obligations related to criminal law, and administrative and other obligations on the parties to the convention. These include obligations to cooperate in an estimate system (which serves to ensure the availability of sufficient amounts of narcotic drugs only for medical and scientific purposes),[1] general obligations to combat the cultivation of cannabis for recreational purposes,[2] obligations to criminalize acts – including cannabis

1 See Articles 12–21 of the Single Convention.

2 Article 4 of the Single Convention, Article 14(2) of the Illicit Traffic Convention and Article 38 of the Single Convention.

cultivation – that are aimed at or are related to recreational use of cannabis, with a view to achieving a total ban of these acts,[3] obligations resulting both explicitly and implicitly from the conventions to prosecute for cannabis cultivation that is not small-scale and not intended for personal use, a total ban on the possession of narcotic drugs including cannabis intended for recreational use,[4] obligations to seize cannabis intended for recreational use,[5] and the obligation to implement and participate in a system of international cooperation in criminal matters.[6] The fulfilment of all these obligations should result in a situation where no cannabis for recreational use is in circulation.

The most serious provisions in the conventions are those about the obligations to criminalize specific acts. These obligations cover both small-scale cultivation for personal use[7] and cultivation that is not small-scale and/or is not intended for personal use.[8] Given these obligations, legalization or decriminalization of the cultivation of cannabis for recreational use is not an option. The question then is whether it is permissible to adopt a general policy of refraining from prosecution of these punishable offences (penal tolerance). The obligations to prosecute for essentially serious criminal offences, ensuing implicitly from the Single Convention, make it hard to argue that a policy of tolerating cannabis cultivation for the supply of retail shops is permissible on the basis of the expediency principle under the Single Convention. More specifically, such a policy of penal tolerance would contravene Article 3(6) of the Illicit Traffic Convention, which imposes an obligation to ensure maximum efficiency in criminal investigation and law enforcement. It is only for this provision – not with reference to the Single Convention nor with other provisions pertaining to cannabis in the Illicit Traffic Convention – that the Netherlands formulated a reservation. In view of the content and background of the reservation, international public law according to which reservations are fixed with respect to the law applicable at the time that they are formulated as well as the 'object and purpose' of the convention, the Dutch reservation does not leave sufficient room for adopting a policy of permitting cannabis cultivation. The INCB, also, takes the view that general policy-based penal tolerance of cannabis cultivation for recreational consumption – not designated for personal use – is contrary to the drugs conventions.

---

3 In particular, Article 36 of the Single Convention and Article 3(1) and 3(2) of the Illicit Traffic Convention.

4 Article 33 of the Single Convention.

5 Article 33 of the Single Convention and Article 37 of the Single Convention.

6 See the many provisions in the Single Convention and more particularly, the Illicit Traffic Convention.

7 See Article 36(1) of the Single Convention (which is not entirely clear), and the indisputable Article 3(2) of the Illicit Traffic Convention.

8 Article 36(1) of the Single Convention and Article 3(1) of the Single Convention.

The conclusion that the UN narcotic drugs conventions leave no room for condoning cannabis cultivation for the recreational user market would still hold, even if the Public Prosecutions Service were able to refrain from prosecution for cannabis cultivation intended for the supply of retail shops, with an appeal to the expediency principle under the conventions. The reason for this is that the expediency principle in criminal law cannot diminish the obligations of criminalization nor other obligations that in principle do not pertain to criminal law that arise from the conventions for states parties. Therefore, even in the case of permissible non-prosecution (penal tolerance) those states remain bound by general obligations to combat drugs,[9] obligations to prohibit and seize cannabis,[10] the obligation to take measures against cannabis use,[11] and the obligation to fight the cultivation of cannabis.[12] However, a policy of tolerating and actually permitting cannabis cultivation would imply that these obligations are not fulfilled, whereas the Netherlands is also legally bound to do so. Many of these obligations rest with the government, and also apply to municipalities. This multi-layered system of diverse obligations related to criminal law, administrative and other obligations would be incompatible with legalizing, decriminalizing, tolerating by virtue of a policy and/or otherwise regulating the cultivation of cannabis for recreational use.

Finally, it is important that cannabis cultivation for recreational use cannot be subsumed under the exception of 'medical and scientific purposes'. The scope of the exception is far too limited for that: it only covers the use of narcotic drugs as meaningful and/or effective medicine in concrete cases, the use of narcotic drugs to produce medicines for such cases, and scientific research for medicinal use, the production of medicines or medical science. The exception, therefore, does not comprise public health in a broad sense, so arguments that legalization, decriminalization or regulation of the cannabis market for recreational use would serve public health interests, founder on the conventions. The observation that the conventions reveal a limited, one-sided and rigid view of public health interests does not detract in any way from this conclusion. For that matter, the INCB also opposes stretching the exception of medical purposes in order to enable access to cannabis for recreational use.

5.2.2. EUROPEAN LAW

The instruments developed in the European Union to combat the illicit trade in drugs confirm and build on the obligations ensuing from the UN narcotic

9 Article 4 of the Single Convention.
10 Article 33 of the Single Convention and possibly Article 37 of the Single Convention.
11 Article 38 of the Single Convention.
12 Article 14(2) of the Illicit Traffic Convention.

drugs conventions. The Schengen acquis entails, among other things, the obligation 'to do whatever is possible' to prevent and counteract the harmful consequences of the illegal demand for more cannabis.[13] The Joint Action on Illegal Drug Trafficking requires the states to take the most 'appropriate measures' to combat the cultivation of cannabis for recreational use.[14] It would be difficult to maintain that a state meets these obligations if it were to legalize, decriminalize, tolerate by virtue of a policy and/or otherwise regulate the cultivation of cannabis for recreational use.

Furthermore, the Framework Decision on Illegal Drug Trafficking, the basic instrument with regard to such trafficking within the European Union, entails an obligation to criminalize the cultivation of cannabis for recreational use. This illustrates that legalization or decriminalization of such cultivation is not possible under European law either. It seems reasonable to assume that – in view of the considerations of the European Council, the European Commission and a few rulings of the European Court of Justice – the Framework Decision in principle also demands prosecution of large-scale or commercial cultivation of cannabis for recreational use. However, it would appear that in principle, the obligation to prosecute does not apply to joint cultivation and consumption in Cannabis Social Clubs.

5.3. ASSESSMENT OF THE ARGUMENTS AND INITIATIVES IN AND OUTSIDE THE NETHERLANDS

The previous chapter contains an account and categorization of the numerous arguments and initiatives (both in Dutch municipalities and in other countries) for regulating the cultivation of cannabis, witness the material presented for this book. The assessment of these arguments and initiatives in relation to the UN narcotic drugs conventions and European law consists of three parts. The first part is an explanation and evaluation of the legal arguments presented by and from within municipalities. This is followed by an overview and assessment of various factual, social and/or political arguments used by municipalities to justify the regulation of cannabis cultivation. It must be emphasized here that this book has not looked at the accuracy of the content or validity of this category of arguments: we have always assumed that these arguments are sound and on that premise, we have checked only whether regulation of cannabis cultivation on the grounds of these arguments is permissible under the UN narcotic

[13] Article 70(5) of the Schengen Implementation Agreement.

[14] Article 8 of the Joint Action.

drugs conventions and European laws on drugs. The third part constitutes an account, categorization and evaluation of modalities proposed by Dutch municipalities and introduced in countries other than the Netherlands for the regulation of cannabis cultivation for recreational purposes.

5.3.1. LEGAL ARGUMENTS

While it is legally possible for the Netherlands to denounce the Single Convention and the Illicit Traffic Convention, this course of action would also affect the efforts to fight other kinds of narcotic drugs or other forms of cannabis trafficking adversely, in addition to the risk of damage to the country's reputation in the international community, of international isolation and intense international pressure. Moreover, a withdrawal from the UN narcotic drugs conventions does not remove the obligations such as the criminalization of cannabis cultivation imposed on the Netherlands under European law. Another option would be to amend the UN narcotic drugs conventions. The states that are party to the Single Convention currently number 186 in total and those that are bound by the Illicit Traffic Convention number 190.[15] We conclude that this will make it impossible to amend these conventions in the foreseeable future. Nor does the modification of the Schedules of the Single Convention – e.g., removing cannabis from these Schedules – look like a realistic option. Even if cannabis were entirely removed from the Schedules, this will not relieve the Netherlands from its obligation to criminalize cannabis cultivation for recreational use by third parties. This rules out the legalization and decriminalization of the cultivation of cannabis, that is to say, insofar as this would mean commercial or other than small-scale cultivation. Therefore, that applies to cannabis cultivation intended for the supply of coffee shops as well. Finally, we conclude that the Netherlands cannot in good faith use a reservation to escape in a legally sound manner from the obligations pertaining to cannabis cultivation ensuing from the Single Convention and the Illicit Traffic Convention. This also means that the option to leave the Convention so as to re-accede, after having formulated a reservation that makes it possible to regulate cannabis cultivation, can hardly be seen as legally feasible.

Dutch municipalities primarily present arguments to support the claim that regulating the cultivation of cannabis would benefit the protection of public health in all sorts of ways. Among other things, they point out the importance of separating the soft drugs and hard drugs markets. The question arises whether it is legally possible to stretch the exception of 'medical and scientific purposes'

[15] See: http://treaties.un.org/ (Chapter VI, numbers 18 and 19) (status on 1 January 2019).

to such an extent that it would cover the general public health interest. That, however, is not the case. The main obstacles here are the restrictive meaning given to the exception in the Single Convention, the confirmation of that meaning in the INCB reports and the absence of state practice or a generally accepted broad interpretation of the exception. For similar reasons, the exception – and consequently the UN narcotic drugs conventions and European law that builds on them – does not allow for a scientific experiment to be set up that focuses on cannabis cultivation for recreational use. After all, in that case it is not the cannabis that is the subject or instrument of the scientific research, but rather, among other things, the control and organization of the cultivation and the distribution of the yield. Furthermore, the aim of the research is not the advancement of medical science or developing cannabis in order to produce a useful and/or effective medicine.

Also, the expediency principle, whether or not in connection with the current practice of tolerance of the sale of cannabis for recreational use to consumers and/or the Dutch reservation regarding the Illicit Traffic Convention, leaves no room for legalization, decriminalization, policy-based tolerance and/or other forms of regulating cannabis cultivation for recreational use. The Single Convention (implicitly), the Illicit Traffic Convention (explicitly) and European law (through case law) all entail obligations to prosecute serious cannabis-related offences. The question whether a particular case of cannabis cultivation is to be considered serious depends in principle, among other things, on its scale, the quantity of narcotic drugs involved and the possibly organized structure in which that cultivation and the associated distribution and trade take place. Indeed, within the context of the Illicit Traffic Convention, all acts involving cannabis that are not small-scale and/or are not intended for personal use appear to be considered serious. In the case of serious criminal acts, there is no place for a policy of non-prosecution based on expediency considerations. That is also the case if the Public Prosecutions Department were to rely on general public health interests. At any rate, insofar as such penal tolerance applies to the cultivation of cannabis that is not small-scale and not meant for personal use, there is no room for expediency on the basis of the reservation made by the Netherlands with respect to the Illicit Traffic Convention either. As mentioned above, the reservation leaves insufficient room for that, given the content and background of the reservation, international public law according to which reservations are fixed with respect to the law applicable at the time that they are formulated as well as the 'object and purpose' of the convention. In addition to this, the reservation has no bearing on the Single Convention, European law and all sorts of criminalization obligations, general obligations to combat and seize cannabis and prohibit the possession of cannabis included in the Illicit Traffic Convention. Finally, the analysis in previous chapters also led to the rejection of the reasoning that to extend the permissive policy on coffee shops so as to include cannabis cultivation for coffee shops is such a small step that, if the current policy-based tolerance is permissible, that extension must also be permissible. In view of European law and in particular the UN narcotic drugs conventions (while taking into account the reservation with respect to the Illicit Traffic Convention), it is hard to defend that the current state of affairs in the Netherlands, where the sale of cannabis by coffee shops to customers on a serious scale is condoned as a matter of general policy, is permissible within international law. Moreover, it is difficult to maintain that extension of the policy of tolerance to cover cannabis cultivation would not constitute an essential change, but merely a difference of degree. After all, the consequence of such an extension would be that the Netherlands would allow a fully-fledged domestic cannabis economy, from cultivation to sale, aimed at recreational users.

Finally, the UN narcotic drugs conventions contain a few so-called 'safeguard clauses' to protect national law and in some cases, the conventions de facto leave room for implementation. However, none of these clauses and these opportunities for implementation offer the states parties the option of legalizing, decriminalizing, tolerating by virtue of a policy and/or otherwise regulating the cultivation of cannabis for recreational use. The clauses either have no bearing on obligations relevant for cannabis cultivation or cannot actually be used by the Netherlands for that purpose. Contrary to what is sometimes – incorrectly – assumed, some provisions (in particular Article 36(4) of the Single Convention, Article 2(1) of the Illicit Traffic Convention and Article 3(11) of the Illicit Traffic Convention), do not have any 'safeguard clauses' at all.

5.3.2. FACTUAL, SOCIAL AND/OR POLITICAL ARGUMENTS

In addition to the legal arguments discussed above, Dutch municipalities present various factual, social and/or political arguments. Most of these reflect the problems that municipalities face in connection with the cultivation, distribution, trade, sale, purchase and use of cannabis.

As mentioned before, improving public health is an interest featuring in many arguments propounded by municipalities when making the case for regulating cannabis cultivation for recreational use. These are arguments related to controlling the cannabis quality, fire and contamination risks posed by hemp nurseries in residential areas and separating the soft drugs and hard drugs markets. Because of the unilateral and rigid prohibitive approach of the protection of public health adopted in the UN narcotic drugs conventions, the INCB and – albeit a little more moderately – in European law, none of the public health arguments can be accepted under international law to allow the cultivation of cannabis for recreational use in order to supply coffee shops or other distribution points.

Fighting crime that may or may not be organized is another interest that supports many of the arguments used by municipalities. Among other things, municipalities argue that regulating cannabis cultivation for the recreational user market will decrease the level of involvement of organized crime in that market, and will also reduce the cannabis export and indirect crime such as stealing electrical power, threatening citizens and money-laundering. These arguments in themselves tie in with the rationale of the Illicit Traffic Convention, the EU Joint Action on Illegal Drug Trafficking and the EU Framework Decision on Illegal Drug Trafficking in particular. Nonetheless, the way in which the municipalities on the one hand and the UN narcotic drugs conventions and European law on the other hand aim to prevent and combat those criminal activities are diametrically opposed. Under international law, there is an obligation to achieve this objective through prohibitive and repressive action against cannabis cultivation, among other things, in order to stamp out cannabis for recreational use completely as well as the criminal activities associated with the cultivation, trade, distribution, sale, purchase and consumption of cannabis. This approach is explicitly endorsed by the INCB. This flies in the face of the approach proposed by the municipalities to permit a regulation of cannabis cultivation.

For the same reasons, several other arguments cannot qualify the obligations under international law regarding cannabis cultivation for recreational use, let alone invalidate them. These are arguments that regulation of cannabis cultivation for the recreational user market will lead to a reduction in nuisance and damage for third parties, offers fiscal and other economic advantages, increases administrative control and benefits the credibility of the authorities and offers legal certainty and security to coffee shop owners and cannabis users. Some of these arguments are diametrically opposed to considerations of the ECJ and the INCB, among other bodies.

5.3.3. REGULATING MODALITIES IN DUTCH MUNICIPALITIES AND THOSE APPLIED IN COUNTRIES OTHER THAN THE NETHERLANDS

More concrete forms of legalized, permitted or at any rate regulated cannabis cultivation can be found in some other countries than the Netherlands. Pertinent examples in this respect are Belgium, Spain, Uruguay and the federal states of Colorado and Washington in the United States. The value of discussing developments in these countries is that one can see how certain regulating modalities or the arguments on which they are founded relate to the UN narcotic drugs conventions and/or European law. The developments in those countries and federal states, however, do not provide any legal argument that something is permitted under international or European law. The developments in these and some other states parties do not establish generally accepted interpretations or state practice that enables a reading of international law such that regulation of cannabis cultivation can now be deemed to be compliant with it. The number of countries that openly came out in favour of or began legalization, decriminalization, policy-based tolerance and/or other forms of regulating cannabis cultivation for recreational use makes up only a small part of the total number of states parties or of the EU member states, in absolute terms or percentage-wise.

i. Regulated Legalization of Cannabis Cultivation

Uruguay is the first and currently the only country in the world that has formally legalized the production, distribution and possession of cannabis for recreational use. Legalization has also taken place in the laws of the federal states of Colorado and Washington in the United States, but all cannabis-related activities there as well as in the rest of the United States are still prohibited under federal legislation. Uruguay, Colorado and Washington have implemented in their laws a licensing scheme for cannabis cultivation. The legalization runs counter to the criminalization obligations in the UN narcotic drugs conventions.[16] Were the Netherlands to legalize cannabis cultivation for the recreational users market, this would also contravene European law, in particular the Joint Action on Illegal Drug Trafficking[17] and the EU Framework Decision on Illegal Drug Trafficking.[18] The claim that regulated legalization would come closest to meeting the objectives of the conventions in a substantial way does not alter the fact that the state would be in breach of these conventions. Also, the fact that the law on legalization came about in a democratic process does not detract at all from the obligations undertaken by a state internationally via a treaty or within the European Union.

ii. Cannabis Cultivation and Joint Consumption in Cannabis Social Clubs

Uruguay also legally permits joint cultivation in collectives and/or social clubs. There are also Cannabis Social Clubs (CSCs) in Belgium and Spain but these have not been legalized. With respect to the Netherlands, the city of Utrecht has proposed permitting – an experiment or pilot project with – CSCs like the ones in countries other than the Netherlands. International law leaves no room for legalizing or decriminalizing joint cultivation of cannabis within CSCs. The UN narcotic drugs conventions and the EU Framework Decision on Illegal Drug Trafficking are major obstacles to that.[19] In view of the fact that it

16 See Article 36 of the Single Convention and Article 3 of the Illicit Traffic Convention.

17 See Article 8 of the Joint Action.

18 See Article 2 of the Framework Decision.

19 See Article 36 of the Single Convention, Article 3(1) (not 3(2)) of the Illicit Traffic Convention and Article 2 of the Framework Decision.

is defensible to not treat cultivation within CSCs as a serious criminal offence (given the similarity between joint cannabis cultivation for personal use and personal cultivation for one's own personal use), in principle the Netherlands has the option under the UN narcotic drugs conventions as well as European law to decide whether or not to prosecute CSCs on the basis of expediency considerations. If the Netherlands used the leeway it has for policy-based non-prosecution (penal tolerance) with regard to CSCs, that would not mean that it can tolerate such clubs administratively or de facto (administrative tolerance). Here too, what we see is that the conventions contain all sorts of obligations that in principle do not pertain to criminal law – including the obligation to seize cannabis – and that are intended to combat its cultivation, and they effectively stand in the way of such tolerance.[20] The moment the authorities know precisely where such a cannabis club is located, it is permissible to refrain from prosecuting that club; however, a decision to forgo acting against it in at least a factual or administrative way would conflict with said obligations. There is therefore no place to allow CSCs from an administrative/policy-based perspective also on account of the obligations that do not pertain to criminal law (mostly UN Convention based). However, if a state party disregards the CSC, without regulation, it will be less clearly and at any rate less obviously in breach of the Convention's obligations.

iii. Cannabis Cultivation by Non-Profit or Commercial Producers

Some municipalities envisage a regulating system in which the cultivation of cannabis for the supply of coffee shops is carried out professionally by non-commercial parties that will need to have a licence for that purpose that is granted subject to terms and conditions. Most municipal plans, though, involve cultivation to supply coffee shops through a commercial party, also within a licensing system. The UN narcotic drugs conventions and European law require the criminalization of cannabis cultivation for recreational use by third parties. The obligation does not depend on whether the grower operates on a non-commercial basis or does so for profit, although in the latter case, the criminal cultivation of cannabis will be seen as rather serious. Since the UN narcotic drugs conventions and European law do not make a distinction between commercial and non-commercial growers with respect to any of these obligations, the full range of obligations ensuing from international law also applies when the cultivation of cannabis for recreational use by third parties is non-commercial in nature. This is about the above-mentioned criminalization obligations, obligations to prosecute, obligations to prohibit and seize cannabis,

20 See, among others, the Articles 4, 33, 37 and 38 of the Single Convention, Article 14 of the Illicit Traffic Convention, Article 70(5) of the Schengen Implementation Agreement and Article 8 of the Joint Action.

and the obligation to fight the cultivation of cannabis. However, a distinction that does have relevance is the one between 'serious criminal acts' and those that are not. If a grower's operation is non-commercial, and if he produces truly small quantities of cannabis and these quantities remain within a closed circuit of users and do not end up on the market more or less freely, it can be argued that the cultivation is non-serious. In that case, there would be room under both the UN narcotic drugs conventions and European law to abstain from prosecution, but the government still cannot permit the cultivation, since the criminalization obligation and the various obligations that in principle do not pertain to criminal law are still to be fulfilled.

iv. Cannabis Cultivation for Recreational Use under Medical or Scientific Programmes

In the preceding sections, it has become clear on several occasions that the conventions do not allow the inclusion of 'public health purposes' in the exception of 'medical purposes' so as to permit cannabis cultivation and all other acts aimed at the sale of cannabis for recreational use. Insofar as medical programmes intentionally or unintentionally permit recreational cannabis users access to cannabis, these programmes do not qualify for the exception, and therefore contravene the obligations laid down in both the UN narcotic drugs conventions and the EU laws on drugs. Incidentally, the INCB also urges the states parties not to permit cannabis cultivation for recreational purposes under the guise of medical programmes. In previous sections it has also become clear that the exception of 'scientific purposes' has a limited scope and that it does not allow the cultivation of cannabis for recreational use under that heading either. That means that none of the pilot projects and experiments with regulating the cultivation of cannabis for recreational use as proposed by municipalities can take place under this exception. Consequently, implementation of these projects would conflict with the UN narcotic drugs conventions and by extension with relevant European law.

5.4. SUMMARY

The answer to the central question in this book is that legalization, decriminalization, policy-based tolerance and/or other forms of regulating cannabis cultivation for recreational use is not permissible under the UN narcotic drugs conventions and the EU laws on drugs. This answer is based on detailed explanations and analyses of international law in the preceding chapters. The level of detail was achieved by looking not merely at the key question of this book, but also by approaching it from the many arguments and proposals used by municipalities for regulating cannabis cultivation for recreational use as well as the relevant legislation created and passed in countries other than the Netherlands. The accounts of those Dutch arguments and those in other countries and regulating modalities illustrate the legal complexity of the question whether regulated permission for cannabis cultivation aimed at recreational users is possible under international law. Several of these accounts also provide insight into the problems that authorities face in connection with the cultivation, distribution, trade, sale, purchase and use of cannabis. By systematically assessing the arguments and initiatives in the light of international law, the answer to the central question was reinforced. All these evaluations of arguments and regulating modalities always led to the conclusion that legalization, decriminalization, policy-based tolerance and/or other forms of regulating cannabis cultivation for recreational use is not permissible under the UN narcotic drugs conventions and the EU laws on drugs. In other words: none of the arguments and regulating modalities presented by the Dutch municipalities and in countries other than the Netherlands can legitimize the tolerance of cannabis cultivation for the recreational users market, under the UN narcotic drugs conventions and relevant European law. This also answers the two subquestions formulated in the introduction of this book. The conclusion is that given the international obligations pertaining to the fight against drugs, there is no room for regulating cannabis cultivation intended for the supply of retail shops. The same goes for regulating cannabis cultivation in the context of Cannabis Social Clubs or via other modalities that aim to serve third parties for recreational use.

BIBLIOGRAPHY

INTERNATIONAL DOCUMENTS

UNITED NATIONS

UN General Assembly Resolution 64/182, 'International cooperation against the world drug problem', adopted 65th plenary meeting on 18 December 2009, *UN Doc.* A/RES/64/182, 30 March 2010.
UN General Assembly Resolution 67/193, *UN Doc.* A/RES/67/193, 23 April 2013.
UN General Assembly Special Session on the World Drug Problem, 'Our Joint Commitment to effectively addressing and countering the world drug problem', *UN Doc.* A/RES/S-30-/1, 19 April 2016.
ECOSOC Resolution 914 D (XXXIV), *UN Doc.* E/RES/1962/914(XXXIV)D, 3 August 1962.
ECOSOC Resolution 1993/42, *UN Doc.* E/RES/1993/42, 27 July 1993.

COMMISSION ON NARCOTIC DRUGS

CND, 'Political Declaration and Plan of Action', *UN Doc.* E/2009/28, E/CN.7/2009/12.
——, Report on the fifty-second session (14 March 2008 and 11–20 March 2009), *UN Doc.* E/2009/28, E/CN.7/2009/12.
——, Report on the fifty-third session (2 December 2009 and 8–12 March 2010), *UN Doc.* E/2010/28, E/CN.7/2010/18.
CND Resolution 52/5, *UN Doc.* E/2009/28, E/CN.7/2009/12.
CND Resolution 53/15, *UN Doc.* E/2010/28, E/CN.7/2010/18.
CND Resolution 55/9, *UN Doc.* E/2012/28, E/CN.7/2012/18.
CND Resolution 56/10, *UN Doc.* E/2013/28, E/CN.7/2013/14.
CND Resolution 56/2, *UN Doc.* E/2013/28, E/CN.7/2013/14.

INTERNATIONAL NARCOTICS CONTROL BOARD

INCB, *Report of the International Narcotics Control Board for 1992*, New York: United Nations, 1993.
——, *Report of the International Narcotics Control Board for 1997*, New York: United Nations, 1998.
——, *Report of the International Narcotics Control Board for 2001*, New York: United Nations, 2002.

——, *Report of the International Narcotics Control Board for 2003*, New York: United Nations, 2004.
——, *Report of the International Narcotics Control Board for 2004*, New York: United Nations, 2005.
——, *Report of the International Narcotics Control Board for 2007*, New York: United Nations 2008.
——, *Report of the International Narcotics Control Board for 2008*, New York: United Nations, 2009.
——, *Report of the International Narcotics Control Board for 2009*, New York: United Nations, 2010.
——, *Report of the International Narcotics Control Board for 2010*, New York: United Nations, 2011.
——, *Report of the International Narcotics Control Board for 2011*, New York: United Nations, 2012.
——, *Report of the International Narcotics Control Board for 2012*, New York: United Nations, 2013.
——, 'Uruguay is breaking the International Conventions on Drug Control with the Cannabis Legislation approved by its Congress', UNIS/NAR/1190, 11 December 2013.
——, *Report of the International Narcotics Control Board for 2014*, New York: United Nations, 2015.
——, *Report of the International Narcotics Control Board for 2016*, New York: United Nations, 2017.
——, *Report of the International Narcotics Control Board for 2017*, New York: United Nations, 2018.
Press Release of INCB of 21 June 2018 (*International Narcotics Control Board expresses deep concern about the legalization of cannabis for non-medical use in Canada*), UNIS/NAR/1353.

CONFERENCES UN HUMAN RIGHTS AND DRUGS CONVENTIONS

United Nations, 'Conference for the adoption of a Single Convention on Narcotic Drugs. New York - 24 January–25 March 1961, Official Records, Volume I', *UN Doc.* E/CONF. 34/24/.
——, 'Conference for the adoption of a Single Convention on Narcotic Drugs. New York - 24 January–25 March 1961, Official Records, Volume II', *UN Doc.* E/CONF. 34/24/Add. 1.
——, 'United Nations Conference to consider amendments to the Single Convention on Narcotic Drugs, 1961. Geneva – 6–24 March 1972, Official Records, Volume I', New York, 1974, *UN Doc.* E/CONF. 63/10.
——, 'United Nations Conference to consider amendments to the Single Convention on Narcotic Drugs, 1961. Geneva - 6–24 March 1972, Official Records, Volume II', New York, 1973, *UN Doc.* E/CONF. 63/10/Add. 1.

——, 'Conference for the Adoption of a Convention against Illicit Traffic in Narcotic Drugs and Psychotropic Substances. Vienna, 25 November–20 December 1988, Official Records, Volume I', *UN Doc.* E/CONF. 82/16.

——, 'Conference for the Adoption of a Convention against Illicit Traffic in Narcotic Drugs and Psychotropic Substances. Vienna, 25 November–20 December 1988, Official Records, Volume II', *UN Doc.* E/CONF. 82/16/Add.1.

OFFICIAL COMMENTARY ON UN COVENANTS AND CONVENTIONS

United Nations, *Commentary on the Single Convention on Narcotic Drugs, 1961*, New York: 1973.

——, *Commentary on the Protocol Amending the Single Convention on Narcotic Drugs, 1961*, New York: 1976.

——, *Commentary on the United Nations Convention Against Illicit Traffic in Narcotic Drugs and Psychotropic Substances*, Vienna: 1988.

INTERNATIONAL LAW COMMISSION

ILC, Guide to Reservations and the Commentaries thereto, in: Report of the ILC on the Work of its 63rd session, General Assembly, Official Records, 66th Session, Supplement n° 10, Addendum 1, *UN Doc.* A/66/10/Add.1. (2011).

OTHERS

UNODC, *A Century of International Drug Control*, Vienna: United Nations, 2008.

EUROPEAN UNION

EUROPEAN COMMISSION

Proposal for a Council Framework Decision laying down minimum provisions on the constituent elements of criminal acts and penalties in the field of illicit drug trafficking, Brussels: Commission of the European Communities, 2001/C 304 E/03, *OJ* C 304 E/172, 30 October 2001.

Proposal Framework Decision Illegal Drug Trafficking, Brussels: Commission of the European Communities, 23 May 2001, COM(2001) 259, 2001/0114 (CNS).

Explanatory Statement, Proposal Framework Decision Illegal Drug Trafficking, Brussels: Commission of the European Communities, 23 May 2001, COM(2001) 259, 2001/0114 (CNS).

Report from the Commission on the implementation of Framework Decision 2004/757/JHA laying down minimum provisions on the constituent elements of criminal acts and penalties in the field of illicit drug trafficking, Brussels, 10 December 2009, COM(2009)669 final, SEC(2009)1661.

Proposal for a Directive of the European Parliament and of the Council amending Council Framework Decision 2004/757/JHA of 25 October 2004 laying down minimum provisions on the constituent elements of criminal acts and penalties in the field of illicit drug trafficking, as regards the definition of drug, 17 September 2013, COM(2013) 618 final, 2013/0304 (COD).

European Parliament legislative resolution of 17 April 2014 on the proposal for a directive of the European Parliament and of the Council amending Council Framework Decision 2004/757/JHA of 25 October 2004 laying down minimum provisions on the constituent elements of criminal acts and penalties in the field of illicit drug trafficking, as regards the definition of drug (COM(2013) 0618, C7-0271/2013 – 2013/0304 (COD).

COUNCIL OF THE EUROPEAN UNION

Council Decision 90/611/EEC of 22 October 1990 concerning the conclusion, on behalf of the European Economic Community, of the United Nations Convention against illicit traffic in narcotic drugs and psychotropic substances, *OJ* 1990 L 326/56.

Council Resolution of 20 December 1996 on sentencing for serious illicit drug-trafficking, *OJ*1997, C 10/02.

Council of the European Union, Proposal for the Framework Decision on illegal drug trafficking, Brussels, 27 May 2002, Document 8862/1/02, Rev 1, DROIPEN 31 CORDROGUE 40, file 2001/0114 (CNS).

Council of the European Union, Proposal for the Framework Decision on illegal drug trafficking, Brussels, 2 October 2002, Document 10321/1/02, Rev 1, DROIPEN 42 CORDROGUE 47, file 2001/0114 (CNS).

Declaration for entry in the Council minutes, in: Annex to Council of the European Union, Adoption of the Council Framework Decision on illicit drug trafficking, Brussels: 28 September 2004, 2001/0114 (CNS), 12451/04, DROIPEN 47, CORDROGUE 63.

EUROPEAN PARLIAMENT

The Report on the Proposal Framework Decision on ilegal drug trafficking, Brussels: European Parliament, Committee on Citizens' Freedoms and Rights, Justice and Home Affairs, Rapporteur A.M. Oostlander, A5-0095/2004, 23 February 2004, PE 338.598.

ORGANISATION OF THE AMERICAN STATES

Scenario Team appointed by the Organization of American States, *Scenarios for the Drug Problem in the Americas 2013–2025*, Washington: Organization of American States, 2013.

NATIONAL DOCUMENTS

NETHERLANDS

Kamerstukken II 1990–1991, 22 080 (R 1406), nr. 3 (MvT).
Kamerstukken II 1991–1992, 22 080 (R 1406), nr. 4 (Voorlopig verslag).
Kamerstukken II 1991–1992, 22 080 (R 1406), nr. 6 (MvA).
Kamerstukken II 2002–2003, 23 490, nr. 246 (Ontwerpbesluiten Unie-Verdrag; Brief van de Minister van Justitie).
Kamerstukken II 1994–1995, 24 077, nr. 2 (Drugsbeleid).
Kamerstukken II 1994–1995, 24 077, nr. 3 (Drugsbeleid; Nota).
Kamerstukken II 2005–2006, 24 077, nr. 168 (Drugsbeleid; Brief van de Minister van Justitie).
Kamerstukken II 2012–2013, 24 077, nr. 310 (Drugsbeleid; Brief van de Minister van Veiligheid en Justitie).
Kamerstukken II 2012–2013, 24 077, nr. 312 (Drugsbeleid; Verslag van een algemeen overleg).
Kamerstukken II 2005–2006, 30 339, nr. 3 (MvT).
College van procureurs-generaal openbaar ministerie, 'Aanwijzing Opiumwet (2015A003)', *Stcrt.* 2015/5391.

BELGIUM

Kamer van Volksvertegenwoordigers 2011, Beknopt Verslag Commissie voor de Justitie, *CRABV* 53 COM 190 (Antwoord Staatssecretaris Carl Devlies op Vraag van de heer Bert Schoofs aan de minister van Justitie over 'de Cannabis Social Club' (nr. 3651)).

CANADA

Senate, *Cannabis: Our Position for a Canadian Public Policy. Report of the Senate Special Committee on Illegal Drugs*, 2002.

URUGUAY

'Statement' of 4 February 2014, Minister of Foreign Affairs of Uruguay, to the Members of the International Narcotics Control Board, about the relationship between the INCB and Uruguay in recent months and the newly enacted law number 19.172.

LITERATURE

B. Arp, 'Denunciation Followed by Re-accession with Reservations to a Treaty: A Critical Appraisal of Contemporary State Practice', *Netherlands International Law Review*, vol. 1 (2), 2014.

D. Barrett, *'Unique in International Relations'? A Comparison of the International Narcotics Control Board and the UN Human Rights Treaty Bodies*, London: International Harm Reduction Association, 2008.

——, *Drugs and the Convention on the Rights of the Child*, Stockholm: Stockholm University, 2018.

D.R. Bewley-Taylor, 'Challenging the UN drug control conventions: problems and possibilities', *The International Journal of Drug Policy*', vol. 14 (2), 2003.

——, 'Towards revision of the UN drug control conventions. The logic and dilemmas of Like-Minded Groups', *Series on Legislative Reform of Drug Policies*, Nr. 19, March 2012, pp. 1–16.

——, 'The Contemporary International Drug Control System: A History of the UNGASS Decade', in: John Collins (ed.), *Governing the Global Drug Wars*, London: London School of Economics, 2012.

D.R. Bewley-Taylor & M. Jelsma, 'Fifty Years of the 1961 Single Convention on Narcotic Drugs: A Reinterpretation', *Series on Legislative Reform of Drug Policies*, Nr. 12, March 2011, pp. 1–20.

——, 'Regime change: Re-visiting the 1961 Single Convention on Narcotic Drugs', 23 *International Journal of Drug Policy* 2012, pp. 72–81.

——, 'The Limits of Latitude. The UN drug control conventions', *Series on Legislative Reform of Drug Policies*, Nr. 18, March 2012.

T. Blickman, 'European Cannabis Policies Under Attack', *TNI Briefing*, April 2002, beschikbaar op: http://www.undrugcontrol.info/en/issues/cannabis/item/2400-european-cannabis-policies-under-attack (laatst bezocht februari 2014).

T. Blom, *Drugs in het recht, recht onder druk* (diss. Rotterdam), Deventer: Gouda Quint 1998.

——, *Opiumwetgeving en drugsbeleid*, Deventer: Kluwer, 2008.

N. Brett Boister, *The Suppression of Illicit Drugs Through International Law*, Nottingham: University of Nottingham, 1998.

M. Bossuyt & J. Wouters, *Grondlijnen van internationaal recht*, Antwerpen/Oxford: Intersentia, 2005.

S.K. Chatterjee, *Legal Aspects of International Drug Control*, The Hague,/Boston/ London: Martinus Nijhoff Publishers, 1981.

Commissie-Van de Donk, *Geen deuren maar daden. Nieuwe accenten in het Nederlands drugsbeleid*, Advies Commissie Drugsbeleid, 2009.

Commission G. Le Dain, *Cannabis. A Report of the Commission of Inquiry into the Non-Medical Use of Drugs*, Ottawa, 1972.

J. Crawford, *Brownlie's Principles of Public International Law*, Oxford: Oxford University Press, 2012.

D. Dupras, *Canada's International Obligations under the Leading International Conventions on the Control of Narcotic Drugs*, Ottawa: Library of Parliament, 1988.

European Monitoring Centre for Drugs and Drug Addiction, *Cannabis legalization in Europe. An overview*, Luxembourg: Publications Office of the European Union, 2018.

P. Gallahue, R. Gunawan, F. Rahman, K. El Mufti, N. U. Din & R. Felten, *The Death Penalty for Drug Offences: Global Overview 2012*, London: International Harm Reduction Association, 2012.

W. Geelhoed, 'Europeesrechtelijke eisen aan de beslissing omtrent de omvang van de vervolging', in: J.H. Crijns, P.P.J. van der Meij & J.M. ten Voorde (eds.), *De waarde van waarheid. Opstellen over waarheid en waarheidsvinding in het strafrecht*, Den Haag: Boom Juridische Uitgevers, 2008, pp. 139–161.

——, *Het opportuniteitsbeginsel en het recht van de Europese Unie* (diss. Leiden), Deventer: Kluwer, 2013.

I. Giménez, 'A step back in Spanish drug policies. A de facto criminalisation of cannabis use?', 19 December 2013, http://www.undrugcontrol.info/en/weblog/item/5227-a-step-back-in-spanish-drug-policies.

Th.A. Green (ed.), *Folklore: An Encyclopedia of Beliefs, Customs, Tales, Music, and Art*, vol. 1, Santa Barbara: ABC-CLIO, 1997.

J. Gurulé, 'The 1988 U.N. Convention Against Illicit Traffic in Narcotic Drugs and Psychotropic Substances – A Ten Year Perspective: Is International Cooperation Merely Illusory?', 22 *Fordham International Law Journal* 1998, pp. 74–121.

H. Hennekens, 'Grenzen aan het opportuniteitsbeginsel. Een verkenning in relatie tot het drugsbeleid', in: J.W. Fokkens, P.H.P.H.M.C. van Kempen, H.J.B. Sackers & P.C. Vegter (eds.), *Ad hunc modem. Opstellen over materieel strafrecht* (Machielse-bundel), Deventer: Kluwer, 2013.

R. Hodgkin & P. Newell, *Implementation Handbook for the Convention on the Rights of the Child*, Geneva: UNICEF, 2007.

J. de Hullu, *Materieel strafrecht. Over algemene leerstukken van strafrechtelijke aansprakelijkheid naar Nederlands recht*, Deventer: Wolters Kluwer, 2018.

International Drug Policy Consortium, *The International Narcotics Control Board: Current Tensions and Options for Reform*, IDPC Briefing Paper 7, 2008.

——, 'Bolivia's legal reconciliation with the UN Single Convention on Narcotic Drugs' (Advocacy Note), International Drug Policy Consortium, July 2011, http://papers.ssrn.com/sol3/papers.cfm?abstract_id=1908775.

B. Kilmer, K. Kruithof, M. Pardal, J.P. Caulkins & J. Rubin, *Multinational overview of cannabis production regimes*, RAND Europe/WODC, 2013.

K. Krajewski, 'How flexible are the United Nations drug conventions?', 10 *International Journal of Drug Policy* 4 (1999), pp. 329–338.

A. Lande, 'The Single Convention on Narcotic Drugs, 1961', 16 *International Organization* 4 (1962), pp. 776–797.

R. Lines, '"Deliver us from evil"? – The Single Convention on Narcotic Drugs, 50 years on', 1 *International Journal on Human Rights and Drug Policy* 2010, pp. 1–13.

W.B. McAllister, 'Conflicts of Interest in the International Drug Control System', in: William O. Walker III (ed.), *Drug Control Policy: Essays in Historical and Comparative Perspective*, University Park, Pennsylvania: Pennsylvania State University Press, 1992.

J.H. Mills, 'Science, Diplomacy and Cannabis: The Evidence Base and the International Drugs Regulatory System, 1924–1961', in: John Collins (ed.), *Governing the Global Drug Wars*, London: London School of Economics 2012.

D. Müller, 'Reservations and Time: Is There Only One Right Moment to Formulate and to React to Reservations?', 24 *European Journal of International Law* 4 (2013).

A. Noll, 'Drug abuse and penal provisions of the international drug control treaties', 29 *Bulletin on Narcotics* 4 (1977), pp. 41–57 (par. A).

M. Nougier, 'Informal Drug Policy Dialogue Report. Warsaw, Poland, 14th to 16th February 2013', May 2013, beschikbaar op: http://www.diogenis.info/ckfinder/userfiles/files/Informal%20Drug%20Policy%20Dialogue%20in%20Warsaw_FINAL.pdf (laatst bezocht: februari 2014).

R. Room, 'Reform by subtraction: The path of denunciation of international drug treaties and reaccession with reservations', *The International Journal of Drug Policy*, vol. 23 (5), 2012.

R. Room & S. McKay, *Roadmaps for Reforming the UN Drug Conventions*, Oxford: Beckley Foundation Press, 2012.

R. Room & P. Reuter, 'How well do international drug conventions protect public health?', 379 *The Lancet* 2012 (January 7), pp. 84–91.

E. Shils, *Tradition*, Chicago: University of Chicago Press, 1981.

J. Silvis, 'De internationale juridische speelruimte voor Nederlands drugbeleid', in: T. Blom, H. de Doelder & D.J. Hessing (eds.), *Naar een consistent drugbeleid. Een congresverslag*, Deventer: Gouda Quint, 1996, pp. 215–224.

J. Sinha, *The History and Development of the Leading International Drug Control Conventions*, Ottawa: Library of Parliament, Parliamentary Research Branch, 2001.

T.M.C. Asser Instituut, *Experimenteren met het Gedogen van de Teelt van Cannabis ten Behoeve van de Bevoorrading van Coffeeshops – Internationaal rechtelijke en Europees rechtelijke aspecten*, Den Haag: 2005.

P.H.P.H.M.C. van Kempen, 'Communautaire doorwerking en straf(proces)recht', in: M.J. Borgers, F.G.H. Kristen & J.B.H.M. Simmelink (eds.), *Implementatie van kaderbesluiten*, Nijmegen: Wolf Legal Publishers, 2006.

P.H.P.H.M.C. van Kempen & M.I. Fedorova, *Internationaal recht en cannabis. Een beoordeling op basis van VN-drugsverdragen en EU-regelgeving van gemeentelijke en buitenlandse opvattingen pro regulering van cannabisteelt voor recreatief gebruik*, Deventer: Kluwer, 2014.

—— *International Law and Cannabis II. Regulation of Cannabis Cultivation and Trade for Recreational Use: Positive Human Rights Obligations versus UN Narcotic Drugs Conventions*, Cambridge: Intersentia, 2019.

A.M. Weisburd, 'Customary International Law: The Problem of Treaties', 21 *Vanderbilt Journal of Transnational Law* 1 (1988), pp. 1–46.

G. Zuffa, 'How to determine personal use in drug legislation. The "threshold controversy" in the light of the Italian experience', *Series on Legislative Reform of Drug Policies*, Nr. 15, August 2011.

EXECUTIVE SUMMARY INTERNATIONAL LAW AND CANNABIS II

Are authorities permitted under international law to regulate the cultivation of and trade in cannabis for recreational use? In our first book on *International Law and Cannabis I*,[1] we conclude that this is not the case when the question is considered strictly from the internal perspective of the relevant UN narcotic drugs conventions (the UN 1961 Single Convention and the UN 1988 Illicit Traffic Convention). Whether the answer is different when considered from the external perspective of human rights conventions (ICESCR, ESC, ICCPR, ECHR) is the subject of our second book on *International Law and Cannabis II*.[2] From this external perspective there is a possibility to regulate, even by legalization, the cultivation of and trade in cannabis for the recreational user market.

POTENTIAL RELEVANCE OF HUMAN RIGHTS OBLIGATIONS

Pleas in favour of regulating cannabis cultivations and trade for recreational use are often based on arguments that relate to the interests of individual and public health, the security of citizens and crime control. The essence of these arguments is that regulation of cannabis can better protect these interests than a prohibitive approach. This is interesting from a human rights perspective because health, security and crime control are also covered by the umbrella of human rights. The right to health, the right to life, the right not to be subjected to inhumane treatment and the right to privacy are the source of the so-called positive obligations for the fulfilment of the stated interests. Positive human rights obligations require states to take measures in order to guarantee fundamental human rights of individuals. Central to this study are the obligations to improve actively individual and public health, and to protect

[1] Piet Hein P.H.M.C. van Kempen & Masha I. Fedorova, *International Law and Cannabis I. Regulation of Cannabis Cultivation for Recreational Use under the UN Narcotic Drugs Conventions and the EU Legal Instruments in Anti-Drugs Policy*, Cambridge: Intersentia, 2019.

[2] Piet Hein P.H.M.C. van Kempen & Masha I. Fedorova, *International Law and Cannabis II. Regulation of Cannabis Cultivation and Trade for Recreational Use: Positive Human Rights Obligations versus UN Narcotic Drugs Conventions*, Cambridge: Intersentia, 2019.

actively the lives and physical and mental integrity and privacy of citizens. The so-called negative obligations – that is: obligations that stipulate that a state has to abstain from unlawful interference with rights guaranteed under the human rights conventions – are less relevant for the question whether states are allowed to permit cannabis for recreational use through regulation.

CENTRAL RESEARCH QUESTIONS

In the second book on *International law and Cannabis II*, the first central question is whether states – on the basis of their positive human rights obligations for the protection of individual and public health, the security of citizens and crime control – can be obligated to regulate cannabis cultivation and trade for recreational use if such regulation ensures a better protection of these interests than a prohibitive drug policy in conformity with the narcotic drugs conventions. To the extent that such an obligation can be established, the second question arises whether states can or must prioritize their positive human rights obligations rather than their obligations under the drugs conventions.

CONCLUSIONS OF THIS RESEARCH

Both questions are answered in the affirmative. The regulation of cannabis cultivation and trade for recreational use, because of the interests of individual and public health, security and crime control, can find its basis in positive human rights obligations that arise from international human rights conventions (Chapter 2). Under international law, states must give priority to their human rights obligations over and above any conflicting obligations under the UN drugs conventions (Chapter 3). This means that states have the possibility under international law to regulate cannabis despite their obligations under the UN drugs conventions. However, this applies only when certain conditions are met (Chapter 4).

PRIMARY CONDITIONS FOR REGULATING CANNABIS CULTIVATION AND TRADE FOR RECREATIONAL USE

The possibility for states to regulate cannabis cultivation and trade in view of their positive human rights obligations only exists if at least the following conditions are met:

1. *Relevant human rights-based interest.* First, the regulation of cannabis cultivation and trade should protect interests that are relevant from the

perspective of positive human rights obligations. Otherwise, the potential applicability of such obligations is out of the question.

In the discussion about the possibilities of regulating cannabis cultivation and trade, several arguments in its favour are presented that – assuming their empirical validity – are supported by one or more of those positive obligations. These relevant arguments hold that is it desirable to regulate cannabis because such regulation would better protect the following interests: safeguarding the quality of cannabis; monitoring the cannabis chain; reducing peripheral crime (murder, manslaughter, causing death by negligence, abuse and assault and threats); protection of health, life and the physical and mental integrity of neighbours and local residents (e.g. against fire or seriously harmful infections, such as legionella, that result from the illegal and unsafe installation for illicit cannabis plantations); protection of health of juveniles; reducing substantial nuisance and damage that directly affects the enjoyment of people's private lives (due to, for example, a terrible stench, noise, fire and harmful infections) and the separation of the soft drugs market and the hard drugs market (which would divide the simultaneous availability of and access to soft drugs and hard drugs).

We conclude that regulation of cannabis cultivation and trade for recreational use, under certain conditions is to be considered a positive obligation for the protection of human rights. This conclusion is based on the right to health (ICESCR and ESC) and the right to life, the right not to be subjected to inhumane treatment and the right to privacy (ICCPR and ECHR).

2. *The claim of a more effective human rights protection must be substantiated.* The conclusion that regulation of cannabis cultivation and trade for recreational use can indeed be based on positive human rights obligations does not mean that such regulation is automatically permissible. For this purpose, the state should – in a sincere and convincing manner – demonstrate that regulation would better fulfil the relevant positive human rights obligations (derived from the rights to health, life, physical and mental integrity and privacy) than an approach in which the cultivation and trade of cannabis is prohibited and combatted. Otherwise, it would not be possible to base the regulation of cannabis on positive human rights obligations and the state would be obliged to fully honour its obligations under the narcotic drugs conventions.

Thus, for the potentially relevant positive human rights obligations to be applicable, at least two conditions must be met. First, the regulation of cannabis cultivation and trade for recreational use should provide for a more effective protection of human rights than a policy that is in accordance with the drugs conventions (*the requirement of greater effectiveness*). Second, a state that aspires to regulate cannabis should at a minimum actually substantiate that this regulation would actually lead to a more effective protection of human rights than a prohibitive and repressive approach (*the requirement of substantiation i.e. plausibility*). The substantiation by the state required for this purpose should be based on genuine analysis, argumentation and considerations that are convincing and that are, as far as possible, based on available scientific and other research data.

There is also the question whether a state that intends to regulate cannabis cultivation and trade because of its positive human rights obligations should first collect data on the effects of such regulation through pilot studies rather than introduce nation-wide regulation without any further ado. We conclude that it is up to the state to make a considered and substantiated decision on whether such pilots are meaningful and desirable.

3. *National democratic support and decision-making.* A state's conclusion that regulation of cannabis would lead to more effective protection of human rights should be based on the democratic decision-making process in that state. As states and their societies have their own idiosyncrasies, peculiarities and constellations, the most effective approach in one state does not necessarily work in another state. It is partly for this reason that every state – in accordance with the so-called principle of primarity – in order to fulfil its treaty obligations is first and foremost responsible for determining which means are most adequate. Moreover, in the context of the right to health, the importance of participation of the public in the decision-making process concerning health related issues is emphasized. Furthermore, a measure that cannot count on public support will in many instances also prove to be less effective than in a case where such support exists. Local authorities – or individuals or private organisations – as a rule do not possess the possibility to force national authorities (both the administration and the legislator) to regulate cannabis cultivation and trade when national authorities refuse to take that step.
4. *No disadvantage for other states: a closed system.* When a state proceeds with regulation of cannabis cultivation and trade for recreational use, it should make sure to monitor the regulation to such a degree that other states are not confronted with negative consequences, most importantly with the export from the regulating state. The protection offered in that sense to other states should not be less – and preferably even more effective – than that offered under the prohibitive approach that fully accords with the drugs conventions. Therefore, the state should create a closed national system and/or chain for cultivation, trade and possibly also use of cannabis, i.e. closed in the sense that cannabis cannot leak away to illegal markets.
5. *The obligatory policy of discouragement.* When a state proceeds with regulation of cannabis cultivation and trade for recreational use, it should create an adequate policy to ensure discouragement, limitation and

increased public awareness of the risks associated with recreational use of cannabis. This is necessary not only to ensure that the national drugs policy adequately protects human rights, but also the right to health itself creates an obligation to that end. When developing such a policy of discouragement, the state needs to consider the most effective measures. In this context it is important to underline that obligations do not have to be complied with in any particular manner and should not be implemented so as to backfire in the end.

SUMMARIZING CONCLUSION

This legal research shows that it is possible for states to regulate cannabis cultivation and trade for recreational use by legalization in accordance with international law in spite of the UN drugs conventions. To this end, the state should – in a sincere and convincing manner – demonstrate that regulation would constitute a better protection of human rights than a prohibitive approach in accordance with the drugs conventions. These human rights first and foremost concern positive obligations deriving from the rights to health, life, physical and mental integrity, freedom from inhumane treatment, and privacy to the extent that these obligations serve to ensure individual and public health, security and crime control. The regulation, however, will have to satisfy several requirements and must be accompanied by a policy that discourages recreational cannabis use. If a state is able to satisfy these conditions, under current international law it can legitimately prioritize the human rights obligations over and above any conflicting obligations arising from the UN narcotic drugs conventions.

ABOUT THE AUTHORS

Piet Hein van Kempen is Full Professor of Criminal Law and Criminal Procedure Law and Dean (since 2018) of the Faculty of Law of Radboud University, Nijmegen, the Netherlands. Van Kempen is also Secretary-General of the International Penal and Penitentiary Foundation (IPPF). Furthermore, he has been a Justice (judge) *ad litem* for fifteen years, and as of 2008, in the Court of Appeals, criminal chamber, 's-Hertogenbosch, the Netherlands. Van Kempen has been a member of various editorial boards, including that of *Delikt en Delinkwent*, the major Dutch Journal on criminal law, criminal procedure law and criminology. He is also a member of the Committee Modernization of the Code of Criminal Procedure, established by the Minister of Justice and Security to advise the legislator. Van Kempen (co)authored, amongst others, numerous books and articles, commentaries and case notes in the field of (national, international, European, transnational and comparative) criminal law and criminal procedural law, penitentiary law and human rights law. More specifically, his research and teaching cover themes such as the effect of European, international and transnational criminal law on national criminal justice systems and the interaction between international and national criminal law and procedure; various substantive and procedural criminal law topics, including legality, *mens rea*, justifications and excuses; the basic principles of the criminal justice system; human rights issues, including positive obligations, fair trial, deprivation of liberty, religion, the rights of prisoners, the position of legal persons; transnational criminal law, including terrorism, corruption and trafficking in human beings, drugs and cultural goods; and fundamental legal questions and the dogmatics, foundations and principles of legal regimes and their systemic quality.

Masha Fedorova is Full Professor of Criminal Law and Criminal Procedure Law and Head of the Department of Criminal Law and Criminology at the Faculty of Law of Radboud University, Nijmegen, the Netherlands. Fedorova is also a part-time judge in the criminal law section of the District Court in 's-Hertogenbosch, the Netherlands. Furthermore, she is a member of the Legal Experts Advisory Panel (LEAP) of Fair Trials International and a member of the editorial board of *Nederlands Tijdschrift voor de Mensenrechten (NTM/NJCM Bulletin)*, one of the leading academic journals on human rights in the Netherlands. Fedorova specializes in Dutch substantive criminal law and criminal procedure law; international, transnational and EU criminal law;

and human rights law (with an emphasis on the UN, EU and ECHR framework). Her principal research interest is the interaction between and mutual influence of these different areas of law. Alongside her research on the international drug control system, she conducted research, amongst others, on the appropriateness of certain legislative initiatives in the Netherlands in the fight against the so-called 'foreign terrorist fighters' from the perspective of fundamental principles of substantive criminal law, human rights law and public international law; on the concepts of fairness and equality of arms in international criminal proceedings; on appeal proceedings in Dutch criminal law and on the fair trial concept and the rights of the defense in Article 6 of the European Convention of Human Rights.

www.ingramcontent.com/pod-product-compliance
Ingram Content Group UK Ltd.
Pitfield, Milton Keynes, MK11 3LW, UK
UKHW051922100926
8556IPUK00021B/1319